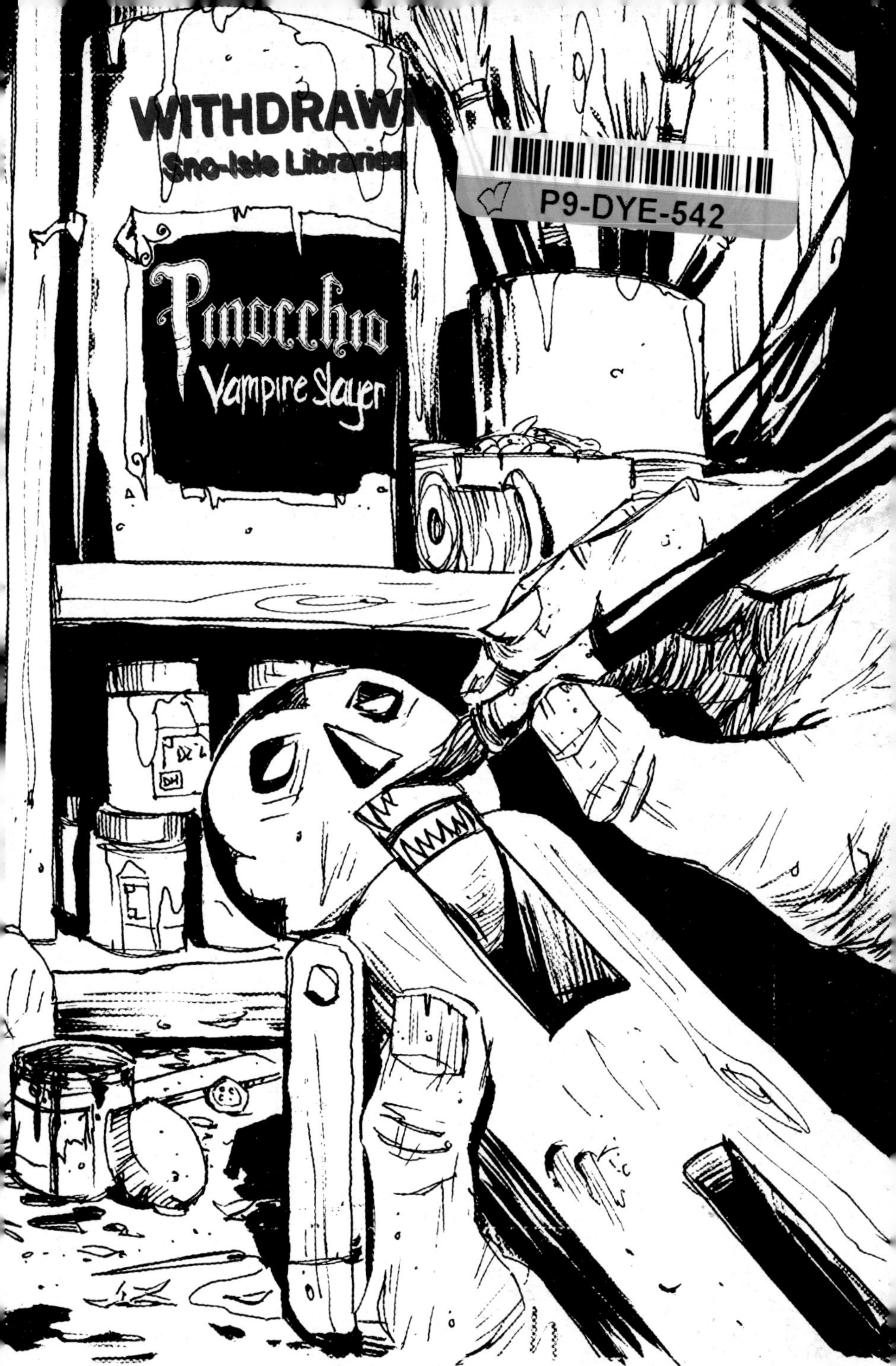
Pinocchio
Vampire Slayer

written by
Van Jensen

created and
drawn by
Dusty Higgins

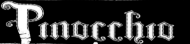

Pinocchio

This book owes a lot to Carlo Collodi's original story, *Pinocchio*. We mean *a lot*. You could say *everything*, and we wouldn't complain. We never could have dreamed up a wooden puppet whose nose grows when he lies. I mean, you can't make that kind of stuff up. Unless your name is Carlo Collodi. Then, apparently, you can.

We humbly beg Collodi's apologies and ask that if he ever rolls over in his grave, and rises, bloodthirsty, that we be spared. This story, after all, is in good fun. And we prefer no real guts be spilled. Especially our guts.

This story is a continuation of Collodi's original. And we stress original, because there are many adaptations that stray far from Collodi's vision. That beloved dancing cricket? He didn't dance or sing and was dead within a few paragraphs. Pinocchio's encounter with the fox and cat ends with him swinging from a tree. And no, they didn't have tire swings back then.

Since we reference the original story within our own, we've created a quick illustrated guide to help you, the reader, catch up to speed with the story thus far. However, we strongly encourage you pick up the original and take a brisk stroll through Collodi's zany, dark and hilarious tale. It's a story that begins with a most perfect phrase:

There was once upon a time a piece of wood...

Vampire Slayer

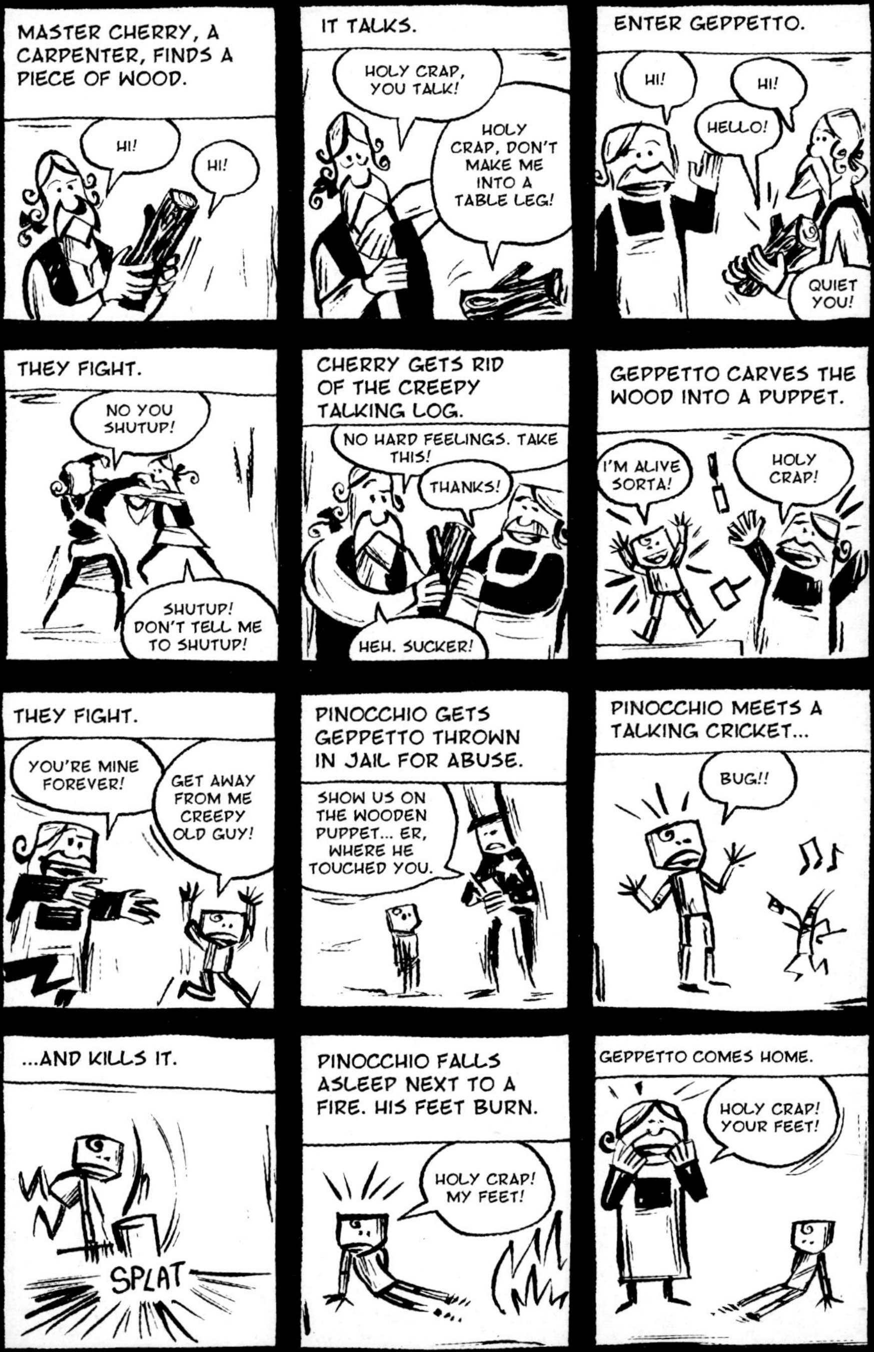
MASTER CHERRY, A CARPENTER, FINDS A PIECE OF WOOD.
HI!
HI!
IT TALKS.
HOLY CRAP, YOU TALK!
HOLY CRAP, DON'T MAKE ME INTO A TABLE LEG!
ENTER GEPPETTO.
HI!
HI!
HELLO!
QUIET YOU!
THEY FIGHT.
NO YOU SHUTUP!
SHUTUP! DON'T TELL ME TO SHUTUP!
CHERRY GETS RID OF THE CREEPY TALKING LOG.
NO HARD FEELINGS. TAKE THIS!
THANKS!
HEH. SUCKER!
GEPPETTO CARVES THE WOOD INTO A PUPPET.
I'M ALIVE SORTA!
HOLY CRAP!
THEY FIGHT.
YOU'RE MINE FOREVER!
GET AWAY FROM ME CREEPY OLD GUY!
PINOCCHIO GETS GEPPETTO THROWN IN JAIL FOR ABUSE.
SHOW US ON THE WOODEN PUPPET... ER, WHERE HE TOUCHED YOU.
PINOCCHIO MEETS A TALKING CRICKET...
BUG!!
...AND KILLS IT.
SPLAT
PINOCCHIO FALLS ASLEEP NEXT TO A FIRE. HIS FEET BURN.
HOLY CRAP! MY FEET!
GEPPETTO COMES HOME.
HOLY CRAP! YOUR FEET!

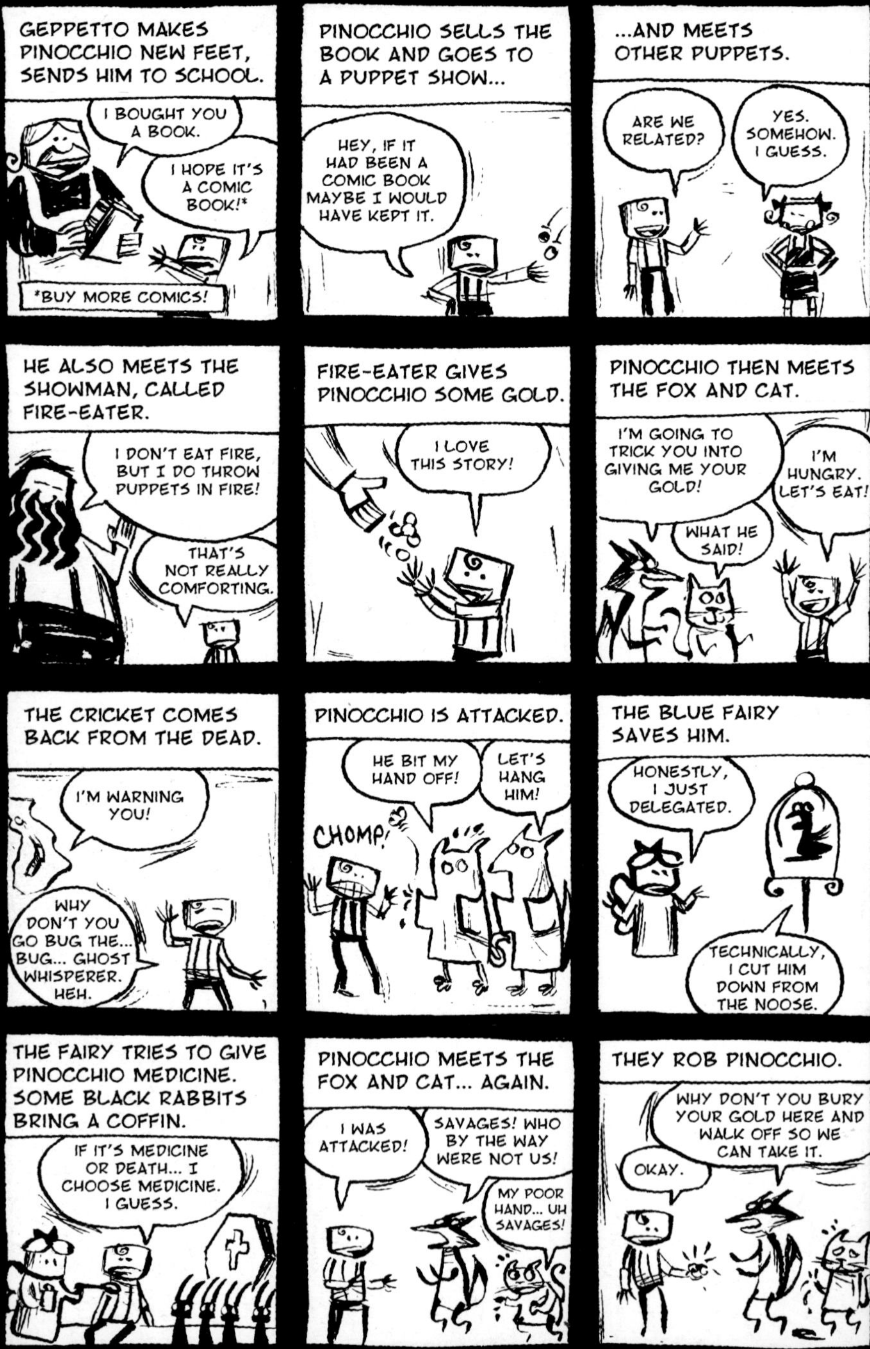
GEPPETTO MAKES PINOCCHIO NEW FEET, SENDS HIM TO SCHOOL.
I BOUGHT YOU A BOOK.
I HOPE IT'S A COMIC BOOK!*
*BUY MORE COMICS!
PINOCCHIO SELLS THE BOOK AND GOES TO A PUPPET SHOW...
HEY, IF IT HAD BEEN A COMIC BOOK MAYBE I WOULD HAVE KEPT IT.
...AND MEETS OTHER PUPPETS.
ARE WE RELATED?
YES. SOMEHOW. I GUESS.
HE ALSO MEETS THE SHOWMAN, CALLED FIRE-EATER.
I DON'T EAT FIRE, BUT I DO THROW PUPPETS IN FIRE!
THAT'S NOT REALLY COMFORTING.
FIRE-EATER GIVES PINOCCHIO SOME GOLD.
I LOVE THIS STORY!
PINOCCHIO THEN MEETS THE FOX AND CAT.
I'M GOING TO TRICK YOU INTO GIVING ME YOUR GOLD!
WHAT HE SAID!
I'M HUNGRY. LET'S EAT!
THE CRICKET COMES BACK FROM THE DEAD.
I'M WARNING YOU!
WHY DON'T YOU GO BUG THE... BUG... GHOST WHISPERER. HEH.
PINOCCHIO IS ATTACKED.
CHOMP!
HE BIT MY HAND OFF!
LET'S HANG HIM!
THE BLUE FAIRY SAVES HIM.
HONESTLY, I JUST DELEGATED.
TECHNICALLY, I CUT HIM DOWN FROM THE NOOSE.
THE FAIRY TRIES TO GIVE PINOCCHIO MEDICINE. SOME BLACK RABBITS BRING A COFFIN.
IF IT'S MEDICINE OR DEATH... I CHOOSE MEDICINE. I GUESS.
PINOCCHIO MEETS THE FOX AND CAT... AGAIN.
I WAS ATTACKED!
SAVAGES! WHO BY THE WAY WERE NOT US!
MY POOR HAND... UH SAVAGES!
THEY ROB PINOCCHIO.
WHY DON'T YOU BURY YOUR GOLD HERE AND WALK OFF SO WE CAN TAKE IT.
OKAY.

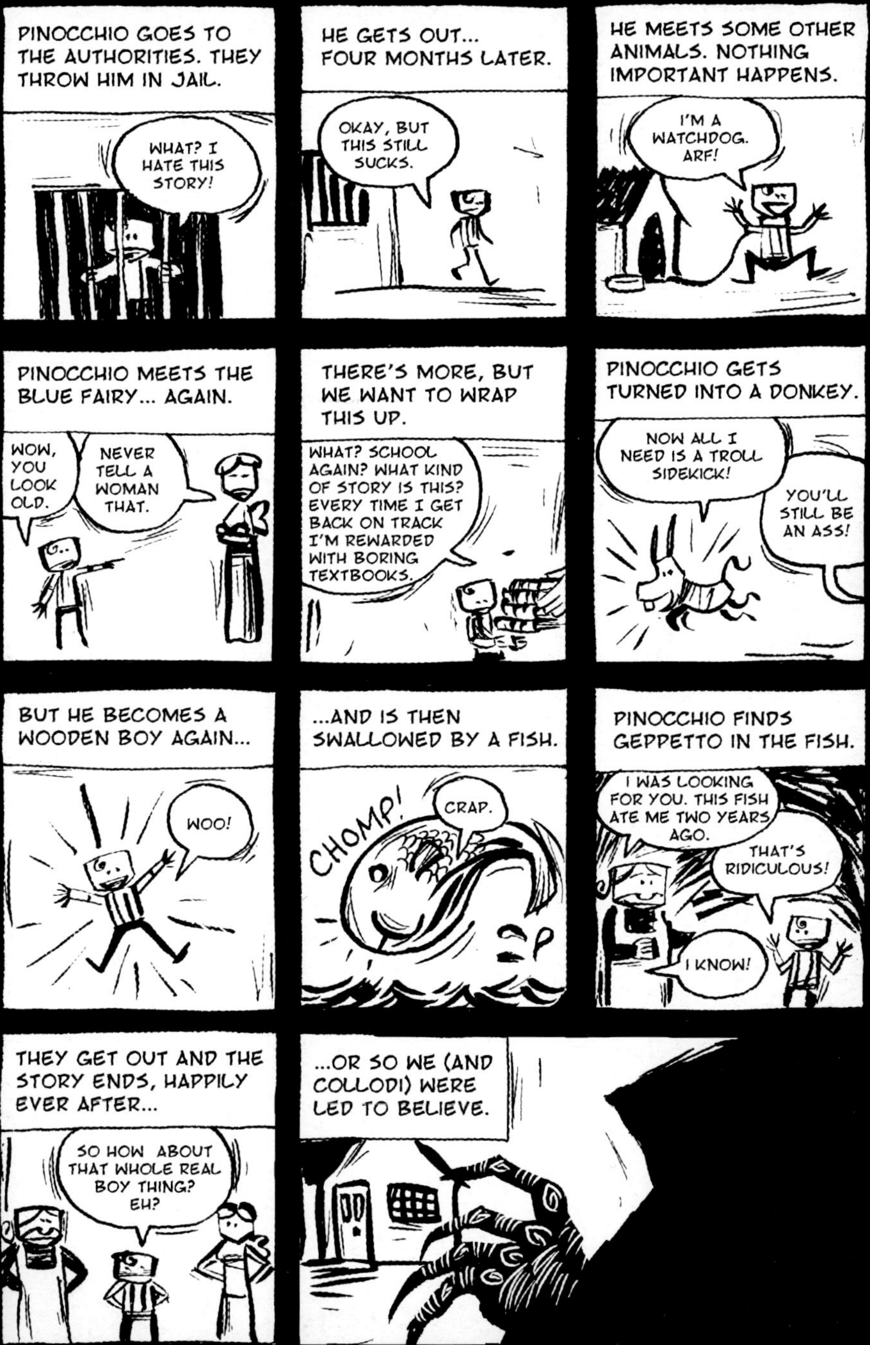
PINOCCHIO GOES TO THE AUTHORITIES. THEY THROW HIM IN JAIL.
WHAT? I HATE THIS STORY!
HE GETS OUT... FOUR MONTHS LATER.
OKAY, BUT THIS STILL SUCKS.
HE MEETS SOME OTHER ANIMALS. NOTHING IMPORTANT HAPPENS.
I'M A WATCHDOG. ARF!
PINOCCHIO MEETS THE BLUE FAIRY... AGAIN.
WOW, YOU LOOK OLD.
NEVER TELL A WOMAN THAT.
THERE'S MORE, BUT WE WANT TO WRAP THIS UP.
WHAT? SCHOOL AGAIN? WHAT KIND OF STORY IS THIS? EVERY TIME I GET BACK ON TRACK I'M REWARDED WITH BORING TEXTBOOKS.
PINOCCHIO GETS TURNED INTO A DONKEY.
NOW ALL I NEED IS A TROLL SIDEKICK!
YOU'LL STILL BE AN ASS!
BUT HE BECOMES A WOODEN BOY AGAIN...
WOO!
...AND IS THEN SWALLOWED BY A FISH.
CHOMP!
CRAP.
PINOCCHIO FINDS GEPPETTO IN THE FISH.
I WAS LOOKING FOR YOU. THIS FISH ATE ME TWO YEARS AGO.
THAT'S RIDICULOUS!
I KNOW!
THEY GET OUT AND THE STORY ENDS, HAPPILY EVER AFTER...
SO HOW ABOUT THAT WHOLE REAL BOY THING? EH?
...OR SO WE (AND COLLODI) WERE LED TO BELIEVE.

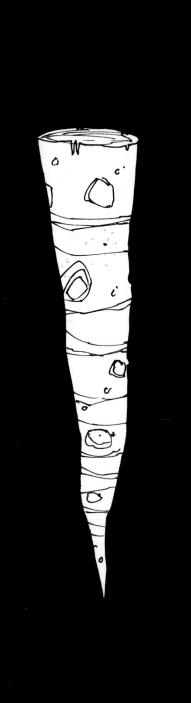

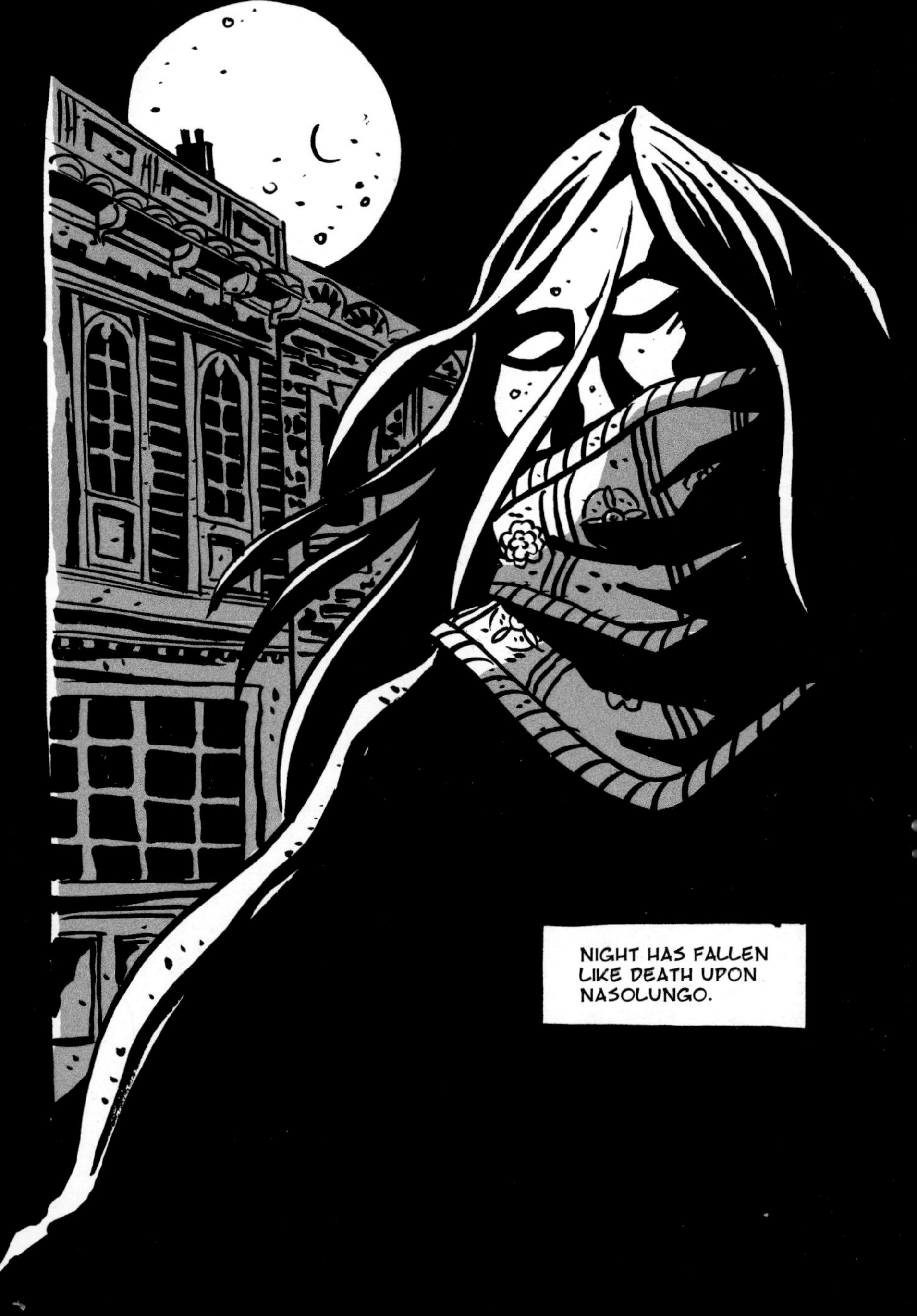
NIGHT HAS FALLEN LIKE DEATH UPON NASOLUNGO.

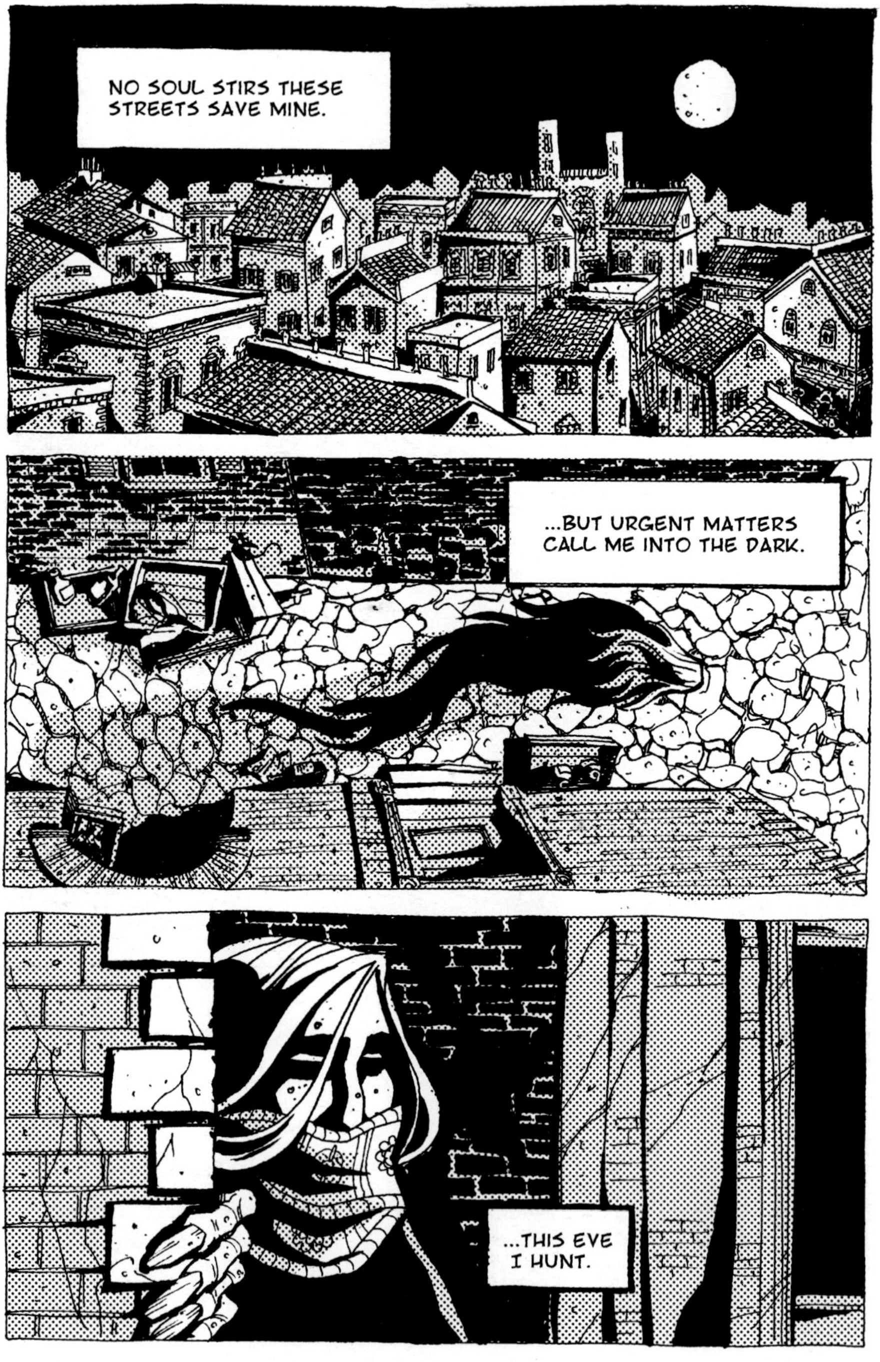
NO SOUL STIRS THESE STREETS SAVE MINE.
...BUT URGENT MATTERS CALL ME INTO THE DARK.
...THIS EVE I HUNT.

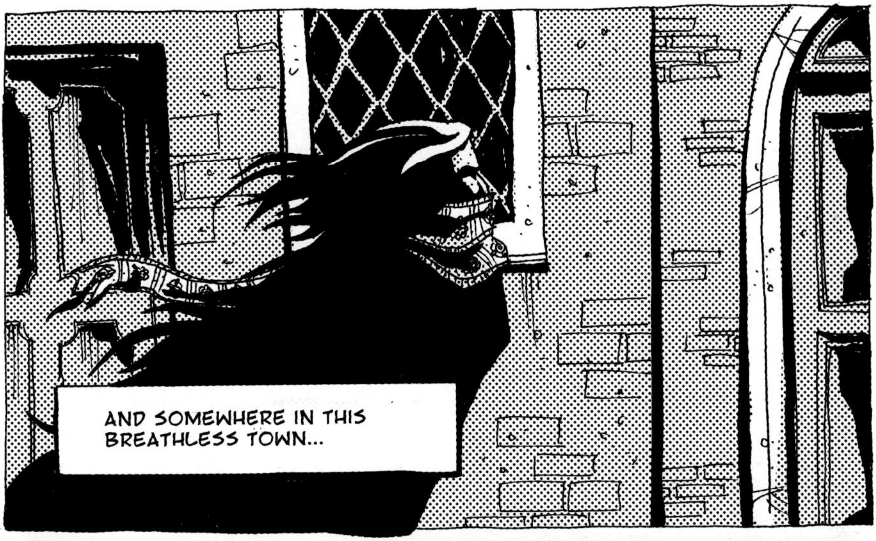
AND SOMEWHERE IN THIS BREATHLESS TOWN...

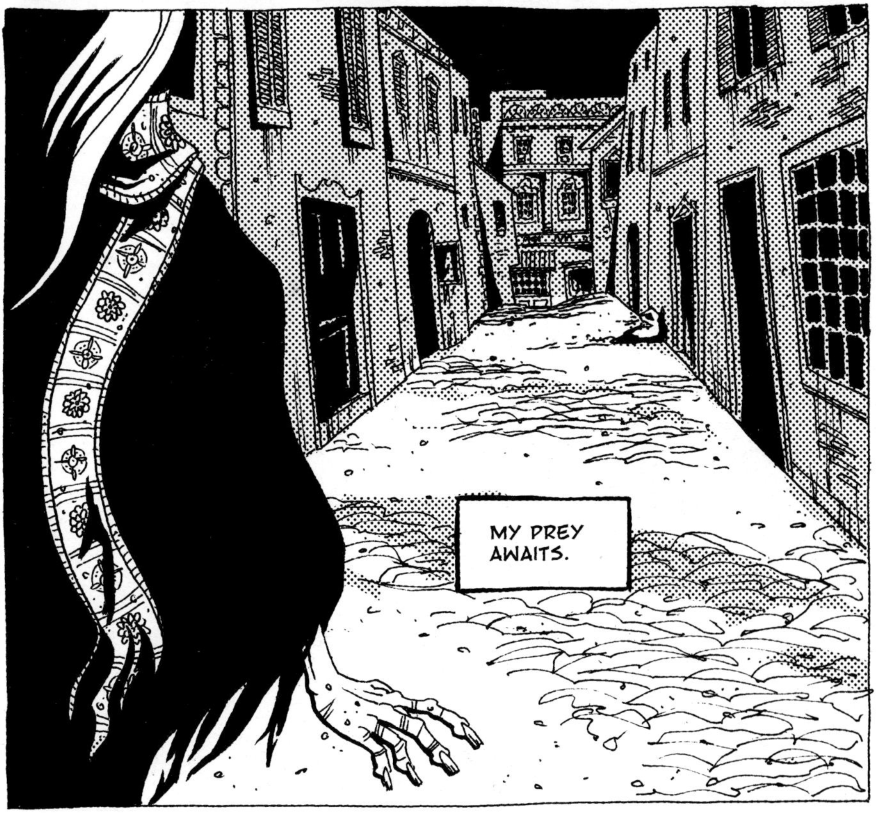
MY PREY AWAITS.

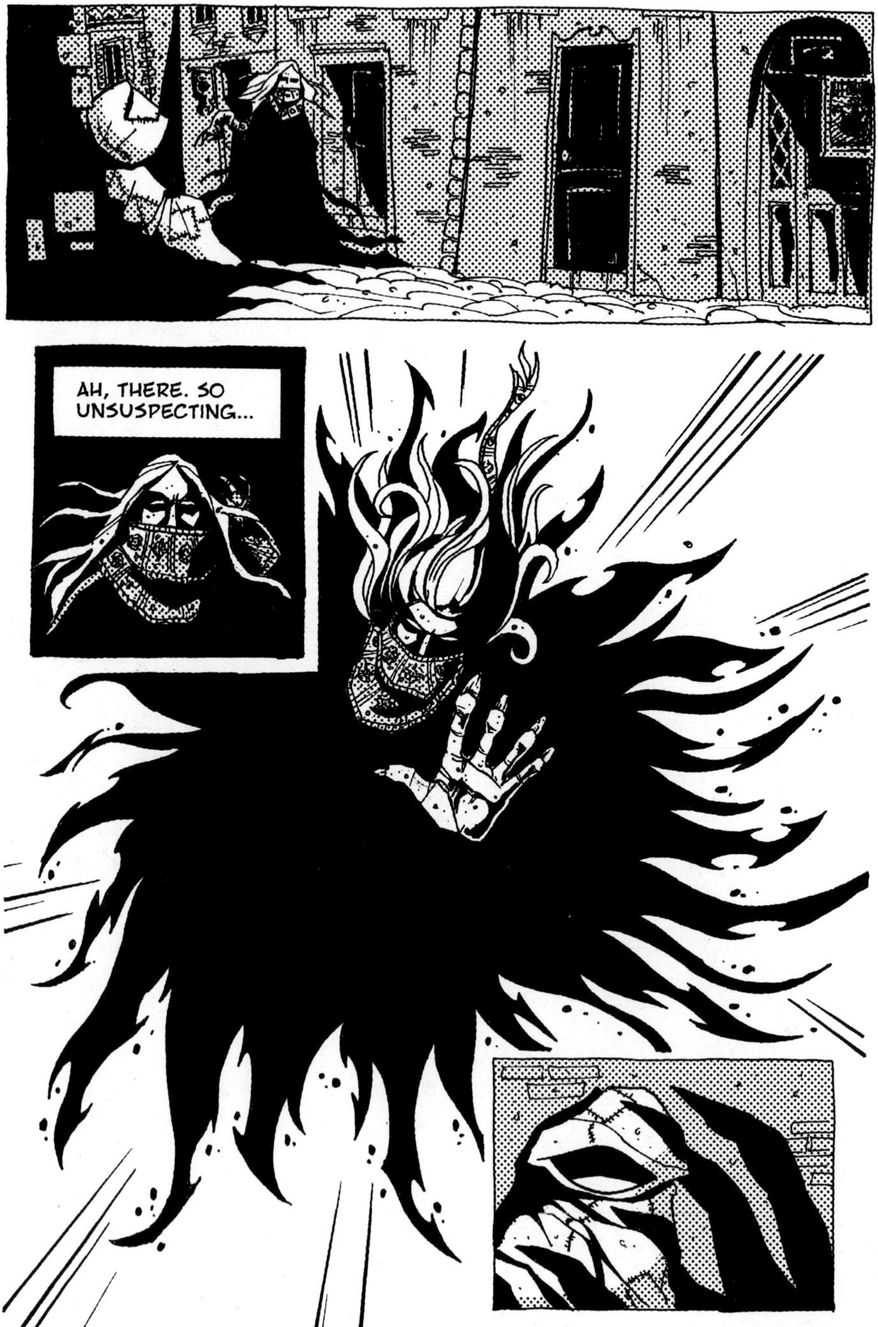
AH, THERE. SO UNSUSPECTING...

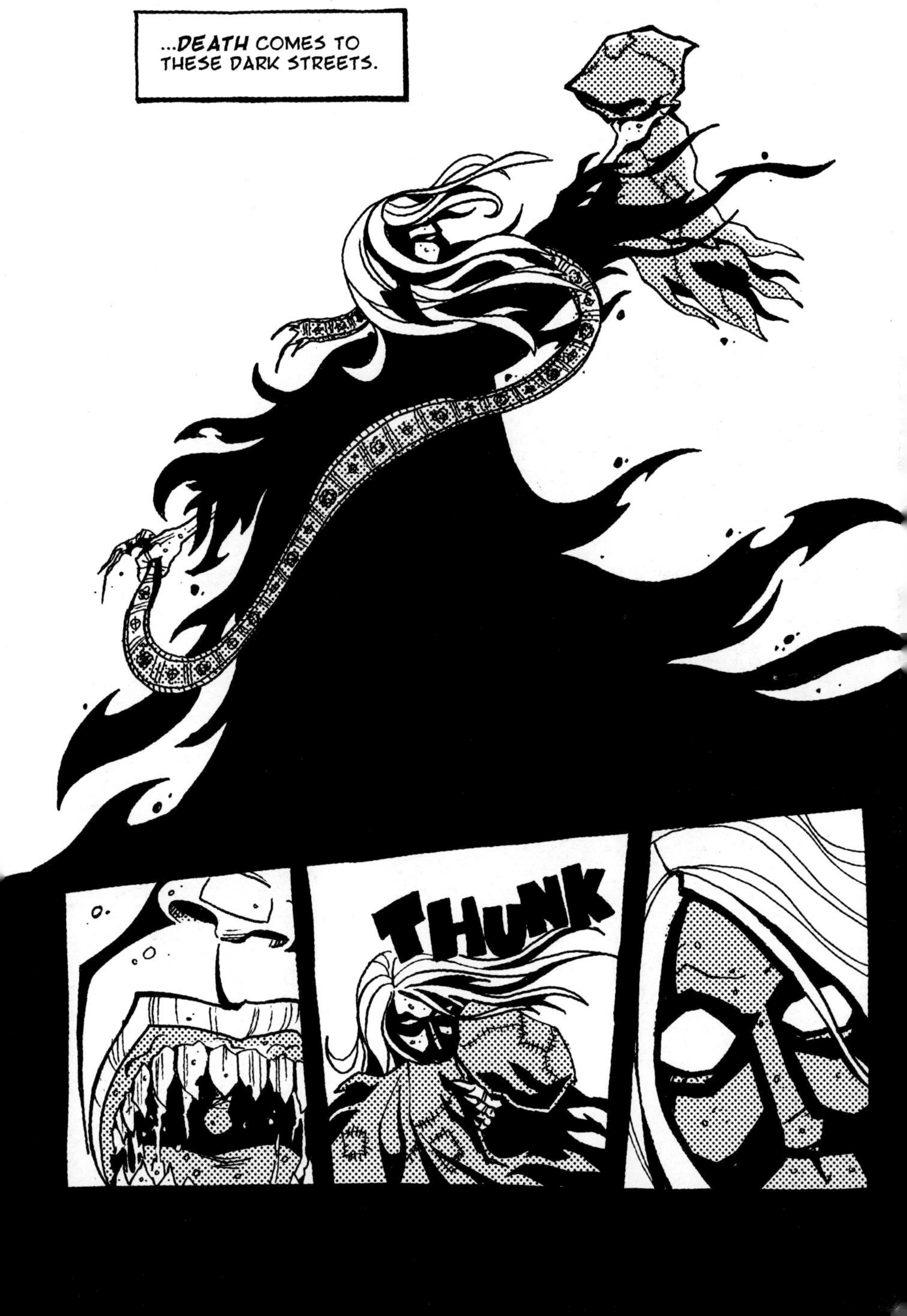

...DEATH COMES TO THESE DARK STREETS.
THUNK

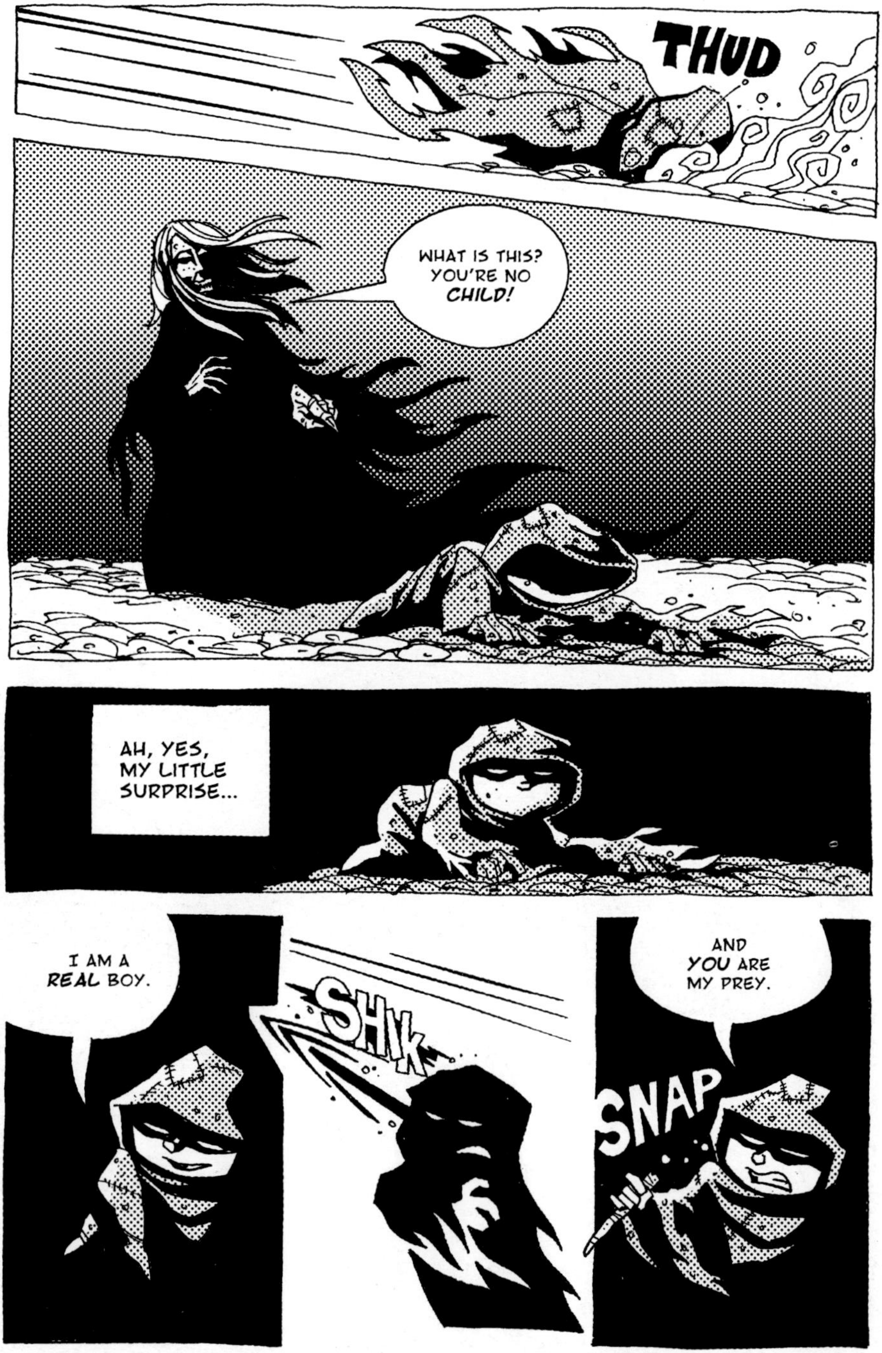
THUD
WHAT IS THIS? YOU'RE NO CHILD!
AH, YES, MY LITTLE SURPRISE...
I AM A REAL BOY.
SHIK
AND YOU ARE MY PREY.
SNAP

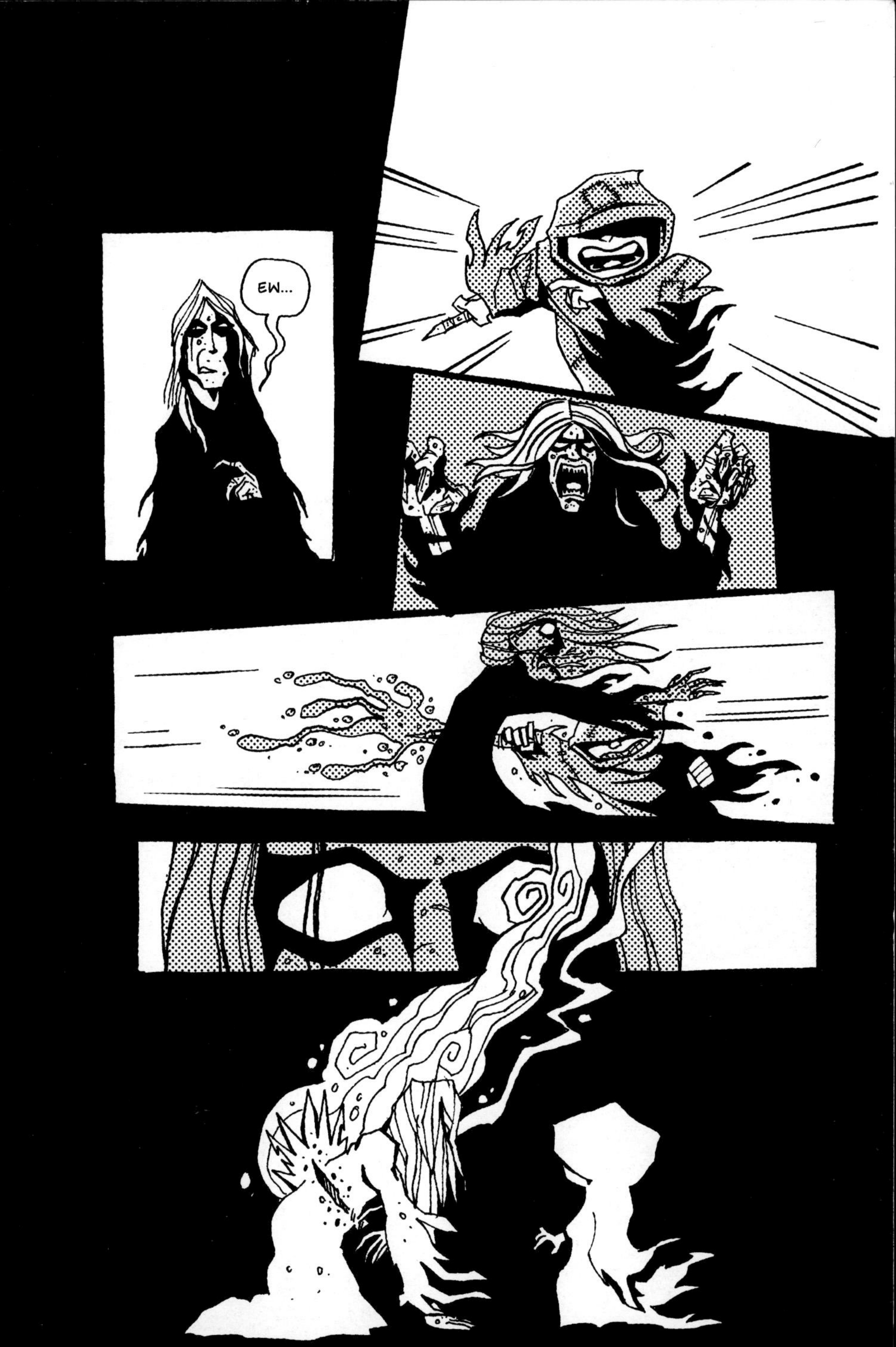
EW...

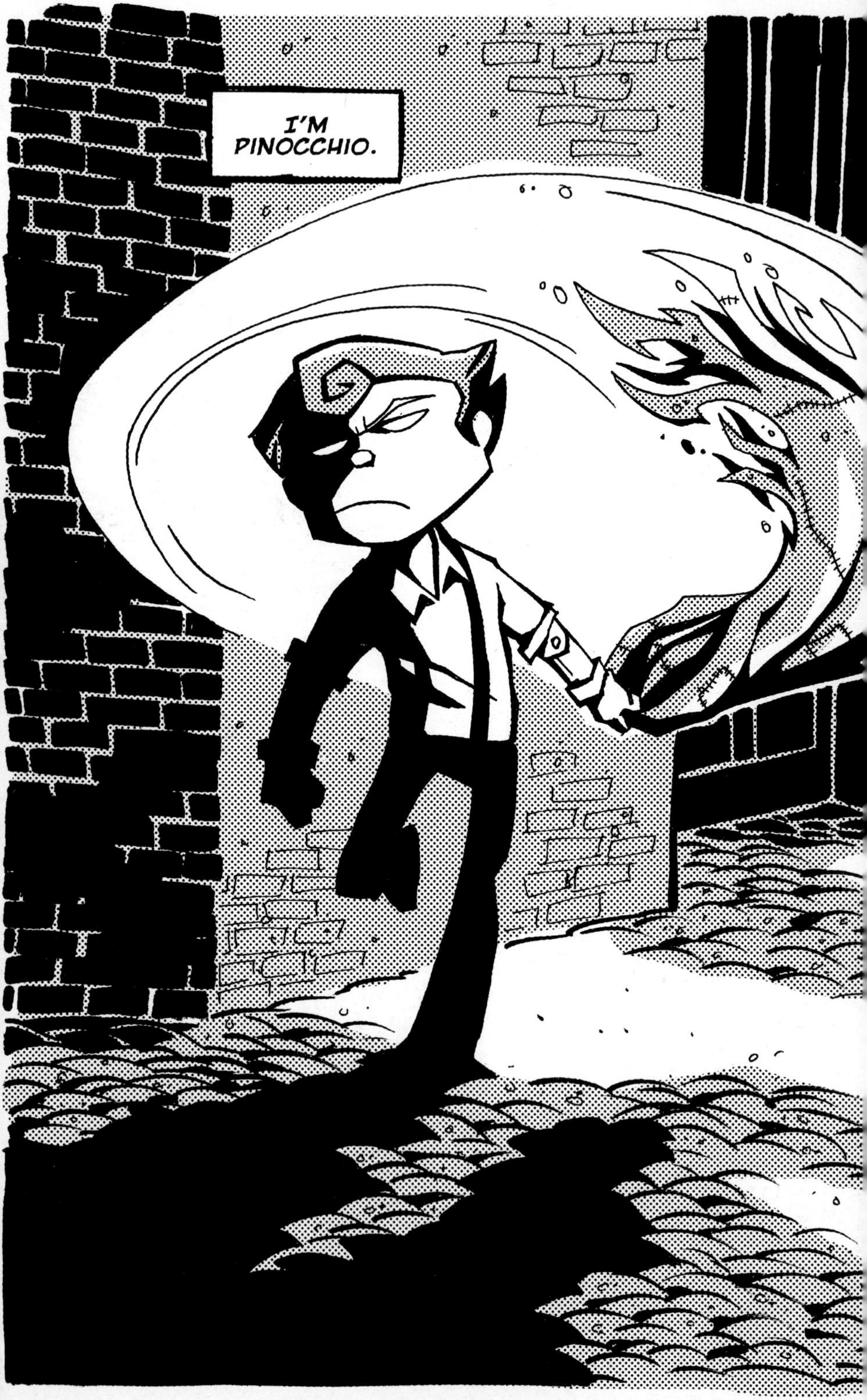
I'M PINOCCHIO.

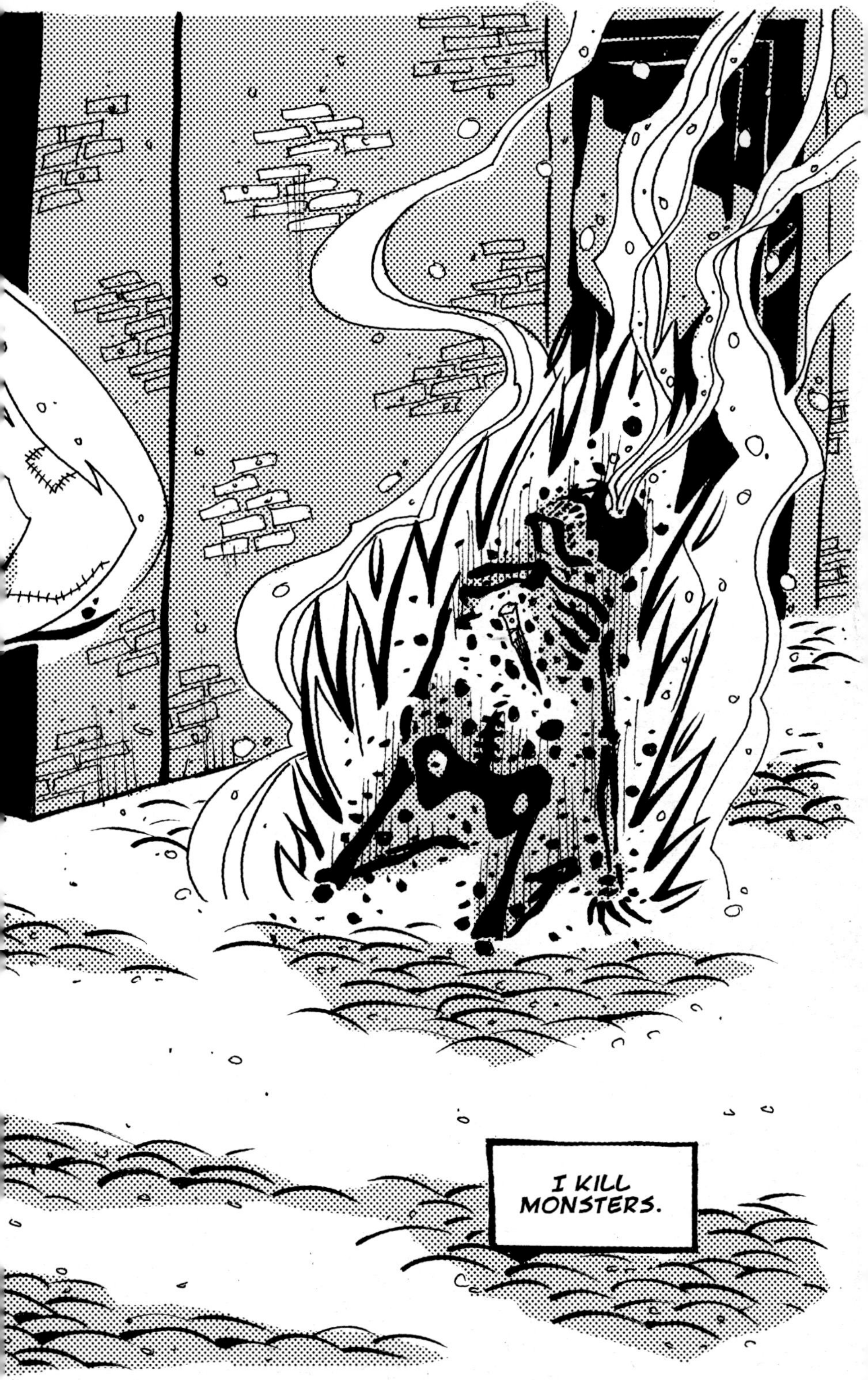
I KILL MONSTERS.

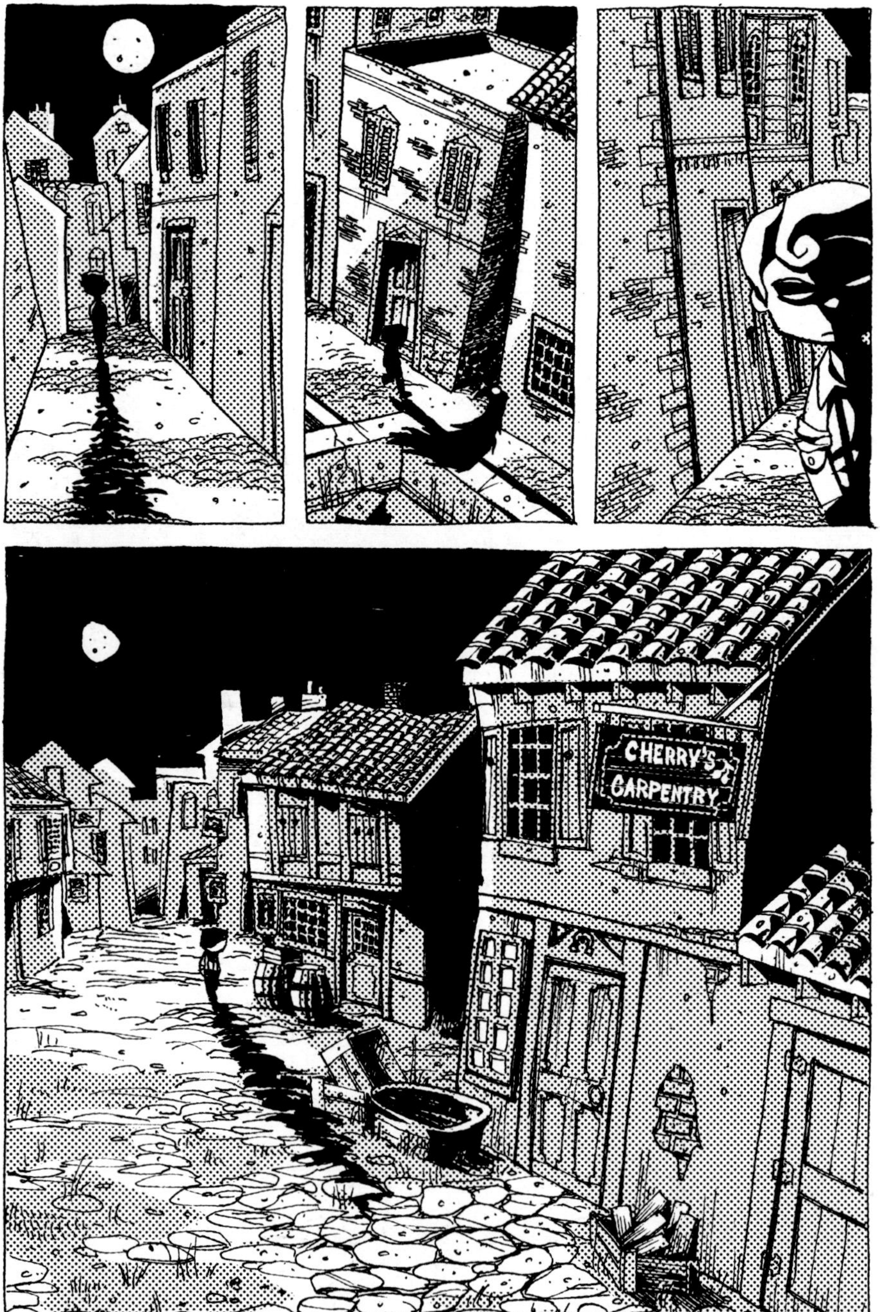
CHERRY'S
CARPENTRY

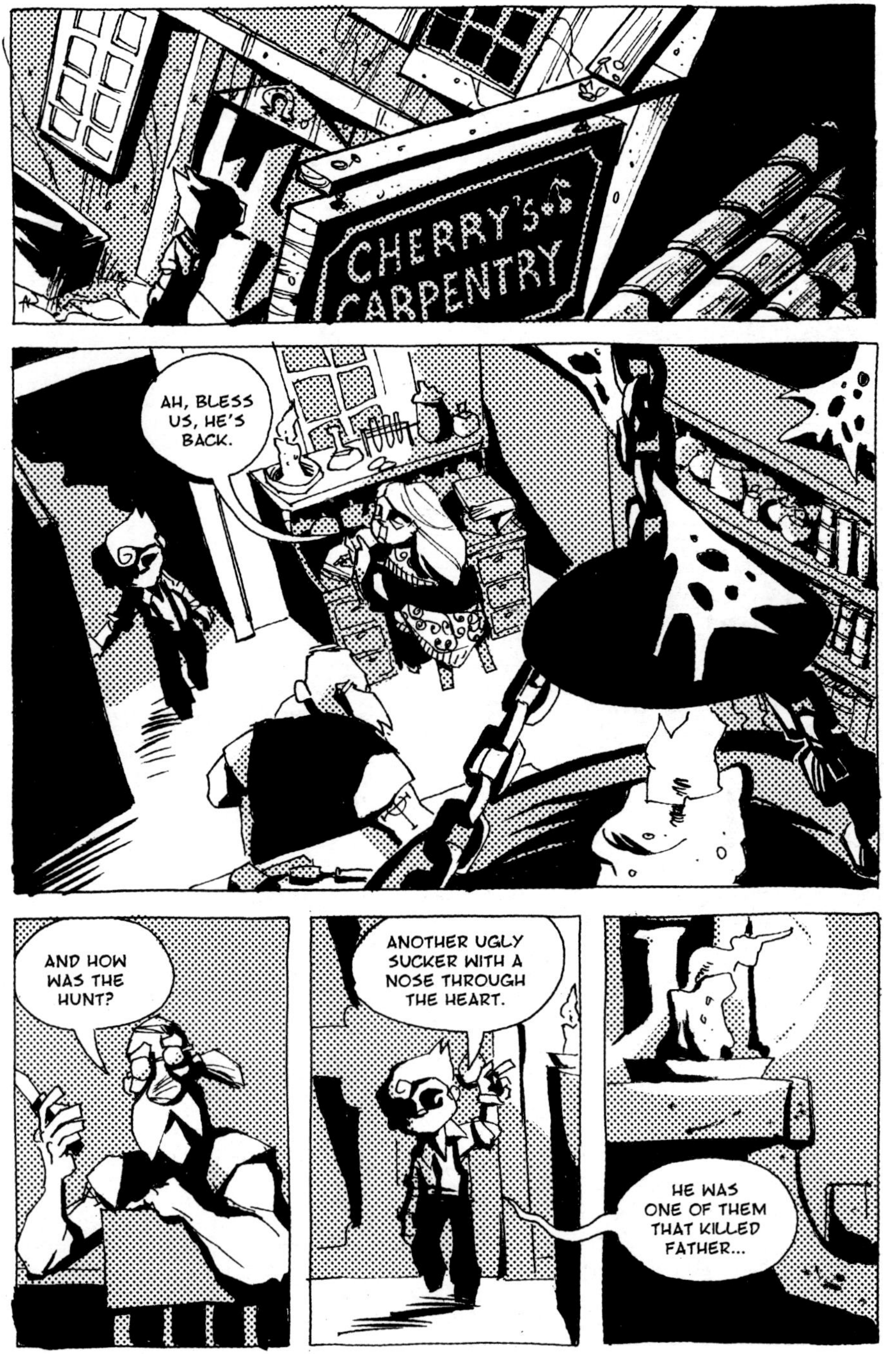
CHERRY'S CARPENTRY
AH, BLESS US, HE'S BACK.
AND HOW WAS THE HUNT?
ANOTHER UGLY SUCKER WITH A NOSE THROUGH THE HEART.
HE WAS ONE OF THEM THAT KILLED FATHER...

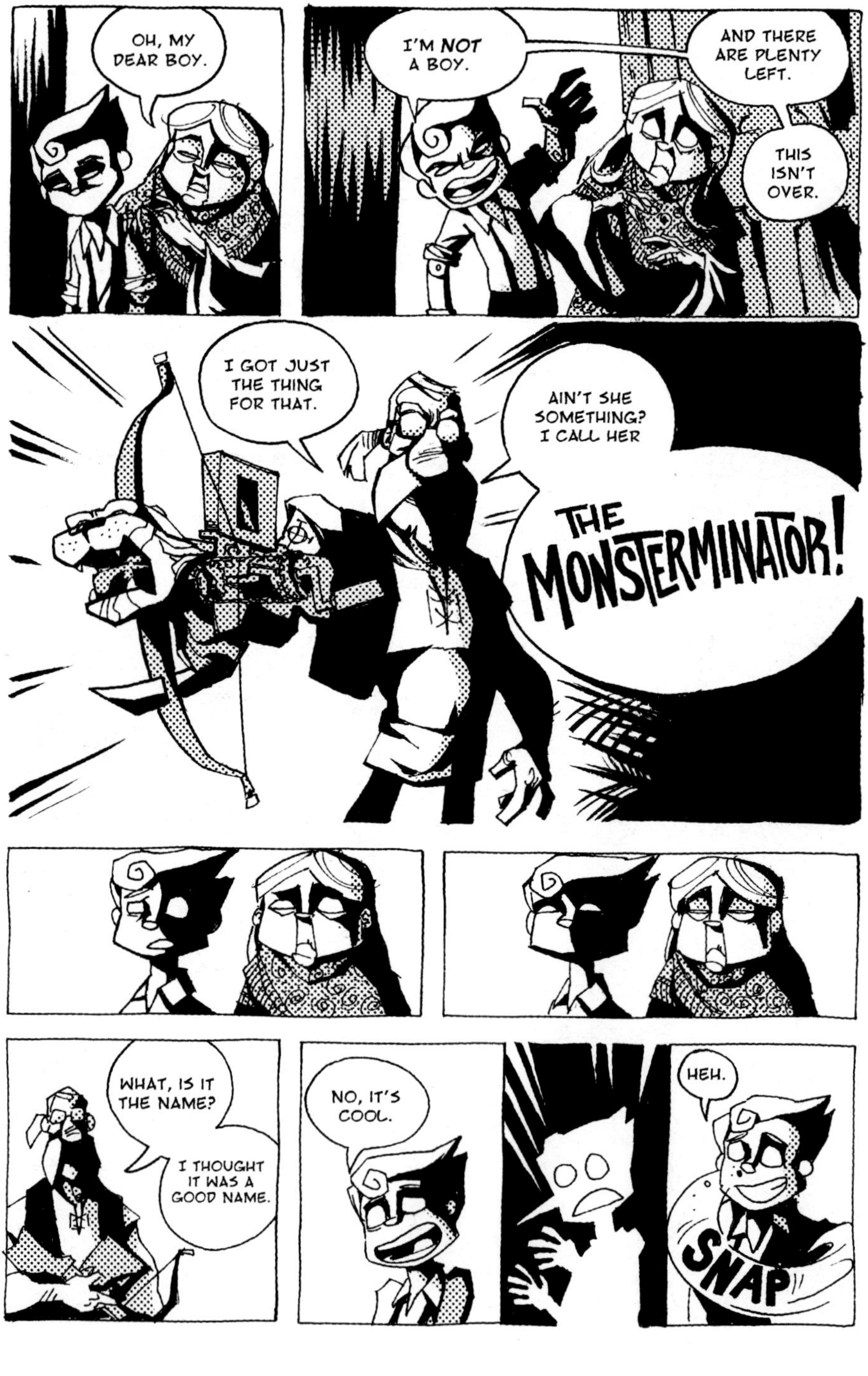

OH, MY DEAR BOY.
I'M NOT A BOY.
AND THERE ARE PLENTY LEFT.
THIS ISN'T OVER.
I GOT JUST THE THING FOR THAT.
AIN'T SHE SOMETHING? I CALL HER
THE MONSTERMINATOR!
WHAT, IS IT THE NAME?
I THOUGHT IT WAS A GOOD NAME.
NO, IT'S COOL.
HEH.
SNAP

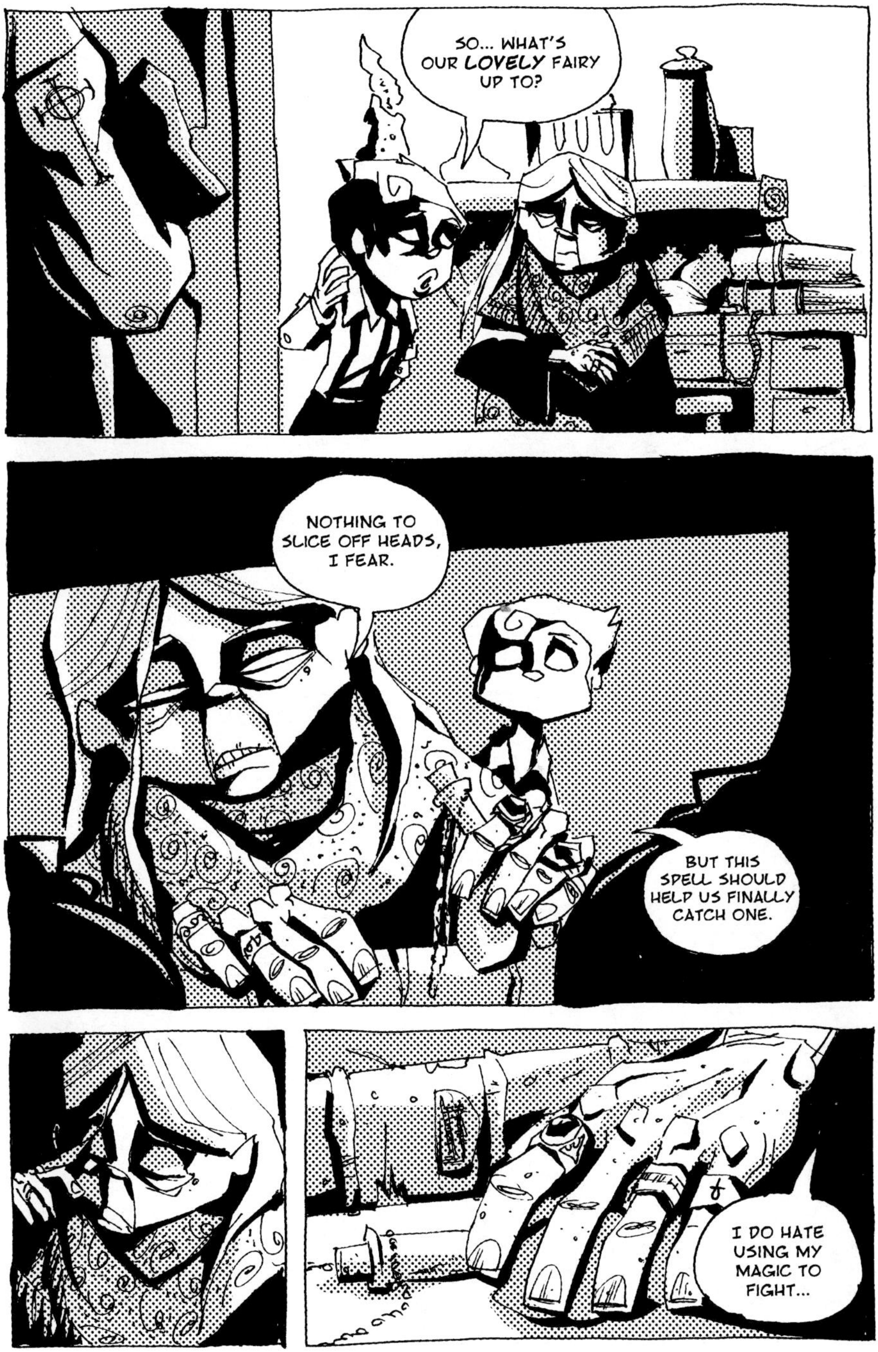
SO... WHAT'S OUR LOVELY FAIRY UP TO?
NOTHING TO SLICE OFF HEADS, I FEAR.
BUT THIS SPELL SHOULD HELP US FINALLY CATCH ONE.
I DO HATE USING MY MAGIC TO FIGHT...

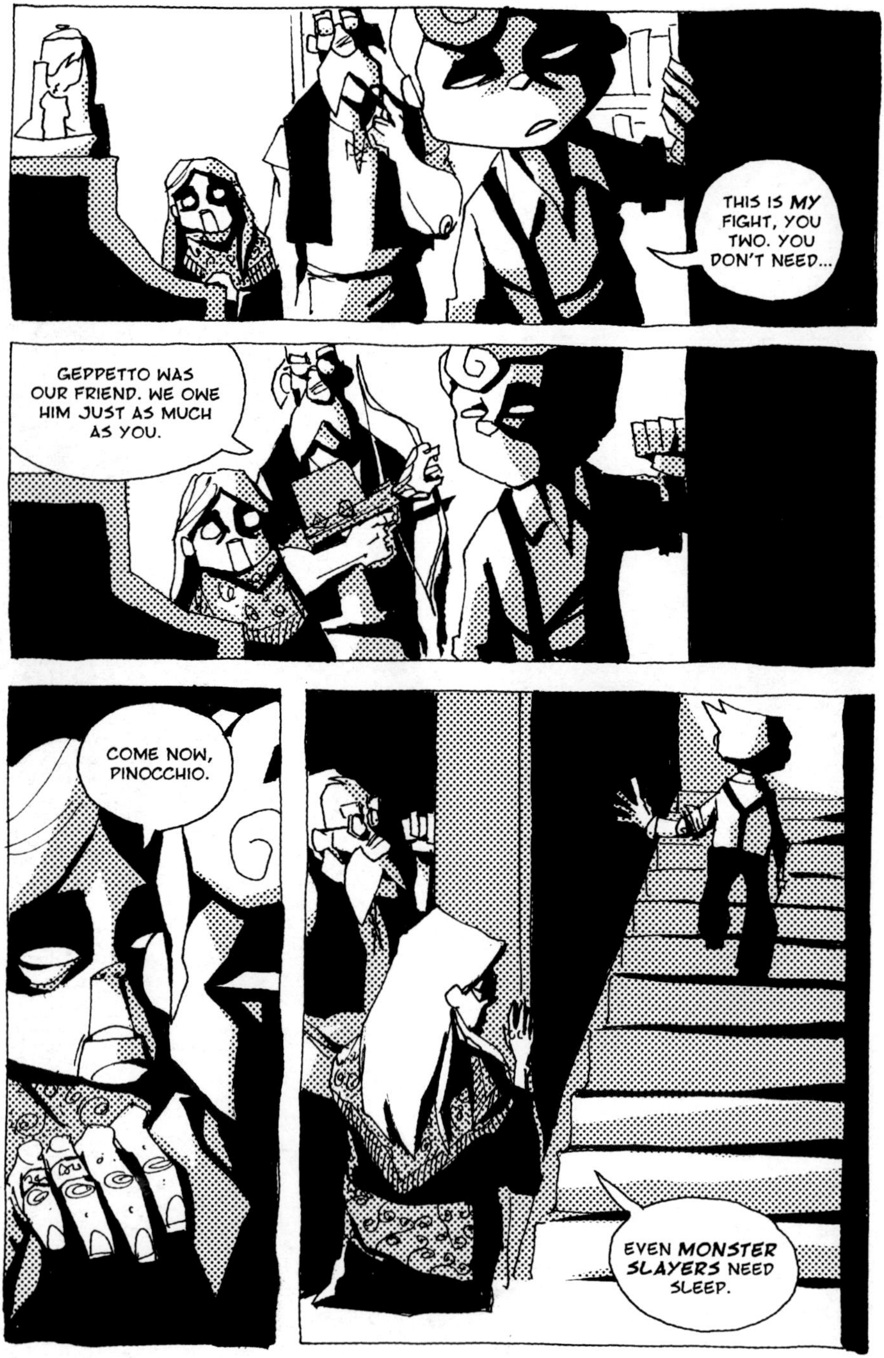
THIS IS MY FIGHT, YOU TWO. YOU DON'T NEED...
GEPPETTO WAS OUR FRIEND. WE OWE HIM JUST AS MUCH AS YOU.
COME NOW, PINOCCHIO.
EVEN MONSTER SLAYERS NEED SLEEP.

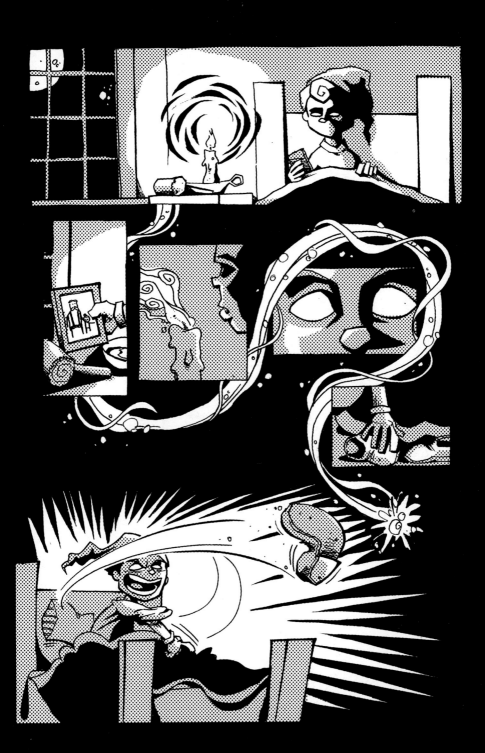

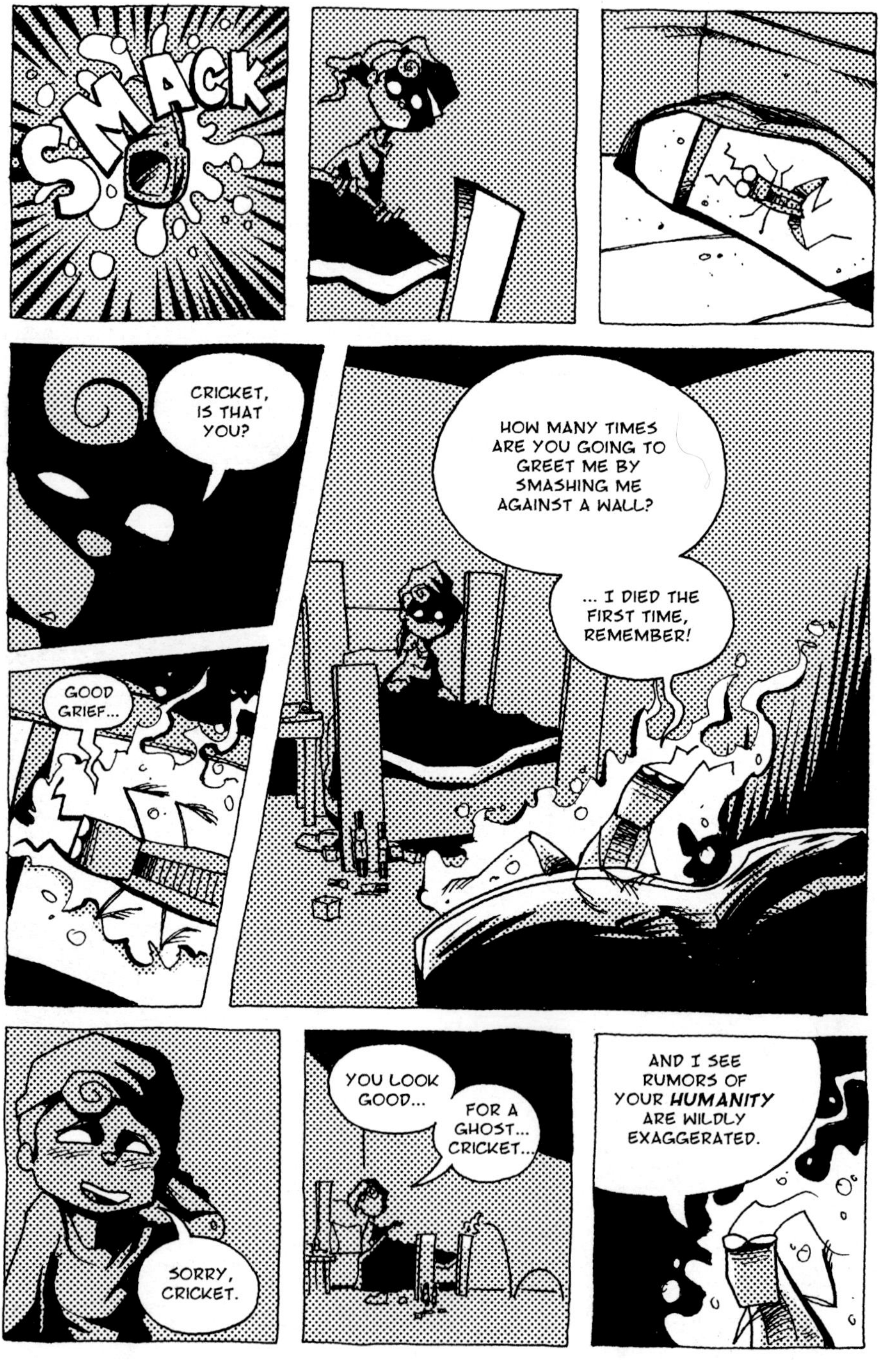
SMACK
CRICKET, IS THAT YOU?
HOW MANY TIMES ARE YOU GOING TO GREET ME BY SMASHING ME AGAINST A WALL?
... I DIED THE FIRST TIME, REMEMBER!
GOOD GRIEF...
SORRY, CRICKET.
YOU LOOK GOOD...
FOR A GHOST... CRICKET...
AND I SEE RUMORS OF YOUR HUMANITY ARE WILDLY EXAGGERATED.

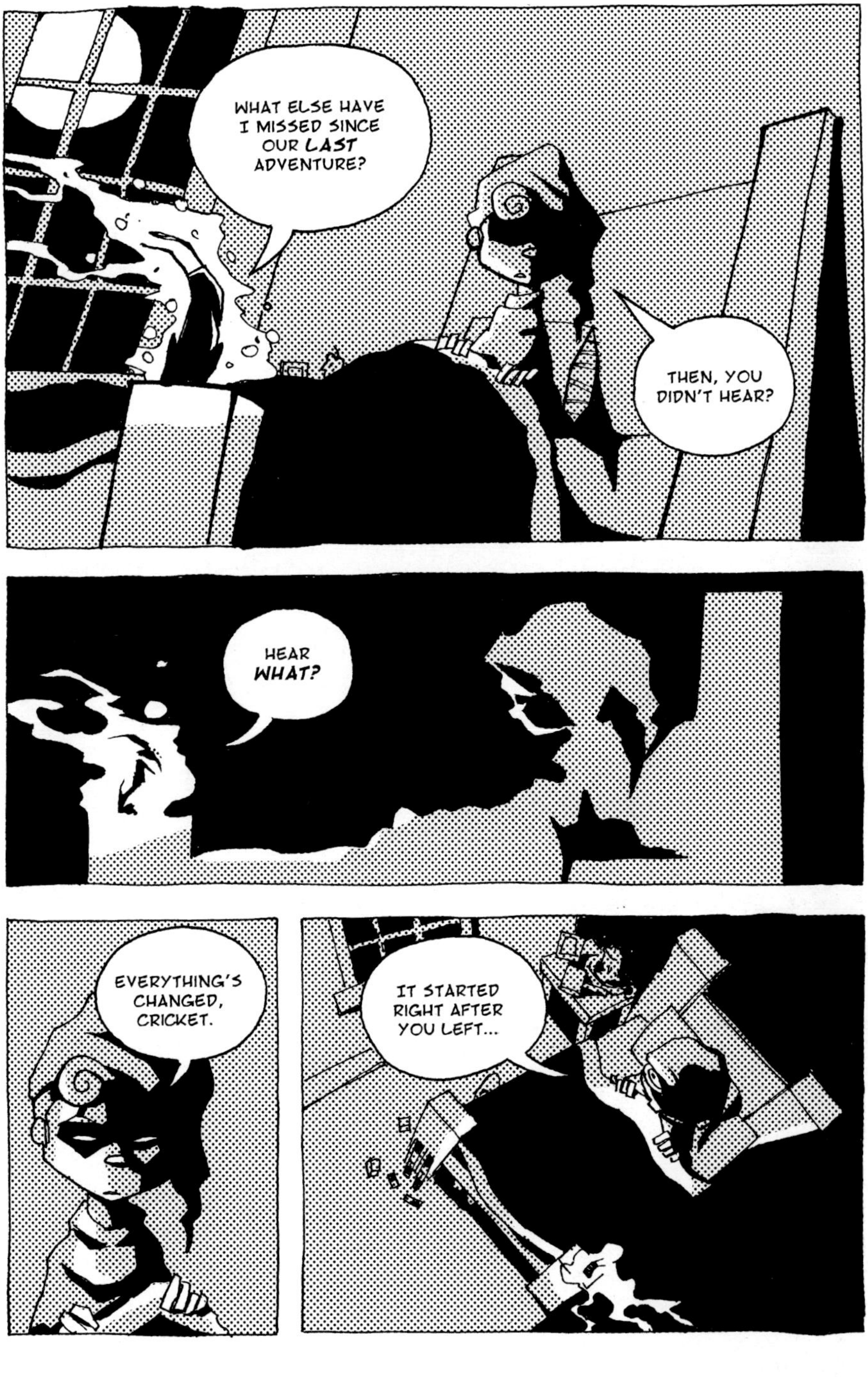
WHAT ELSE HAVE I MISSED SINCE OUR LAST ADVENTURE?
THEN, YOU DIDN'T HEAR?
HEAR WHAT?
EVERYTHING'S CHANGED, CRICKET.
IT STARTED RIGHT AFTER YOU LEFT...

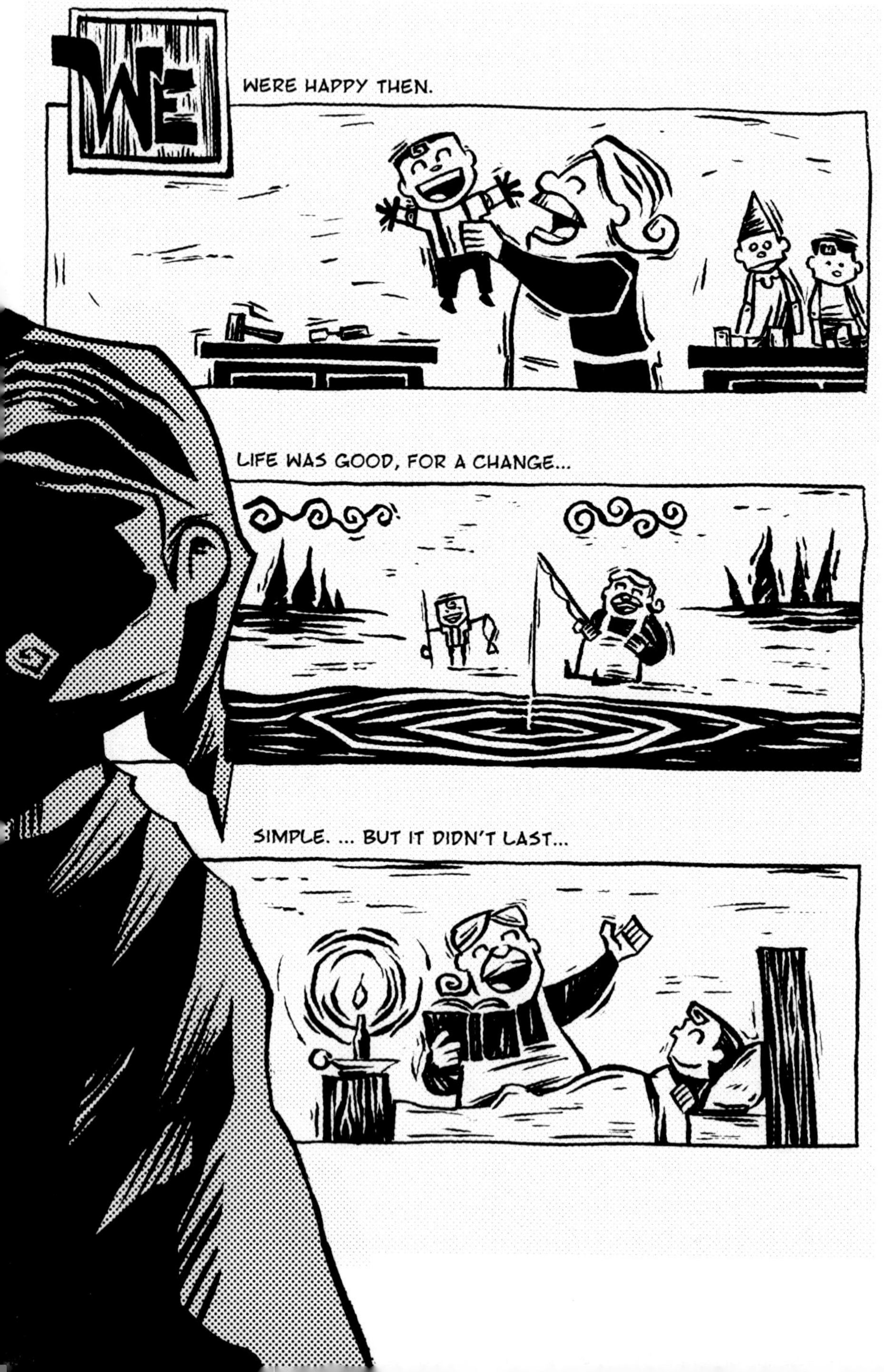
WE WERE HAPPY THEN.
LIFE WAS GOOD, FOR A CHANGE...
SIMPLE. ... BUT IT DIDN'T LAST...

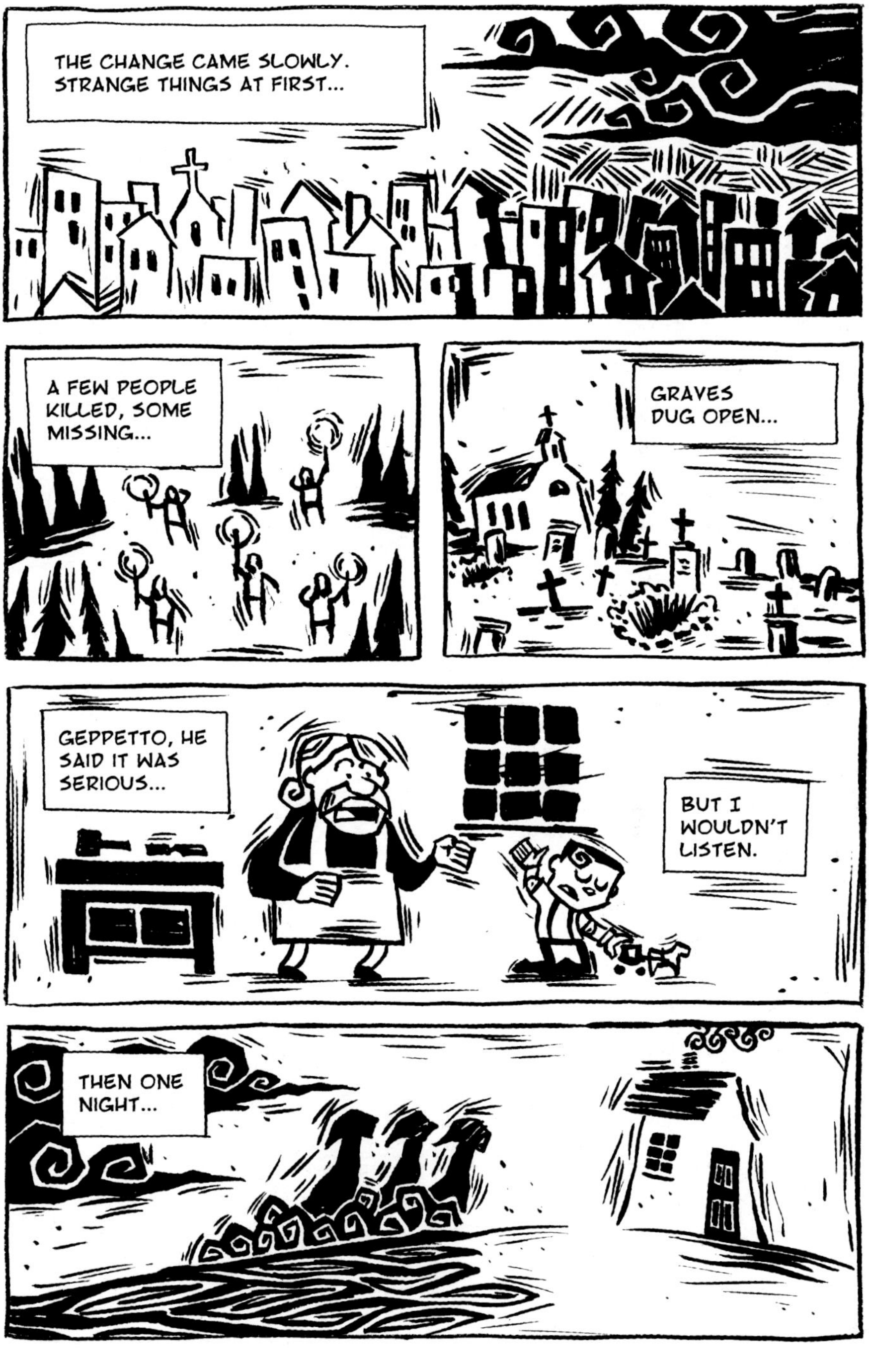

THE CHANGE CAME SLOWLY. STRANGE THINGS AT FIRST...
A FEW PEOPLE KILLED, SOME MISSING...
GRAVES DUG OPEN...
GEPPETTO, HE SAID IT WAS SERIOUS...
BUT I WOULDN'T LISTEN.
THEN ONE NIGHT...

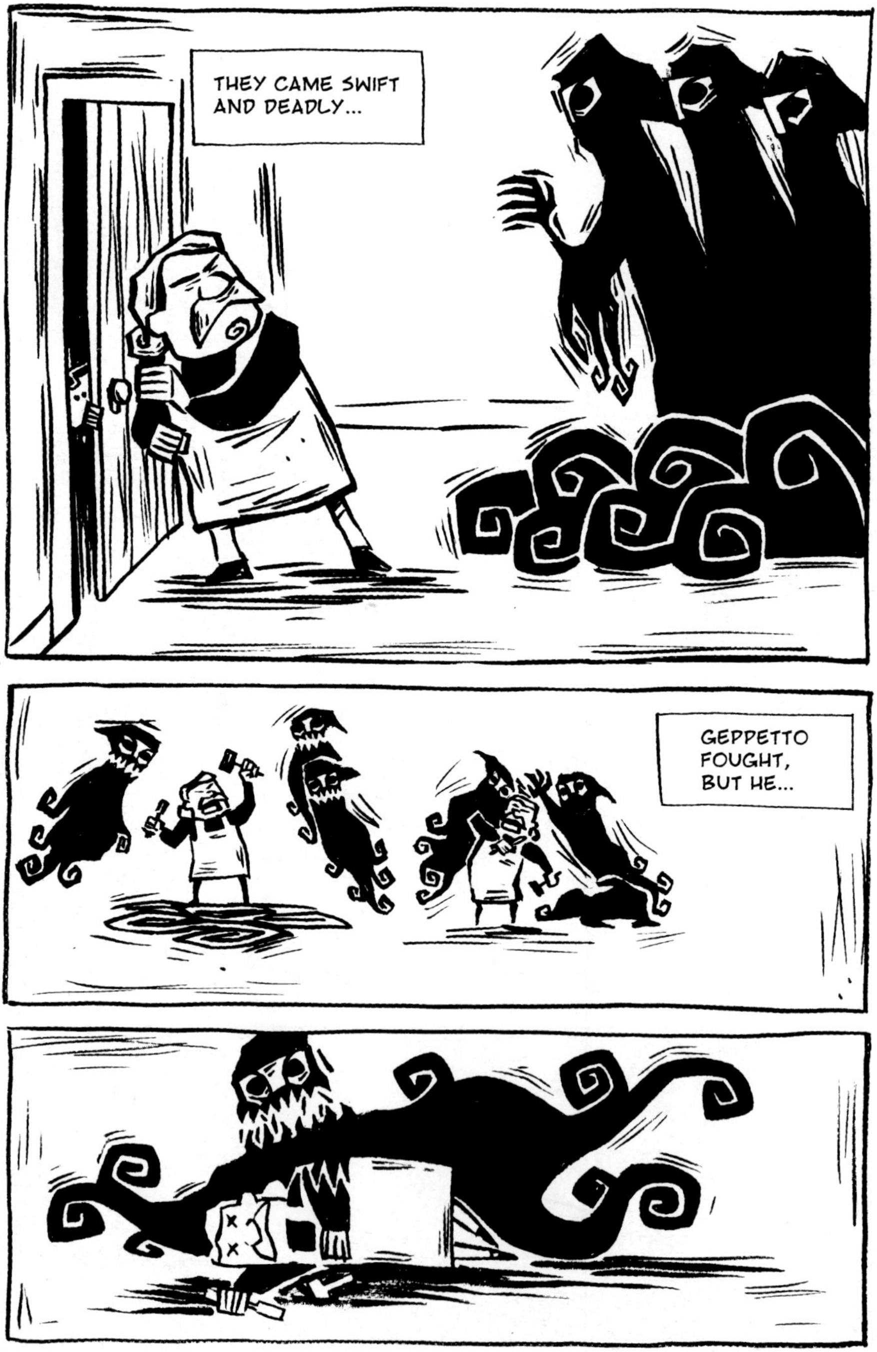
THEY CAME SWIFT AND DEADLY...
GEPPETTO FOUGHT, BUT HE...

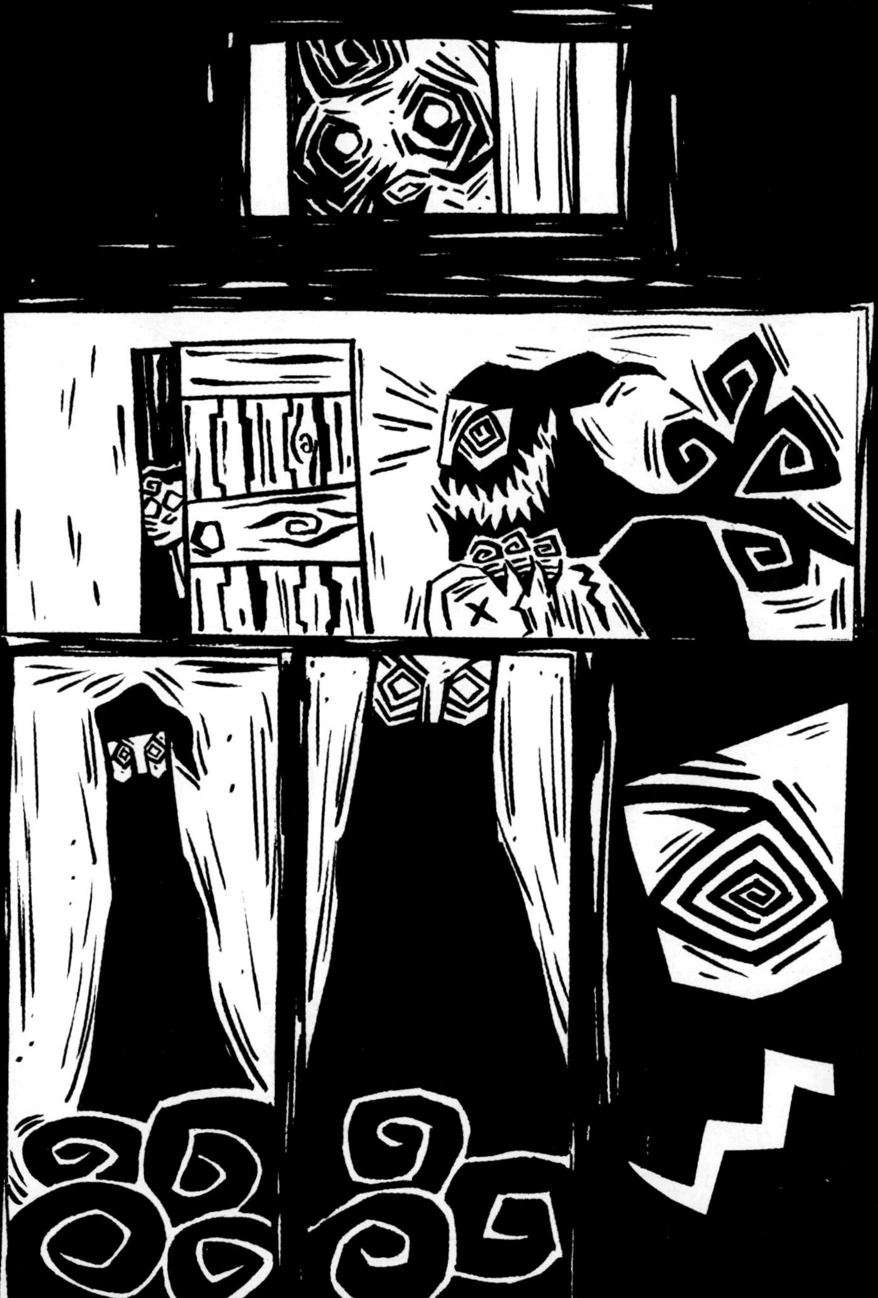

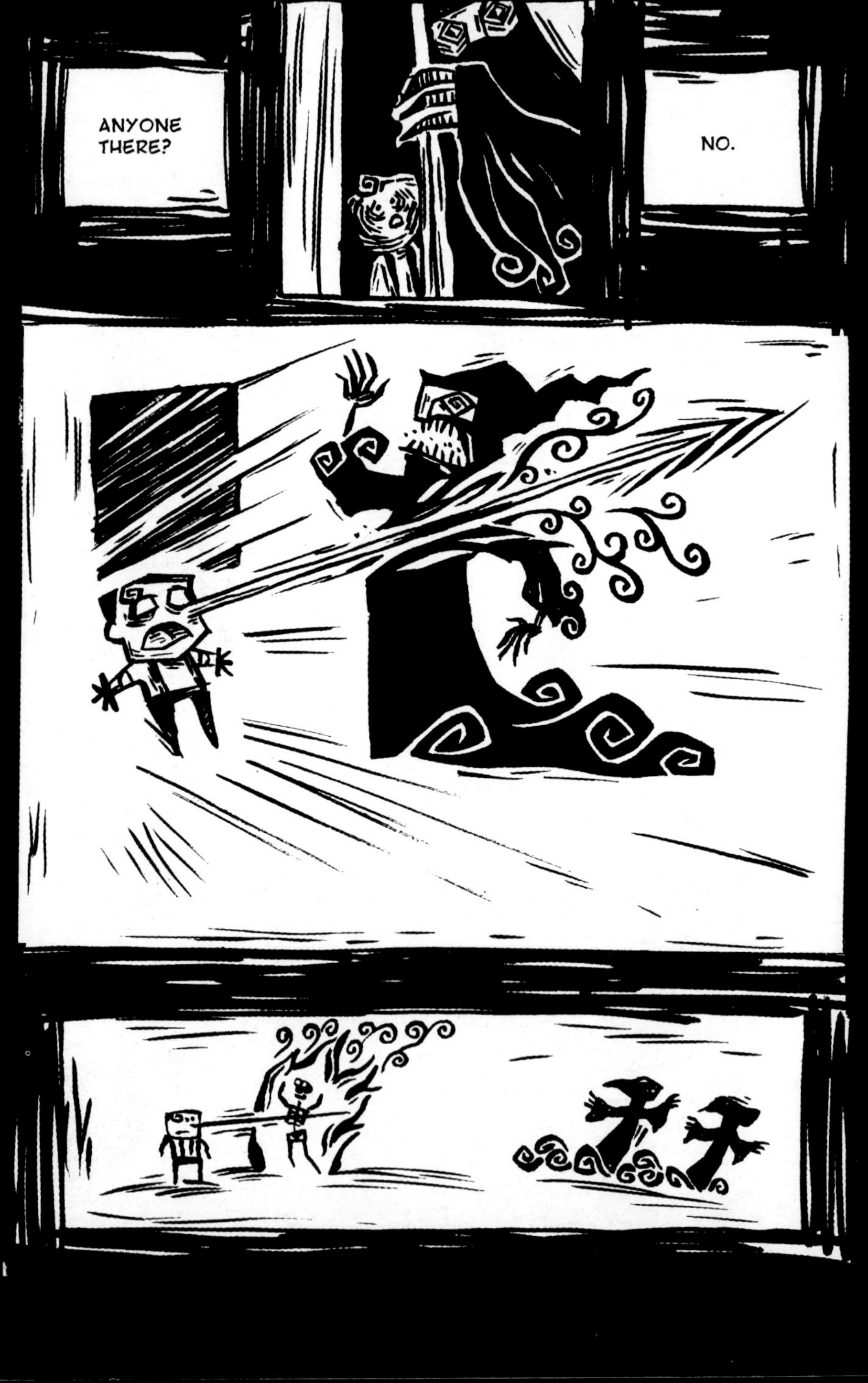
ANYONE THERE?
NO.

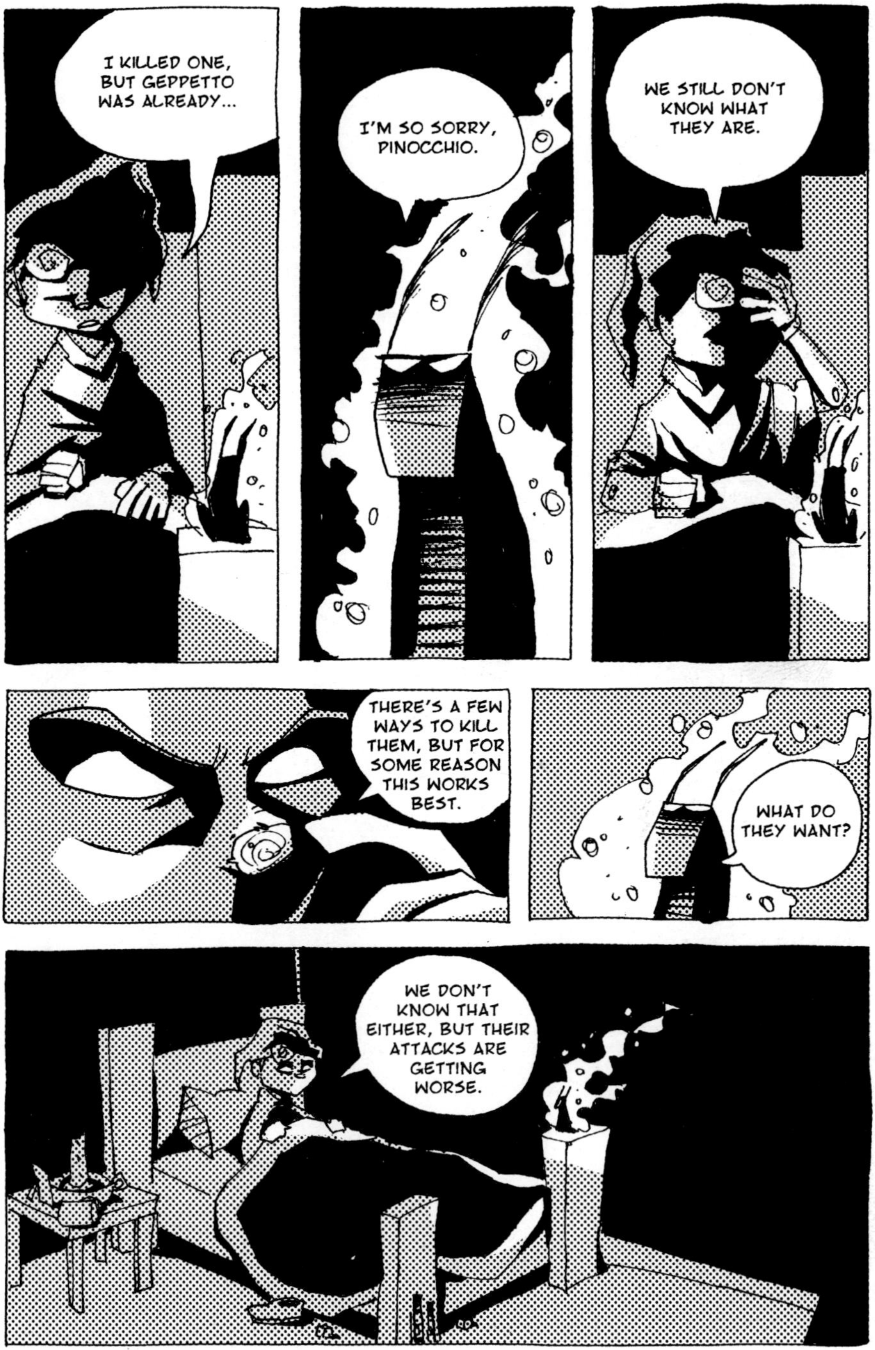
I KILLED ONE, BUT GEPPETTO WAS ALREADY...
I'M SO SORRY, PINOCCHIO.
WE STILL DON'T KNOW WHAT THEY ARE.
THERE'S A FEW WAYS TO KILL THEM, BUT FOR SOME REASON THIS WORKS BEST.
WHAT DO THEY WANT?
WE DON'T KNOW THAT EITHER, BUT THEIR ATTACKS ARE GETTING WORSE.

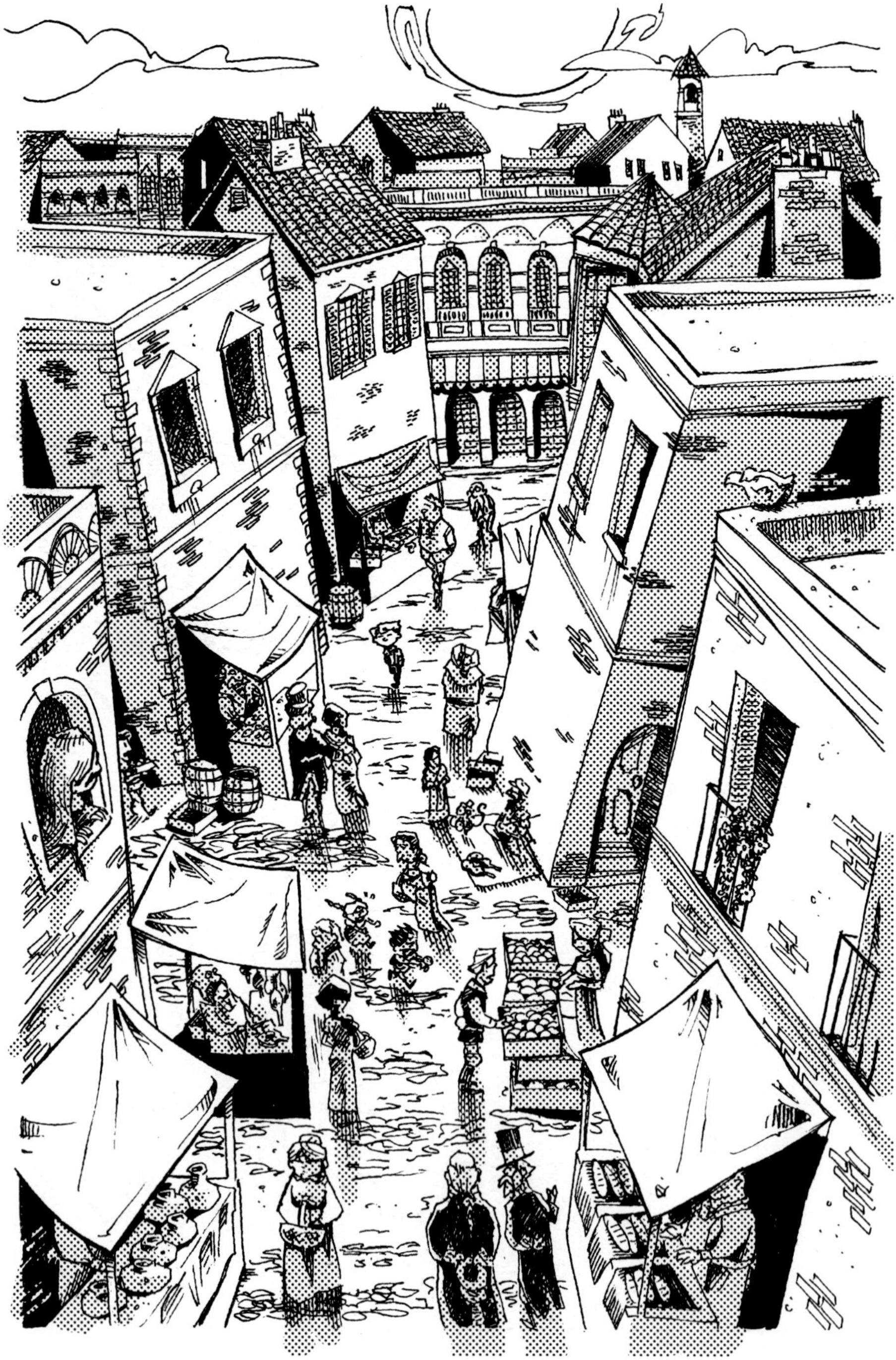

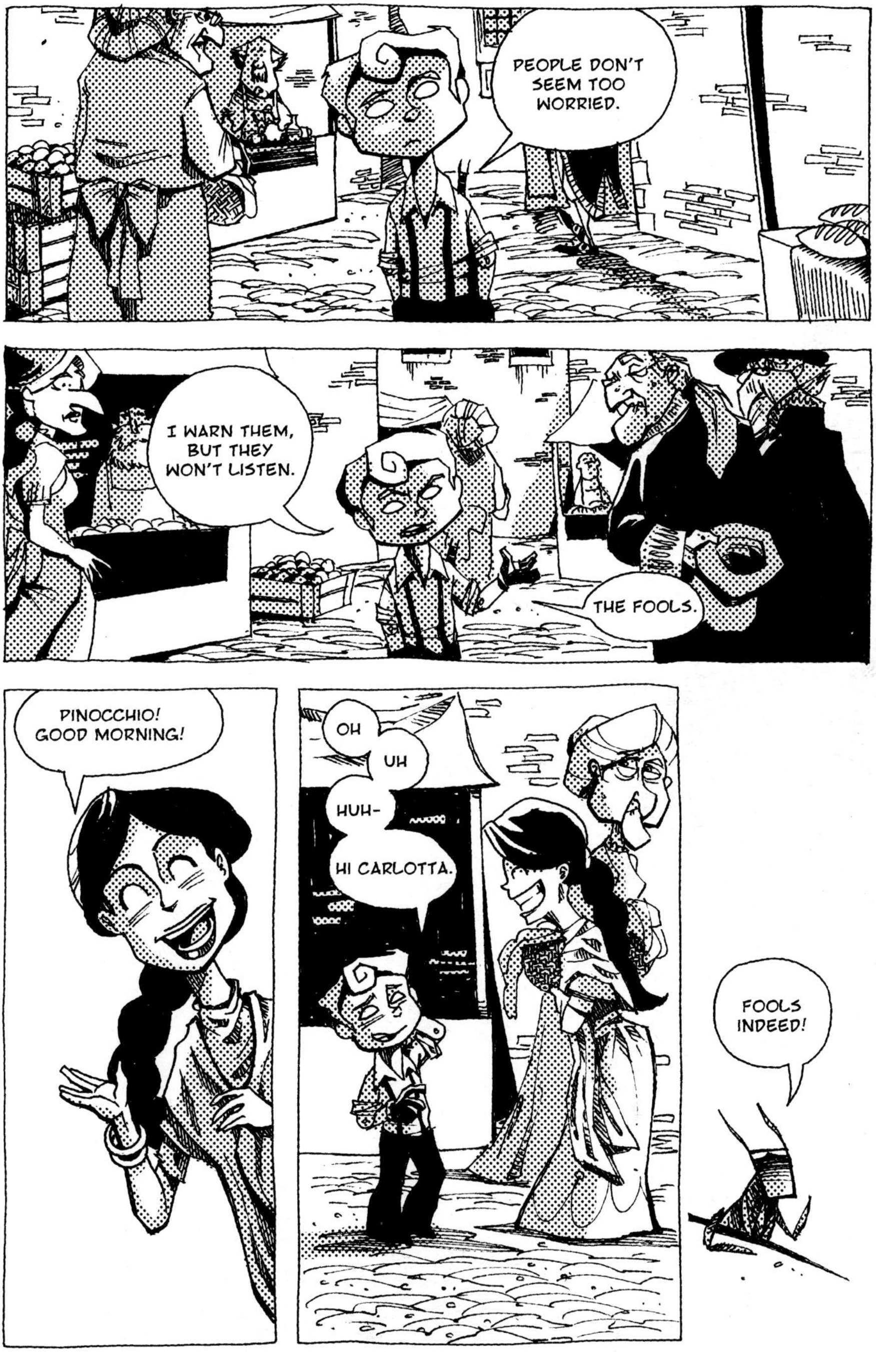
PEOPLE DON'T SEEM TOO WORRIED.
I WARN THEM, BUT THEY WON'T LISTEN.
THE FOOLS.
PINOCCHIO! GOOD MORNING!
OH
UH
HUH-
HI CARLOTTA.
FOOLS INDEED!

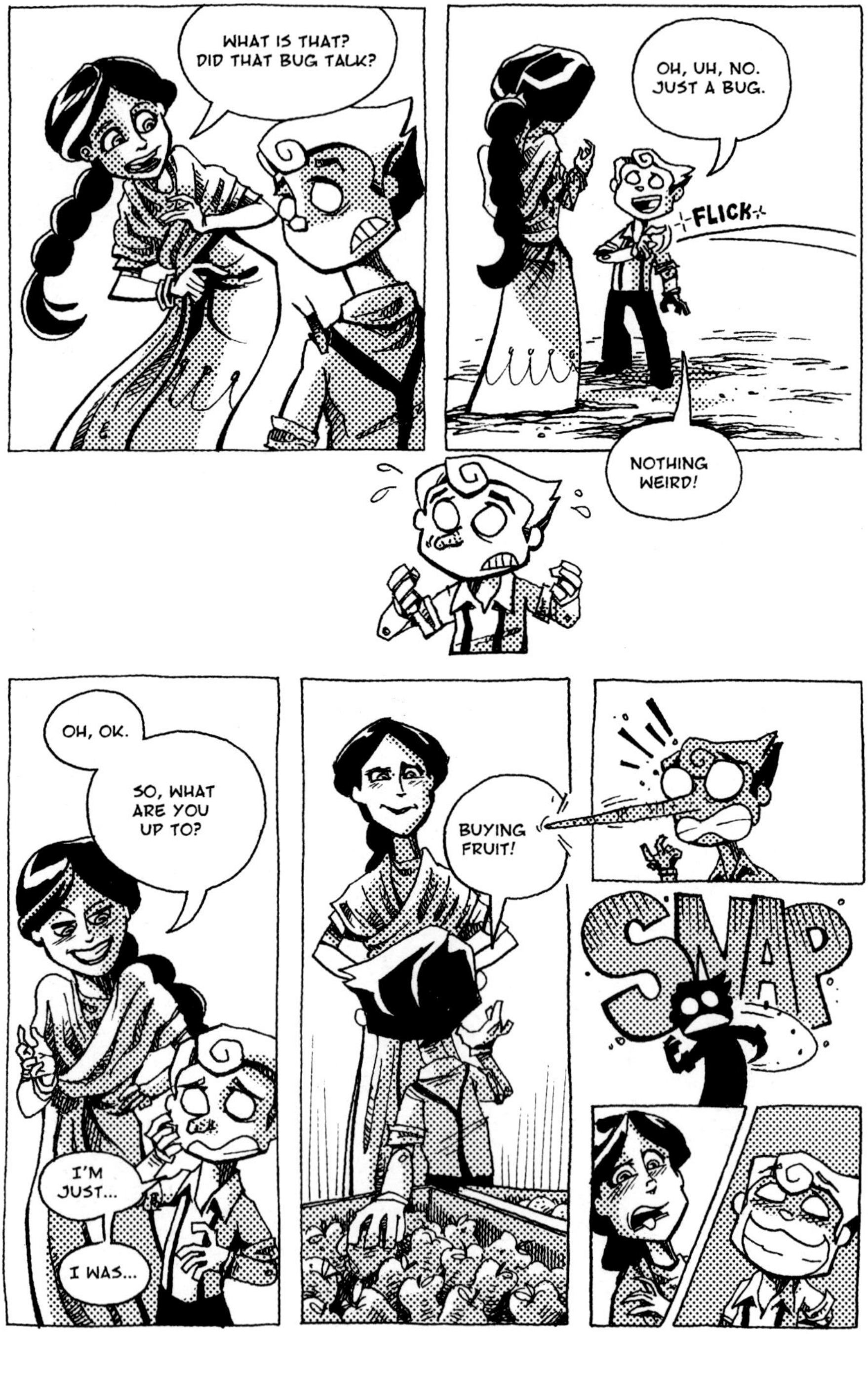
WHAT IS THAT?
DID THAT BUG TALK?
OH, UH, NO.
JUST A BUG.
FLICK
NOTHING
WEIRD!
OH, OK.
SO, WHAT
ARE YOU
UP TO?
I'M
JUST...
I WAS...
BUYING
FRUIT!
SNAP

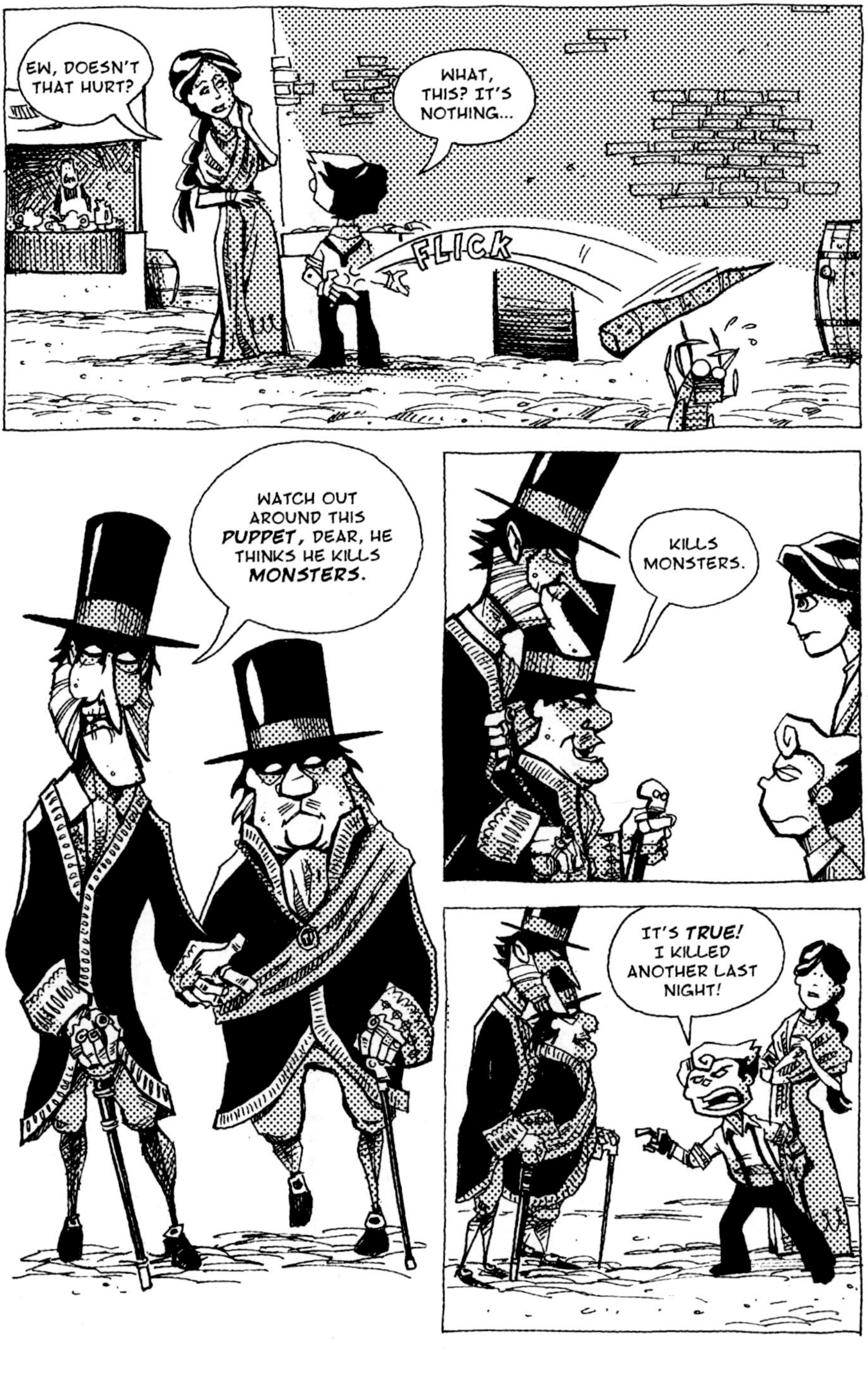
EW, DOESN'T THAT HURT?
WHAT, THIS? IT'S NOTHING...
FLICK
WATCH OUT AROUND THIS PUPPET, DEAR, HE THINKS HE KILLS MONSTERS.
KILLS MONSTERS.
IT'S TRUE! I KILLED ANOTHER LAST NIGHT!

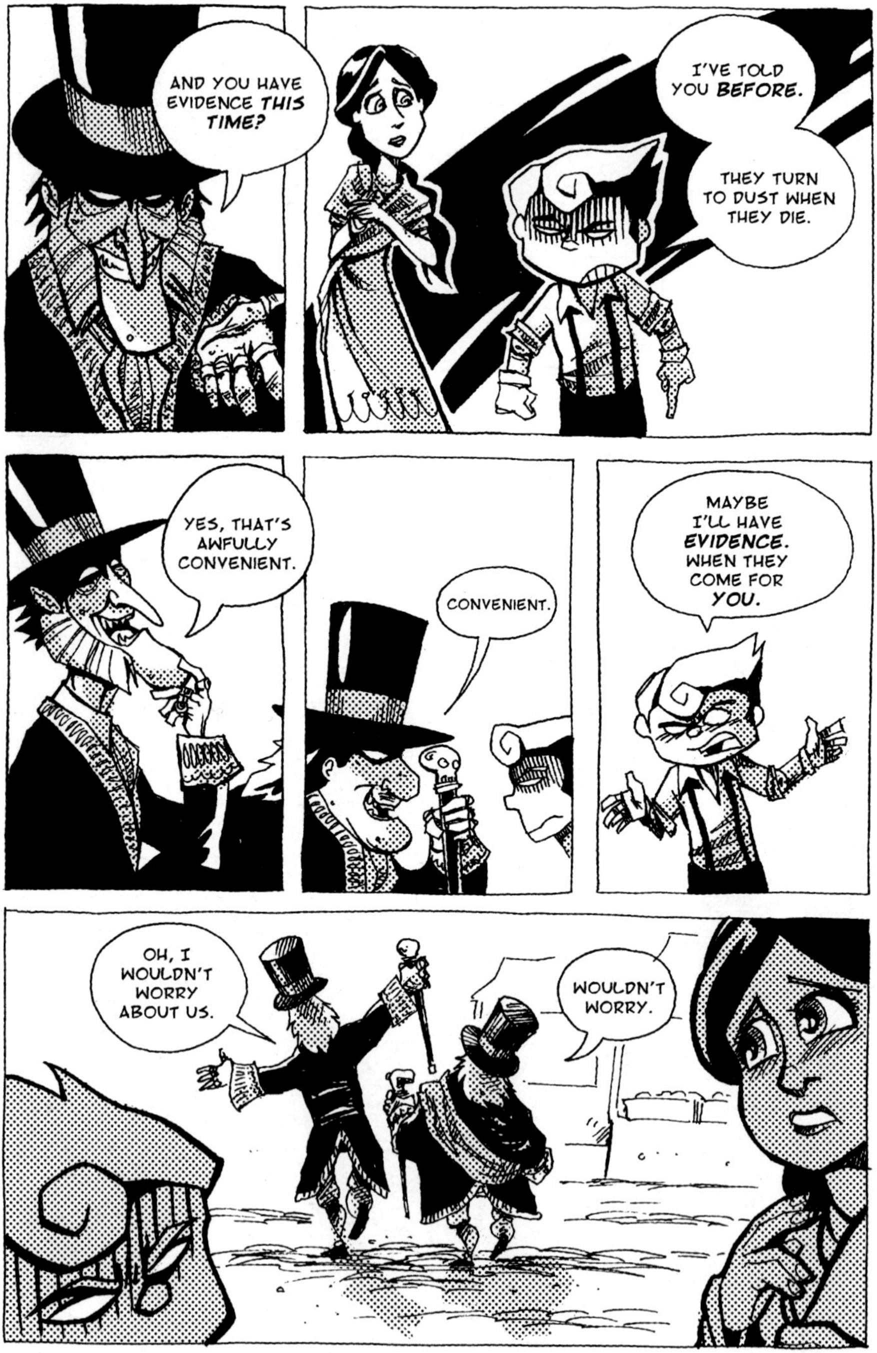
AND YOU HAVE EVIDENCE THIS TIME?
I'VE TOLD YOU BEFORE.
THEY TURN TO DUST WHEN THEY DIE.
YES, THAT'S AWFULLY CONVENIENT.
CONVENIENT.
MAYBE I'LL HAVE EVIDENCE. WHEN THEY COME FOR YOU.
OH, I WOULDN'T WORRY ABOUT US.
WOULDN'T WORRY.

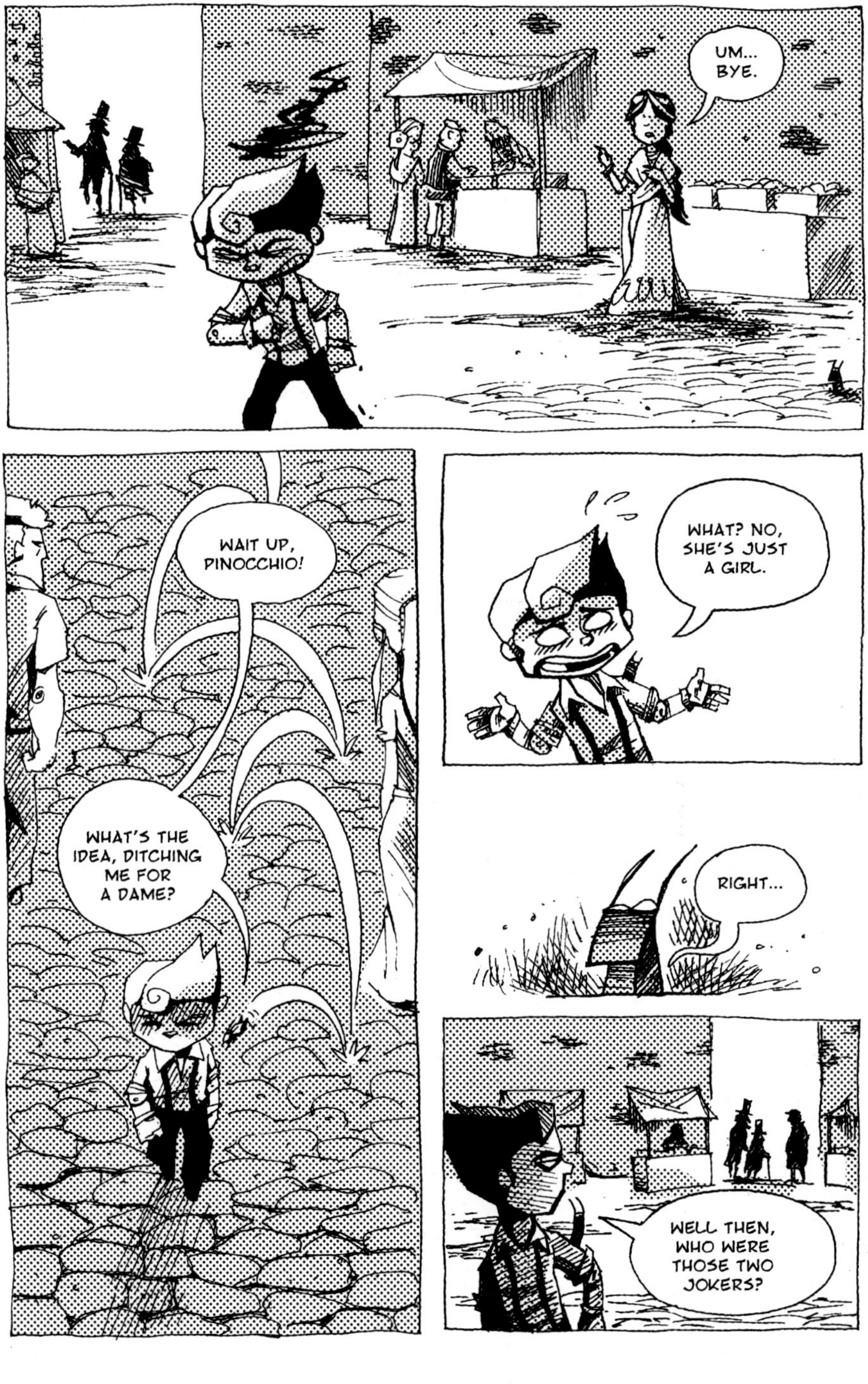
UM... BYE.
WAIT UP, PINOCCHIO!
WHAT'S THE IDEA, DITCHING ME FOR A DAME?
WHAT? NO, SHE'S JUST A GIRL.
RIGHT...
WELL THEN, WHO WERE THOSE TWO JOKERS?

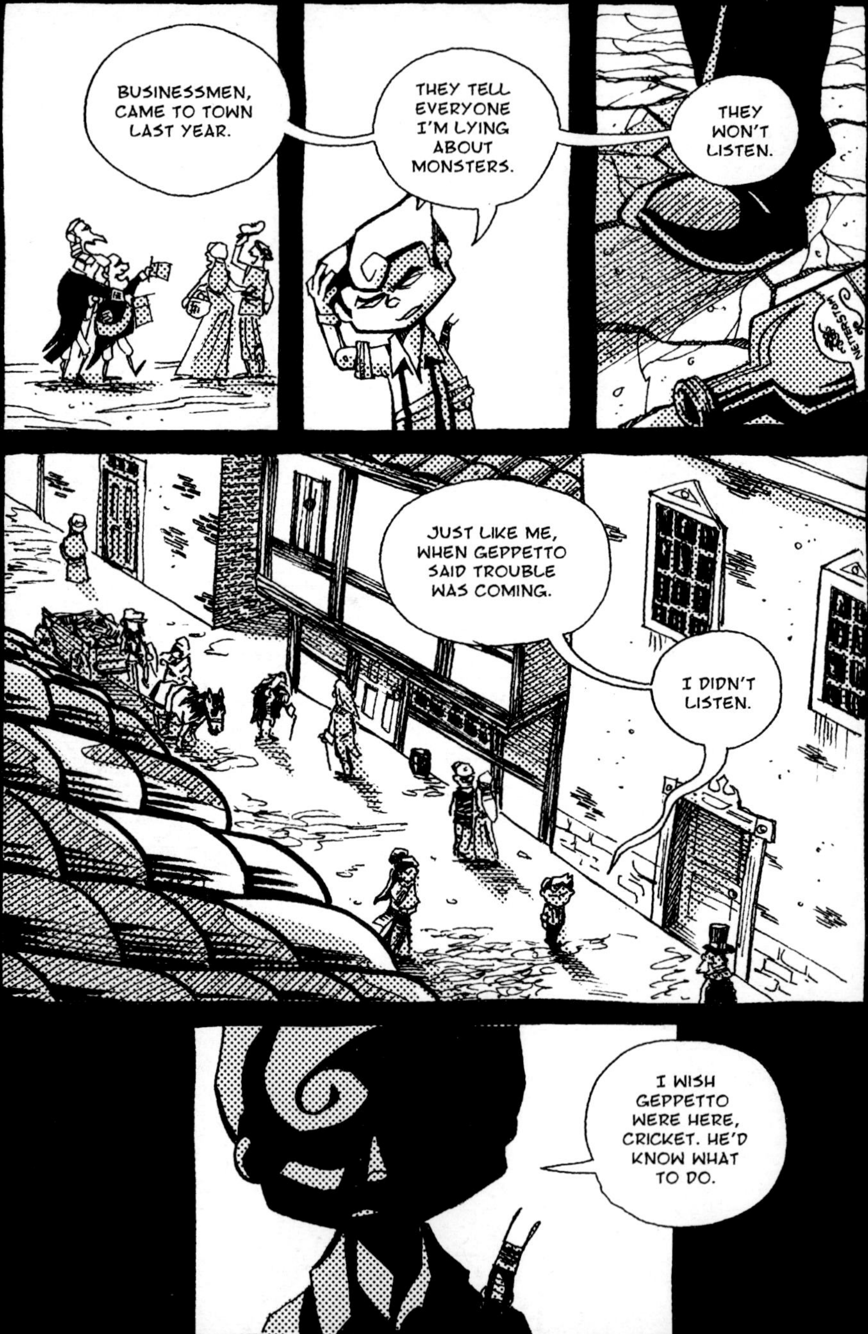
BUSINESSMEN, CAME TO TOWN LAST YEAR.
THEY TELL EVERYONE I'M LYING ABOUT MONSTERS.
THEY WON'T LISTEN.
JUST LIKE ME, WHEN GEPPETTO SAID TROUBLE WAS COMING.
I DIDN'T LISTEN.
I WISH GEPPETTO WERE HERE, CRICKET. HE'D KNOW WHAT TO DO.

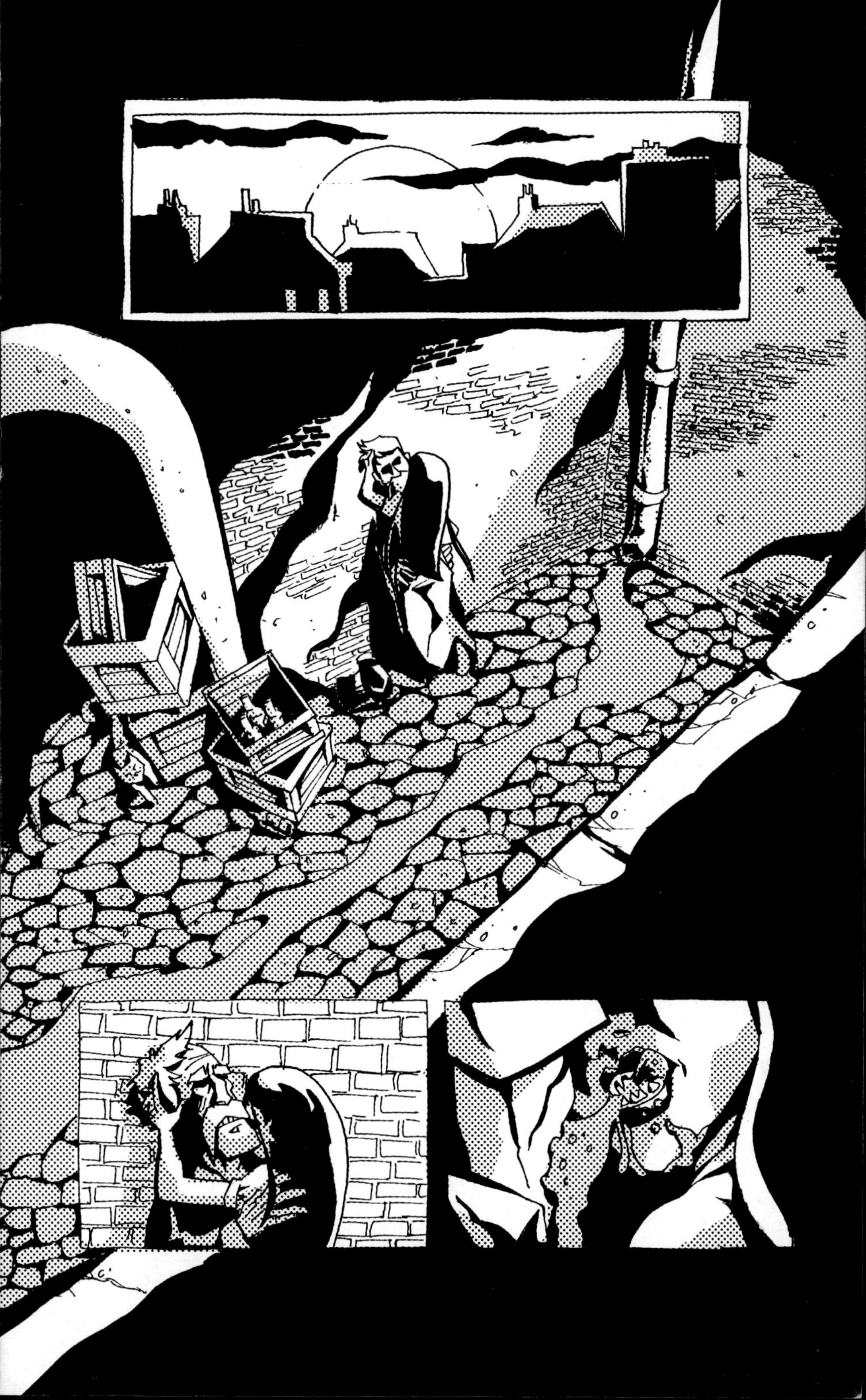

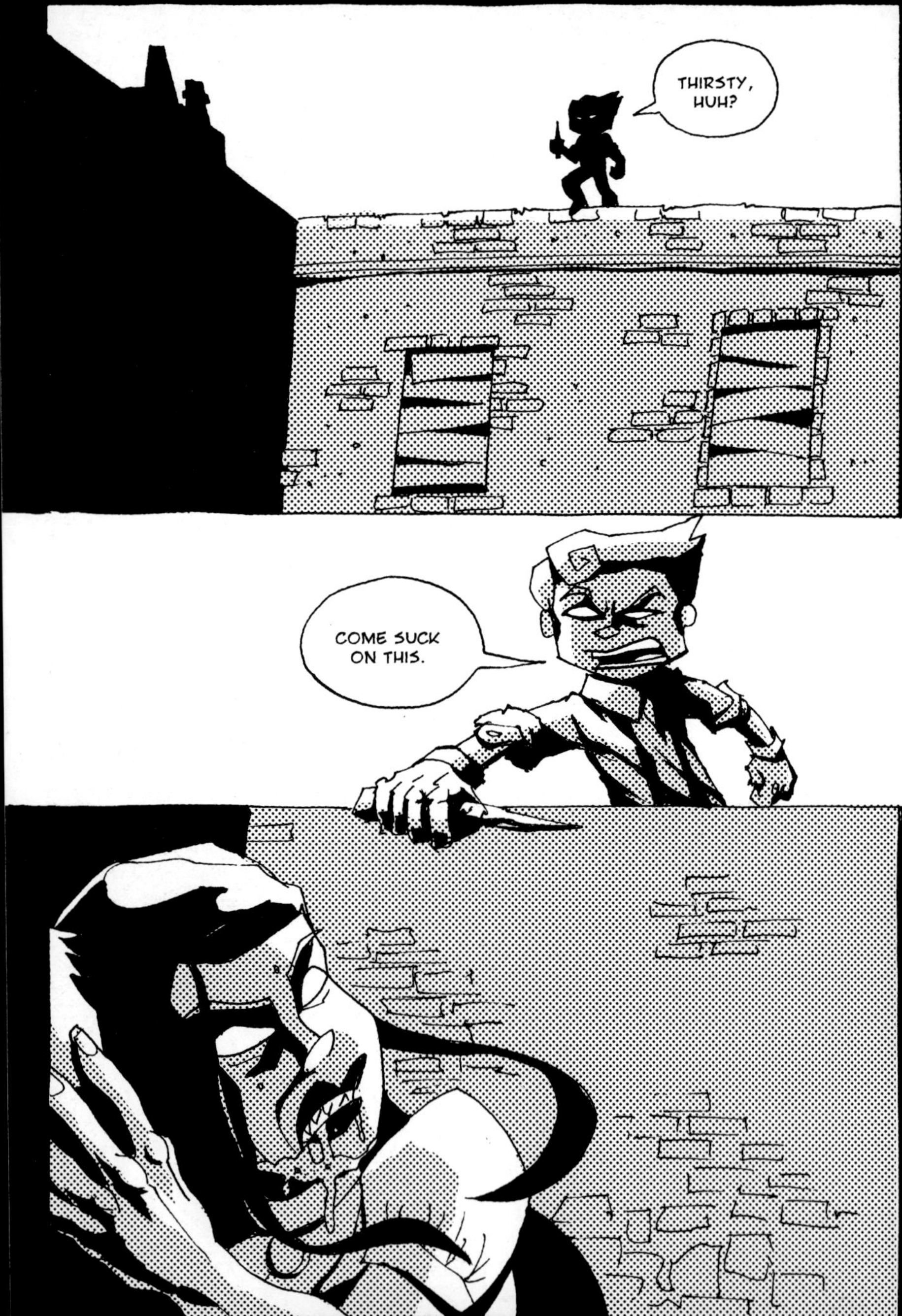
THIRSTY, HUH?
COME SUCK ON THIS.

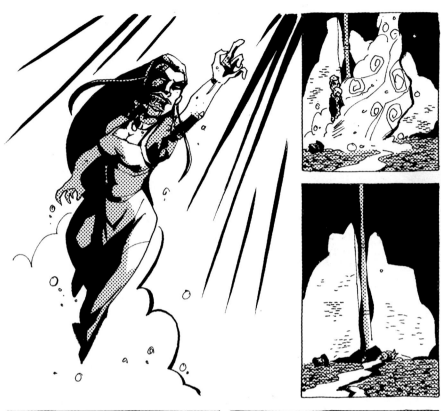

GOTCHA!

NOW, TIME FOR SOME Q&A.

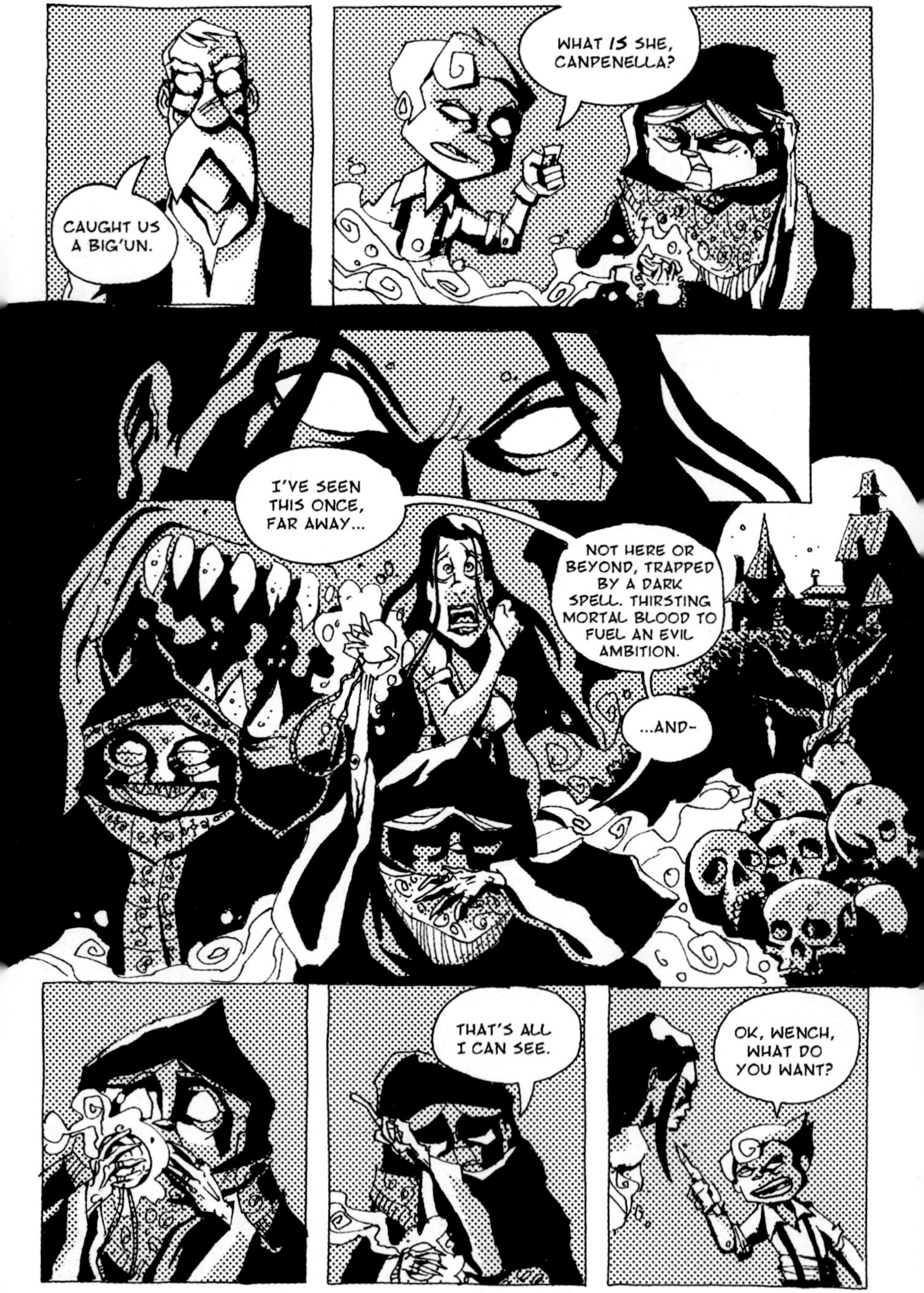
CAUGHT US A BIG'UN.
WHAT IS SHE, CANPENELLA?
I'VE SEEN THIS ONCE, FAR AWAY...
NOT HERE OR BEYOND, TRAPPED BY A DARK SPELL. THIRSTING MORTAL BLOOD TO FUEL AN EVIL AMBITION.
...AND-
THAT'S ALL I CAN SEE.
OK, WENCH, WHAT DO YOU WANT?

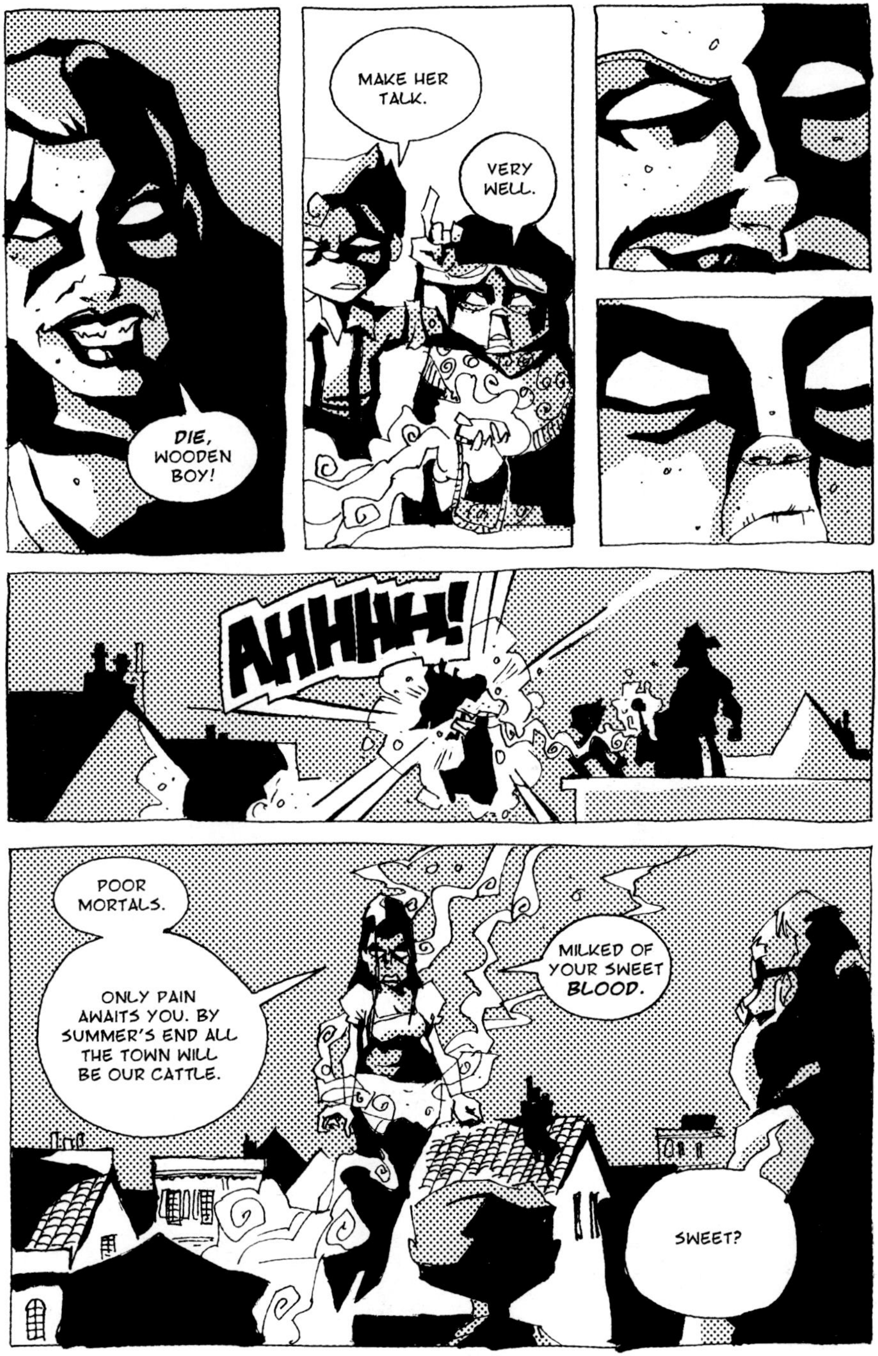
DIE, WOODEN BOY!
MAKE HER TALK.
VERY WELL.
AHHHH!
POOR MORTALS.
ONLY PAIN AWAITS YOU. BY SUMMER'S END ALL THE TOWN WILL BE OUR CATTLE.
MILKED OF YOUR SWEET BLOOD.
SWEET?

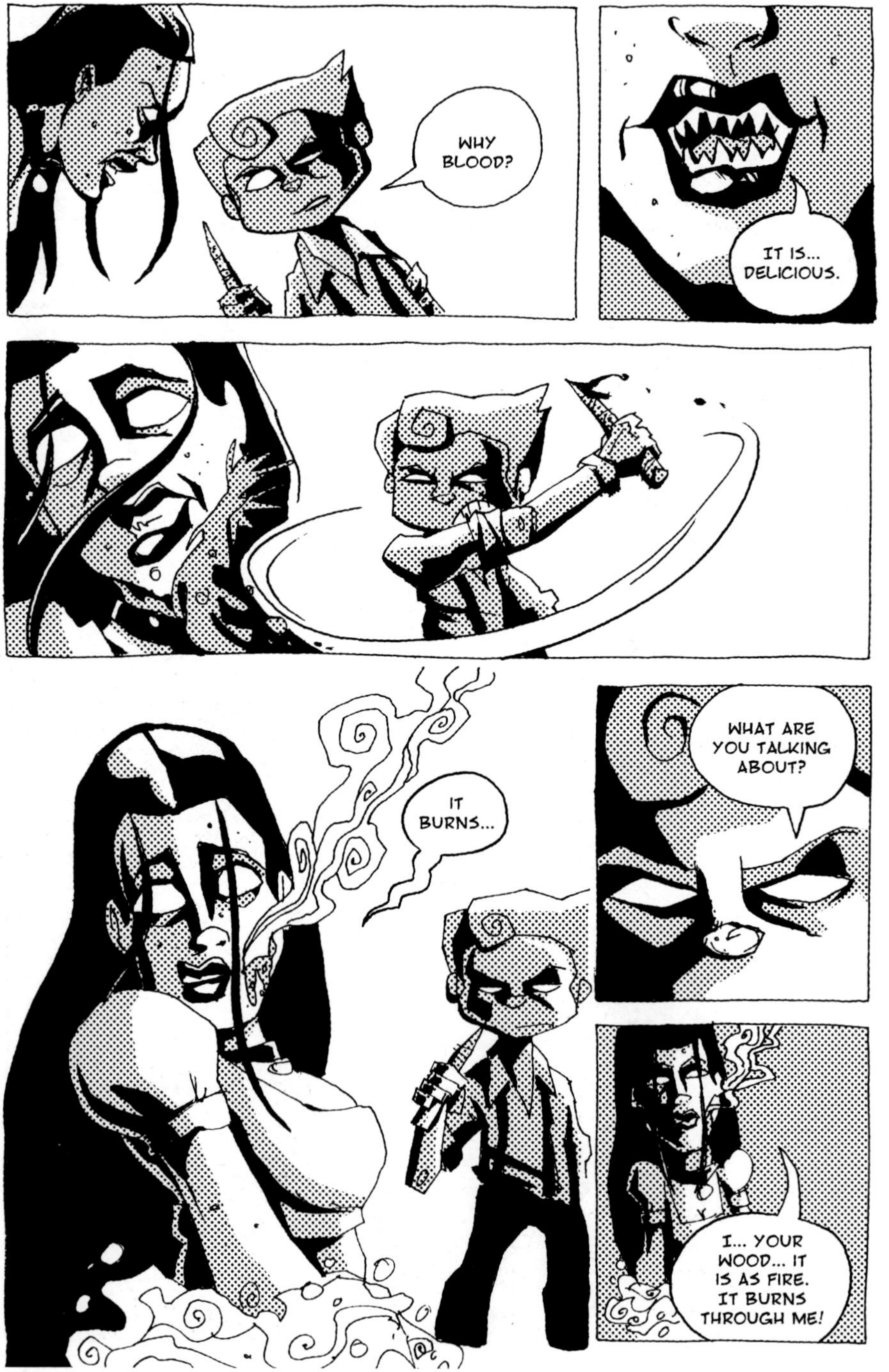
WHY BLOOD?
IT IS... DELICIOUS.
IT BURNS...
WHAT ARE YOU TALKING ABOUT?
I... YOUR WOOD... IT IS AS FIRE. IT BURNS THROUGH ME!

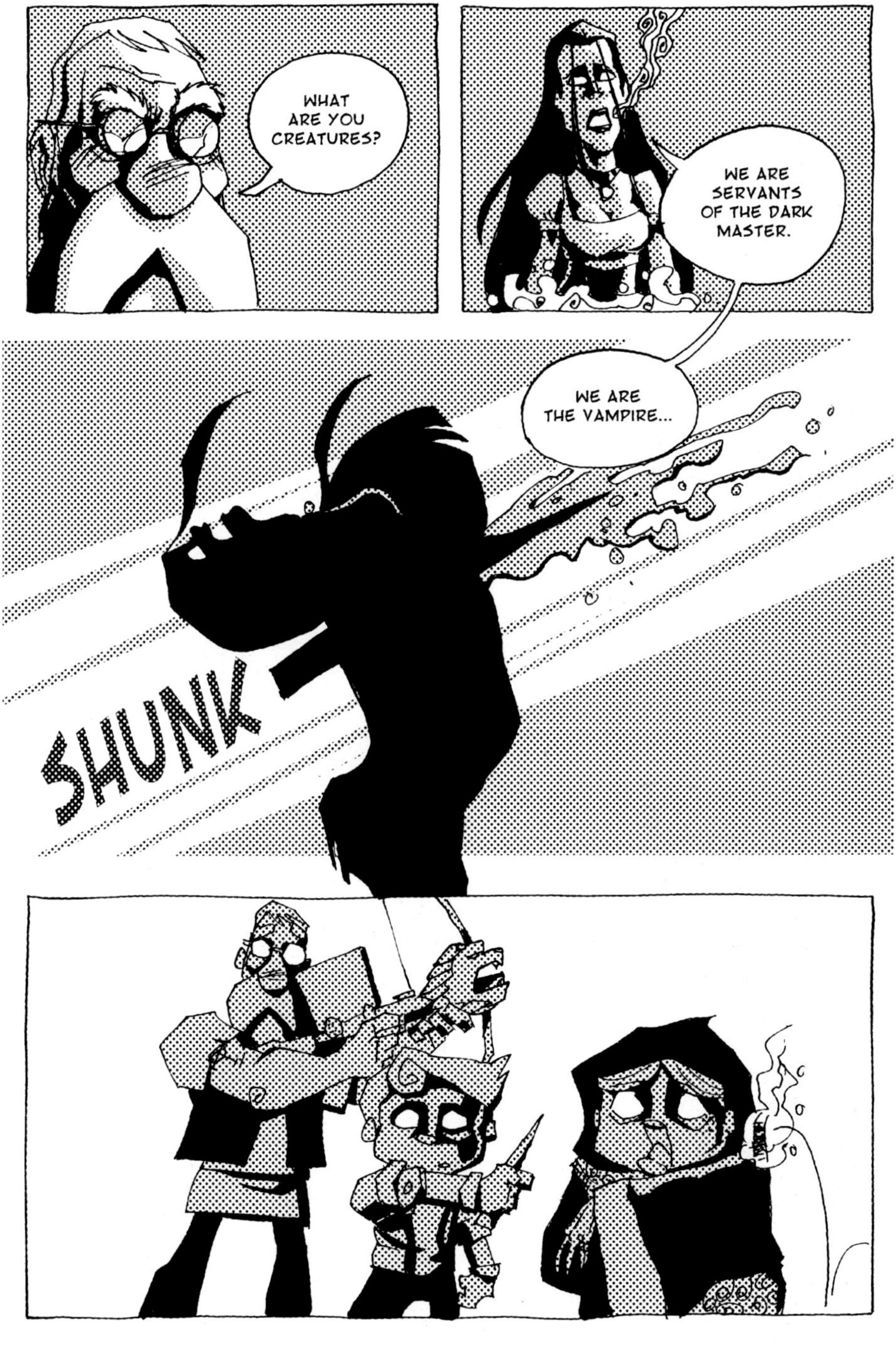
WHAT ARE YOU CREATURES?
WE ARE SERVANTS OF THE DARK MASTER.
WE ARE THE VAMPIRE...
SHUNK

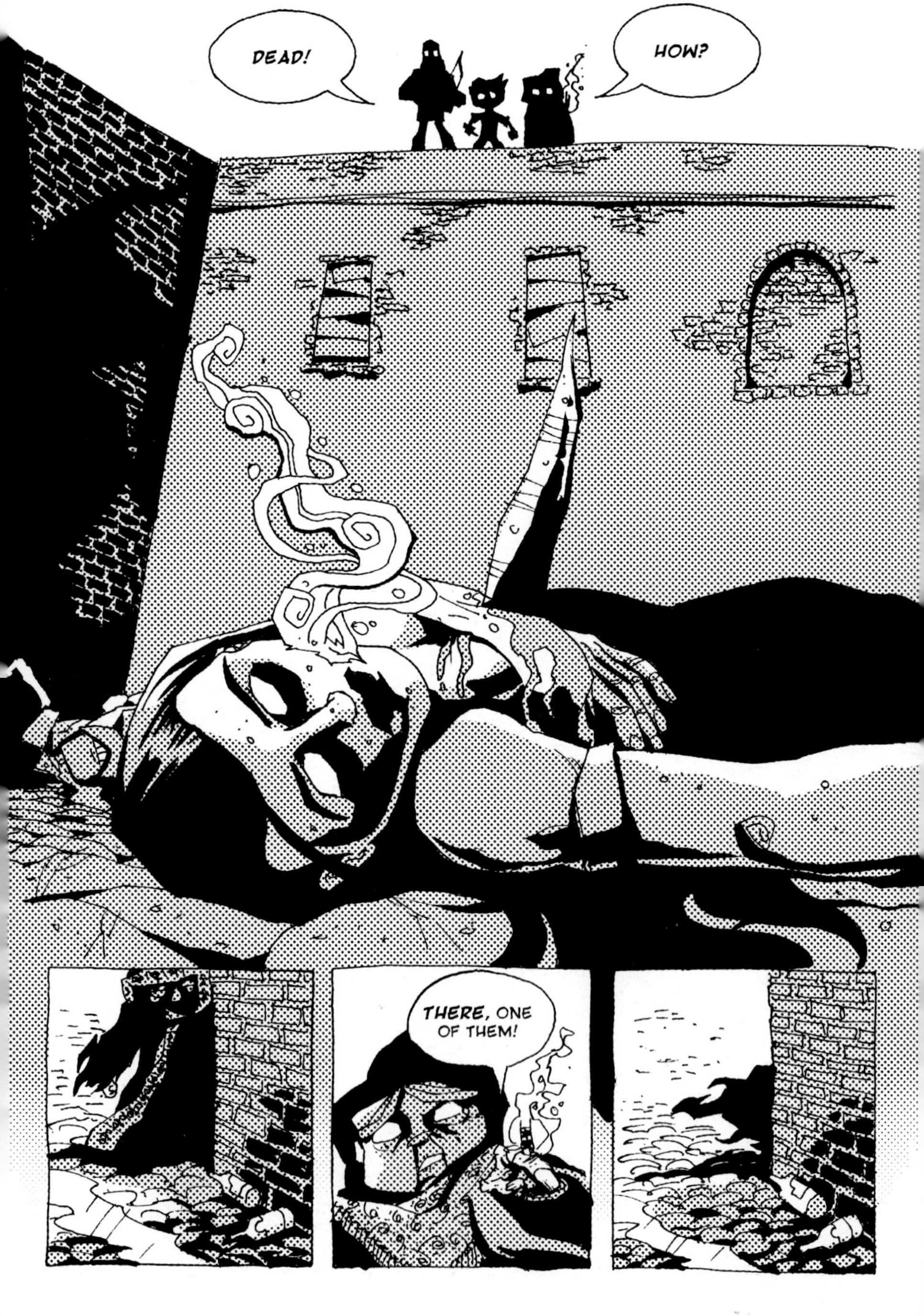

DEAD!
HOW?
THERE, ONE OF THEM!

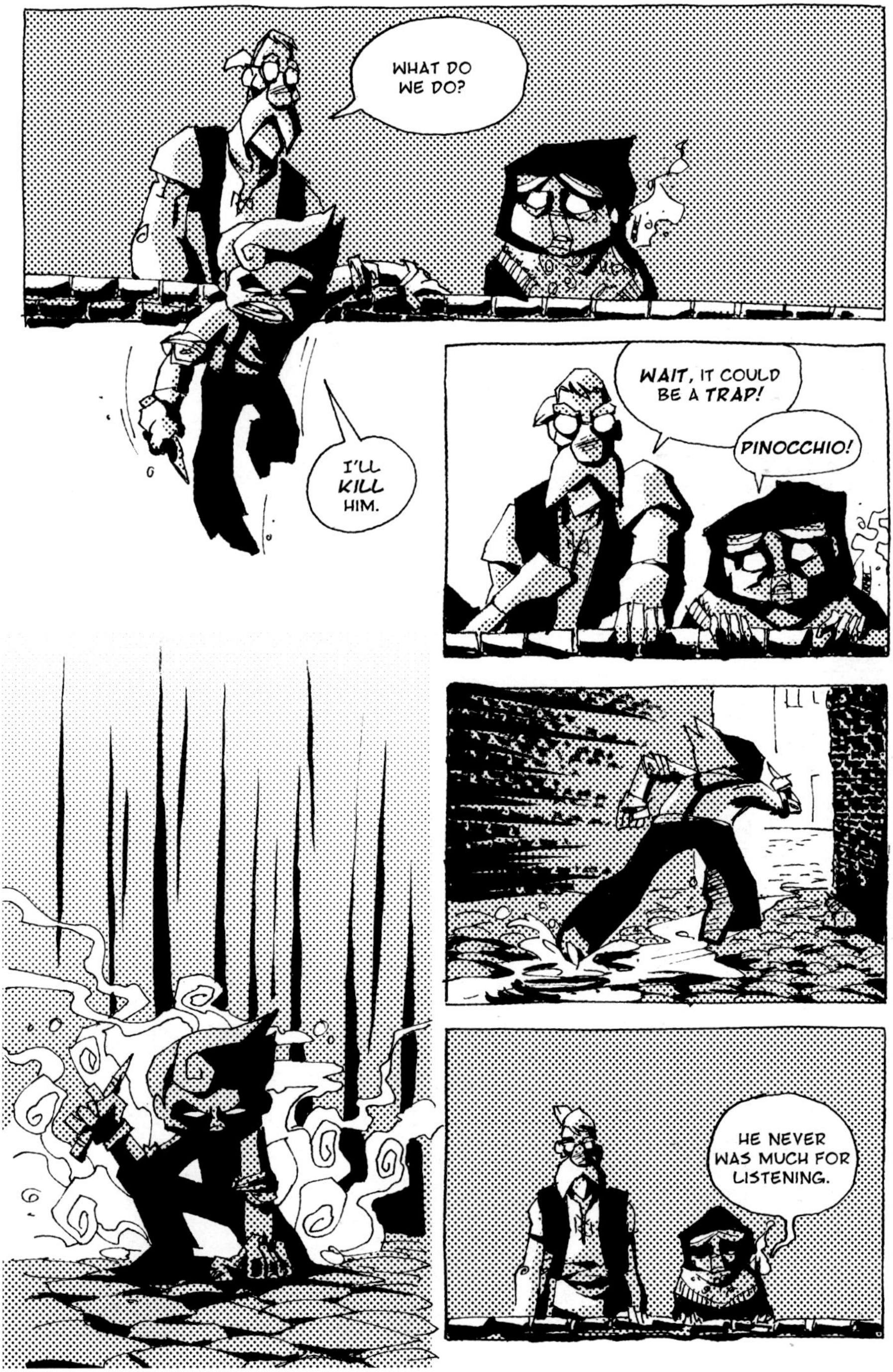
WHAT DO WE DO?
I'LL KILL HIM.
WAIT, IT COULD BE A TRAP!
PINOCCHIO!
HE NEVER WAS MUCH FOR LISTENING.

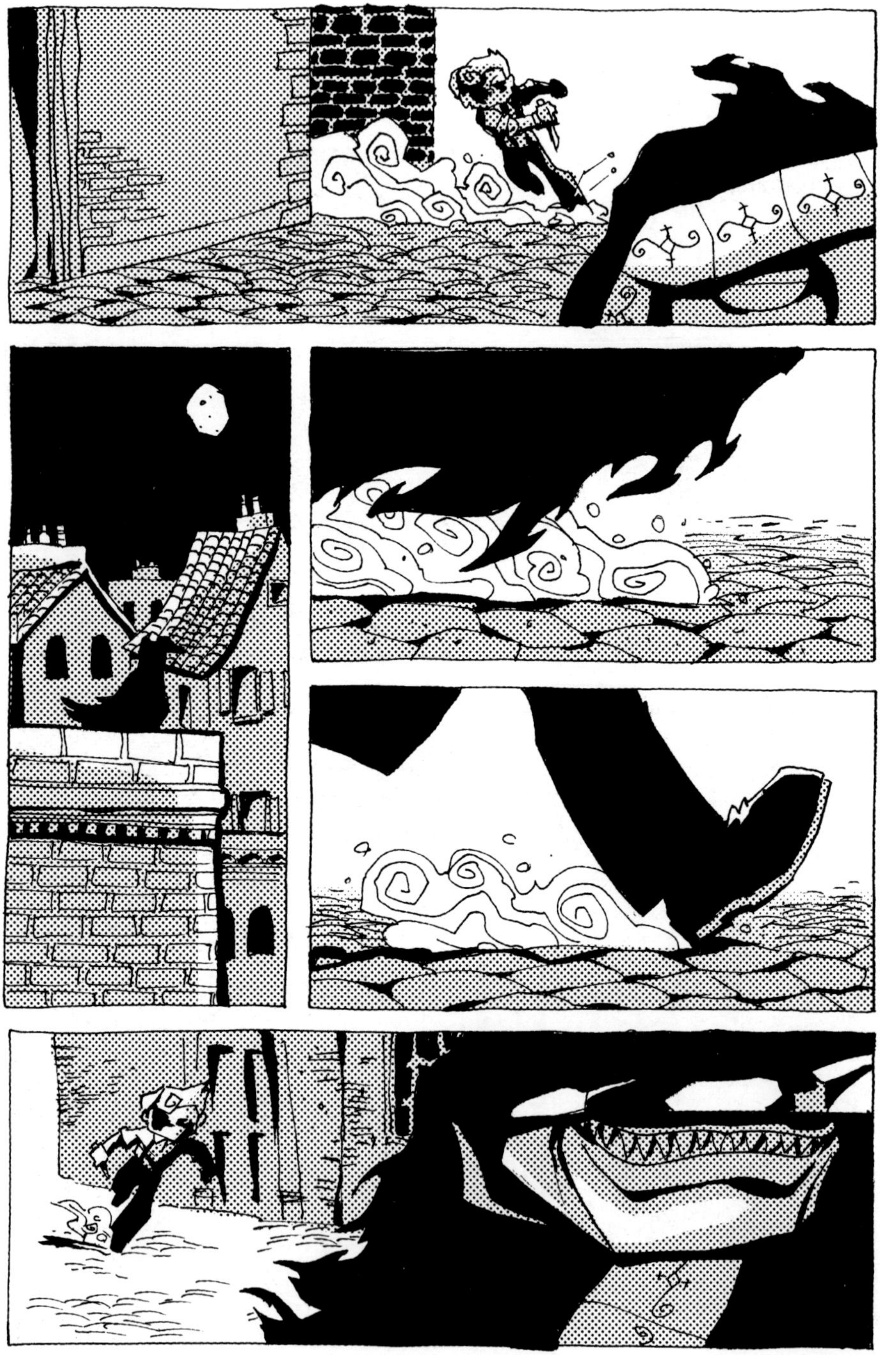

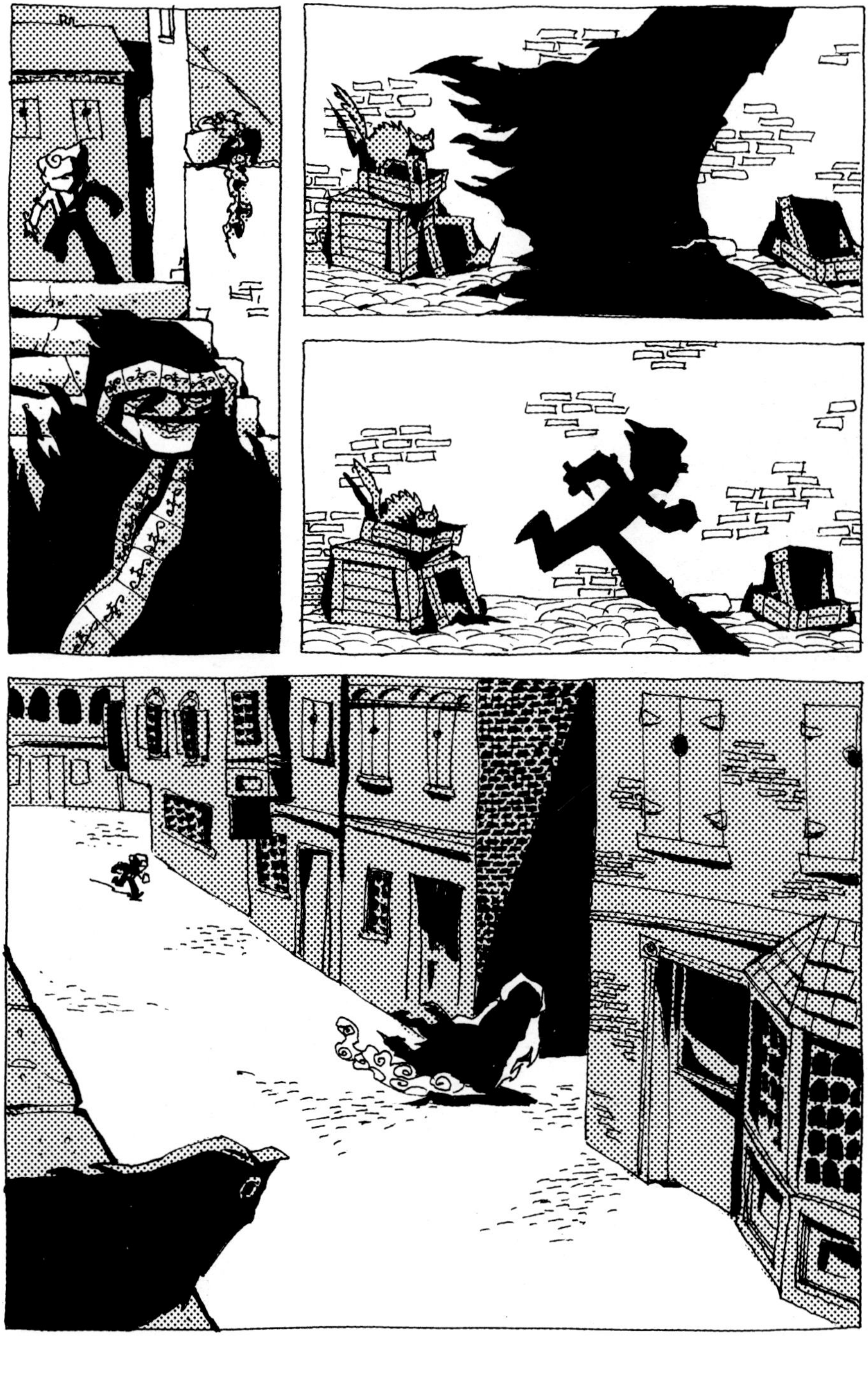

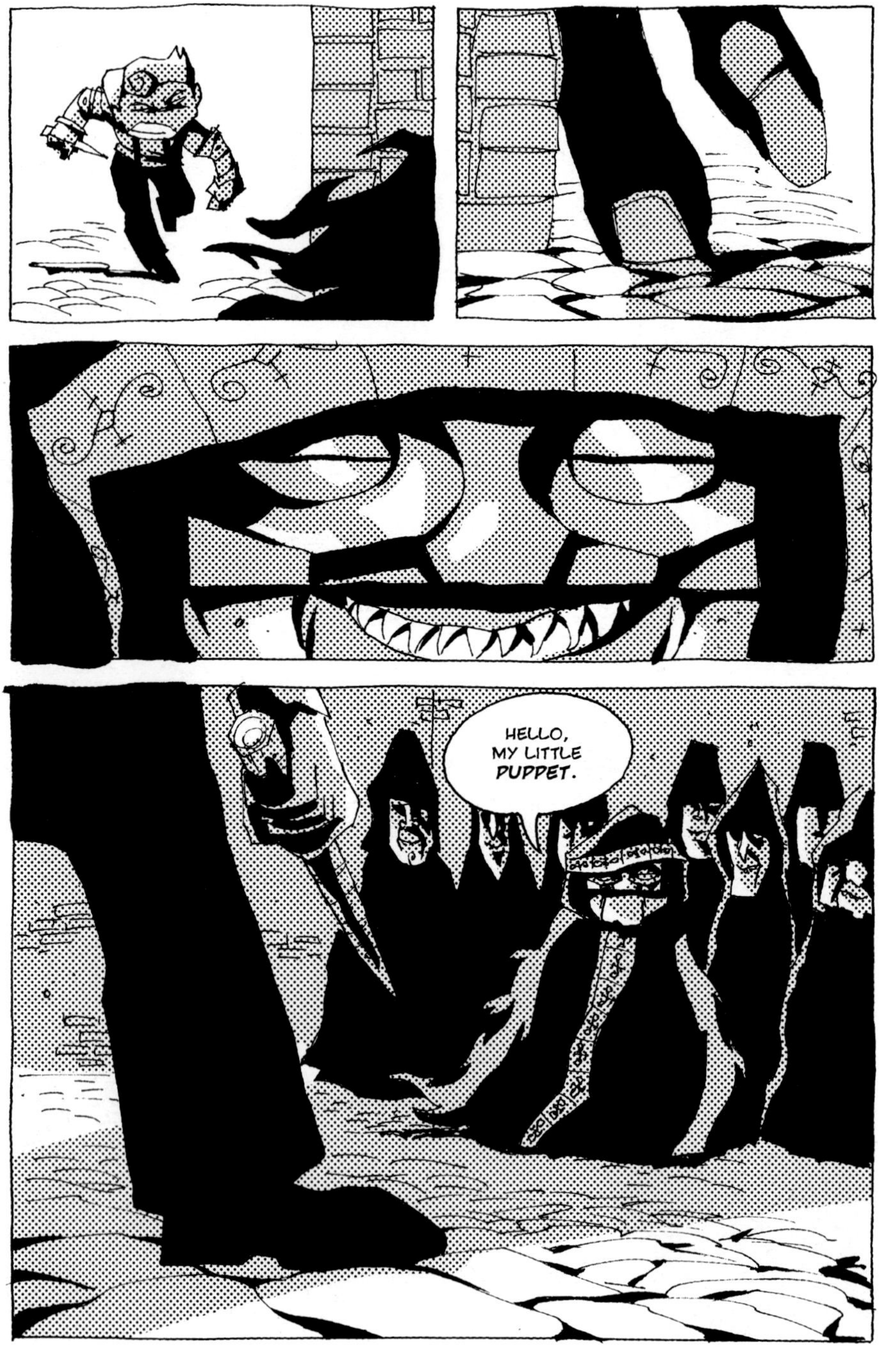
HELLO, MY LITTLE PUPPET.

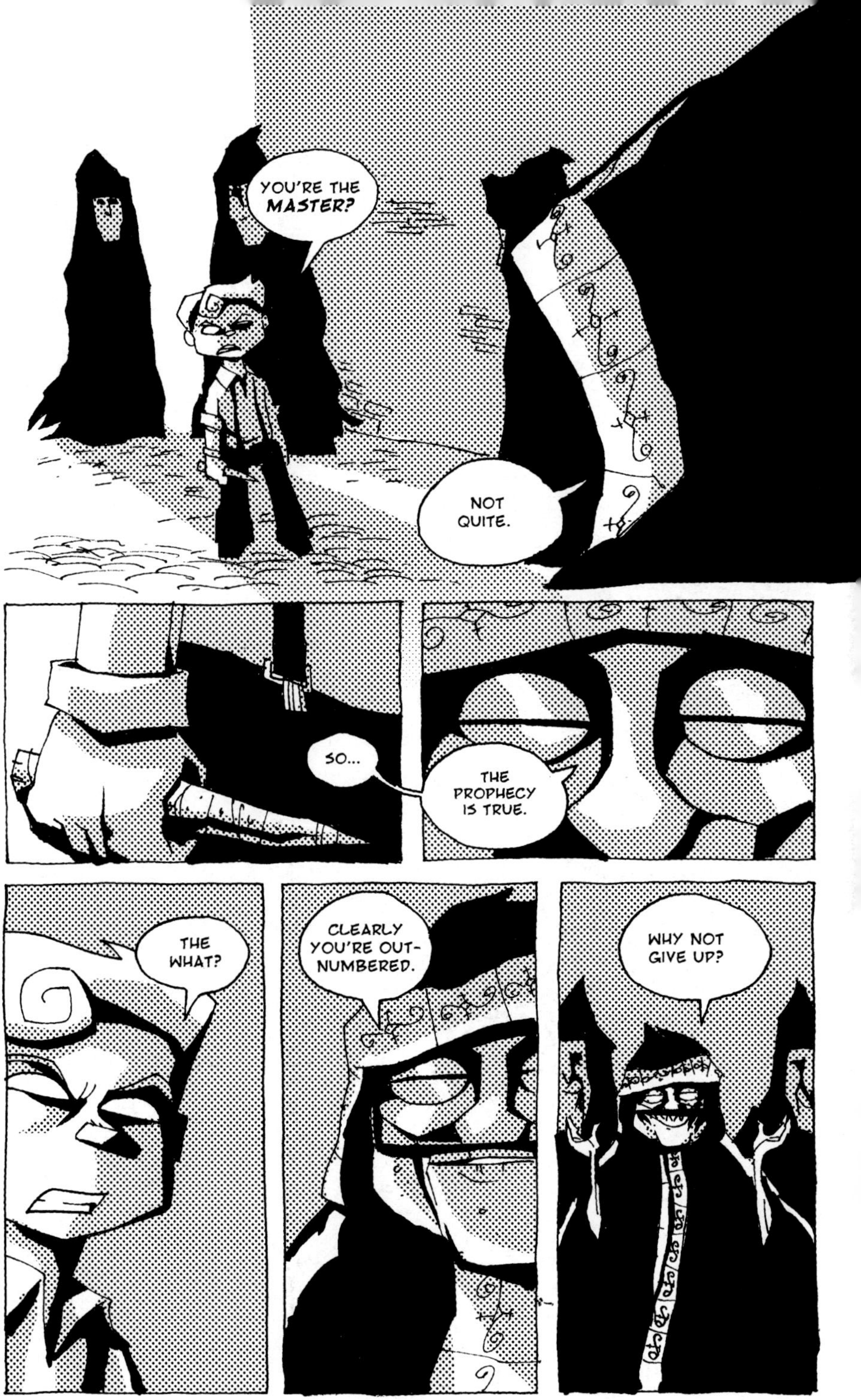
YOU'RE THE MASTER?
NOT QUITE.
SO...
THE PROPHECY IS TRUE.
THE WHAT?
CLEARLY YOU'RE OUT-NUMBERED.
WHY NOT GIVE UP?

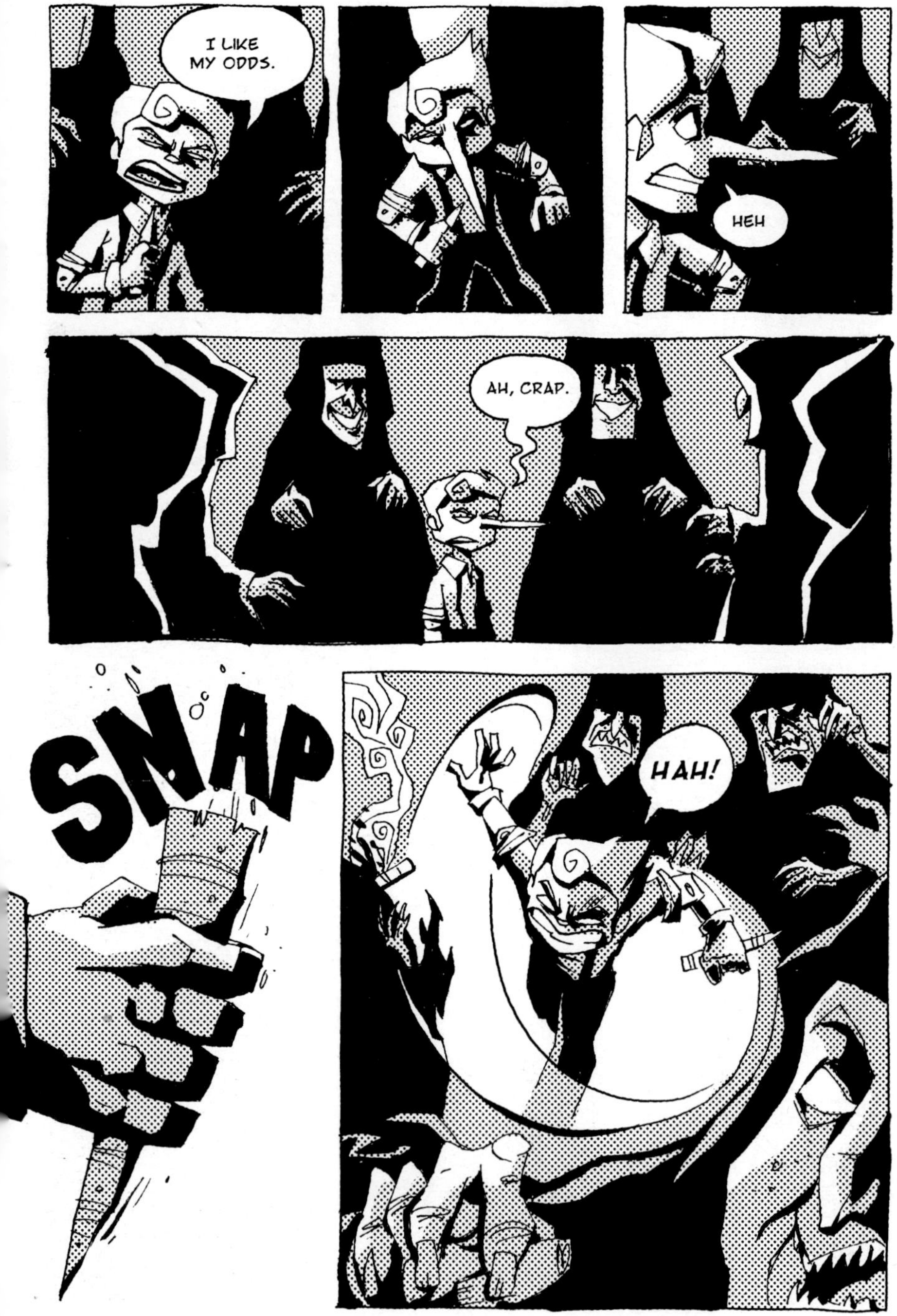
I LIKE MY ODDS.
HEH
AH, CRAP.
SNAP
HAH!

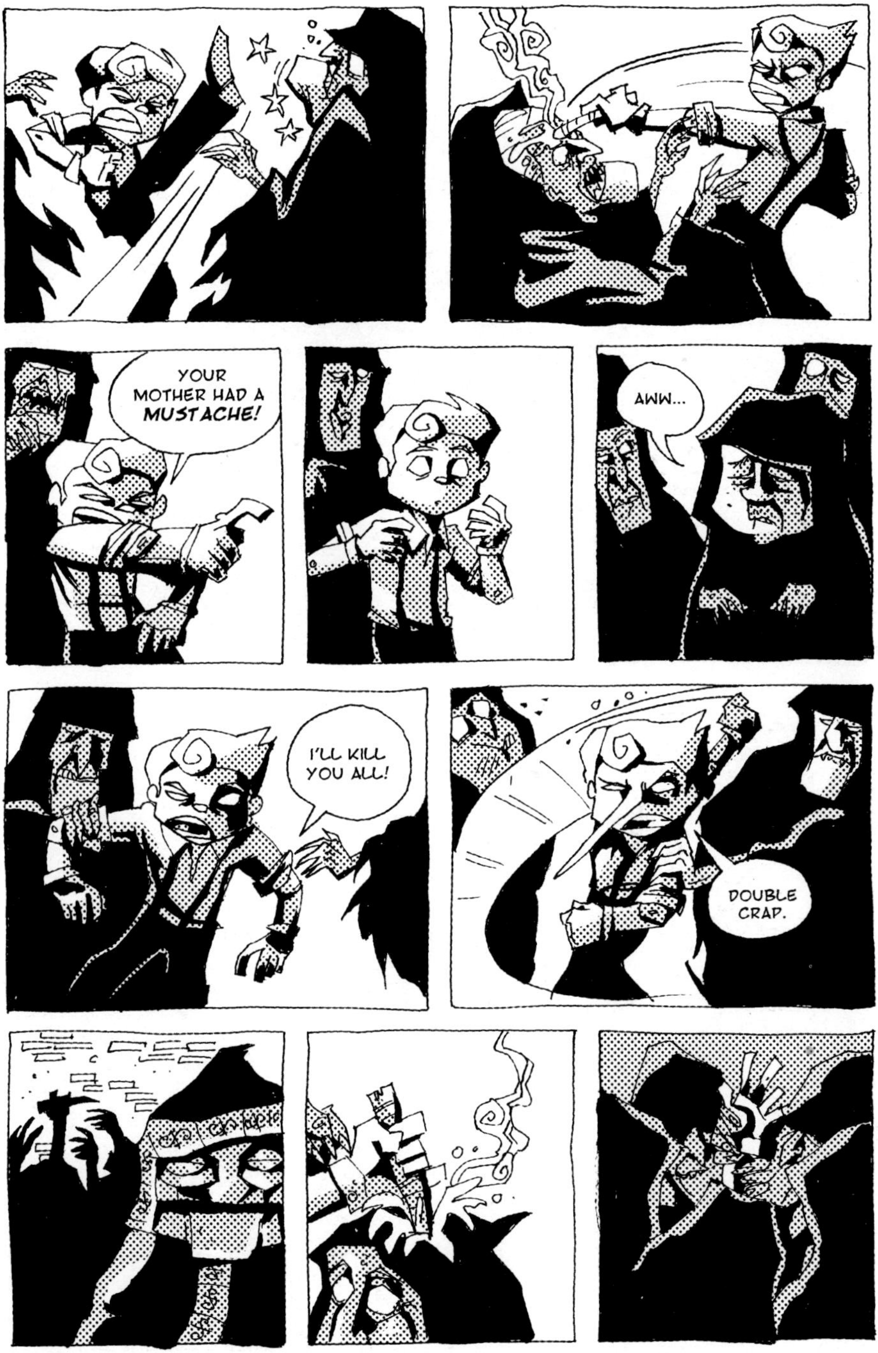
YOUR MOTHER HAD A MUSTACHE!
AWW...
I'LL KILL YOU ALL!
DOUBLE CRAP.

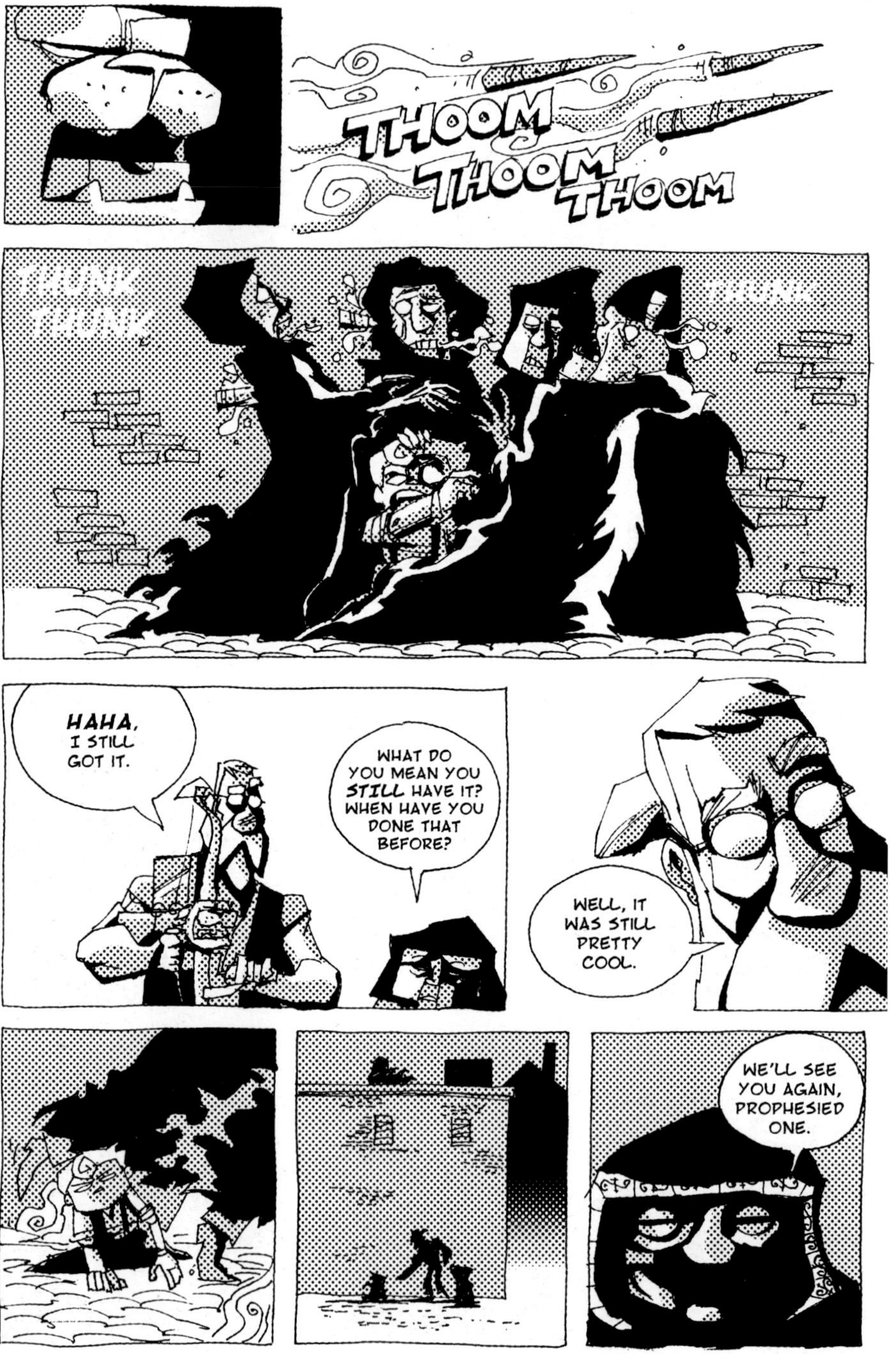
THOOM
THOOM
THOOM
THUNK
THUNK
THUNK
HAHA, I STILL GOT IT.
WHAT DO YOU MEAN YOU STILL HAVE IT? WHEN HAVE YOU DONE THAT BEFORE?
WELL, IT WAS STILL PRETTY COOL.
WE'LL SEE YOU AGAIN, PROPHESIED ONE.

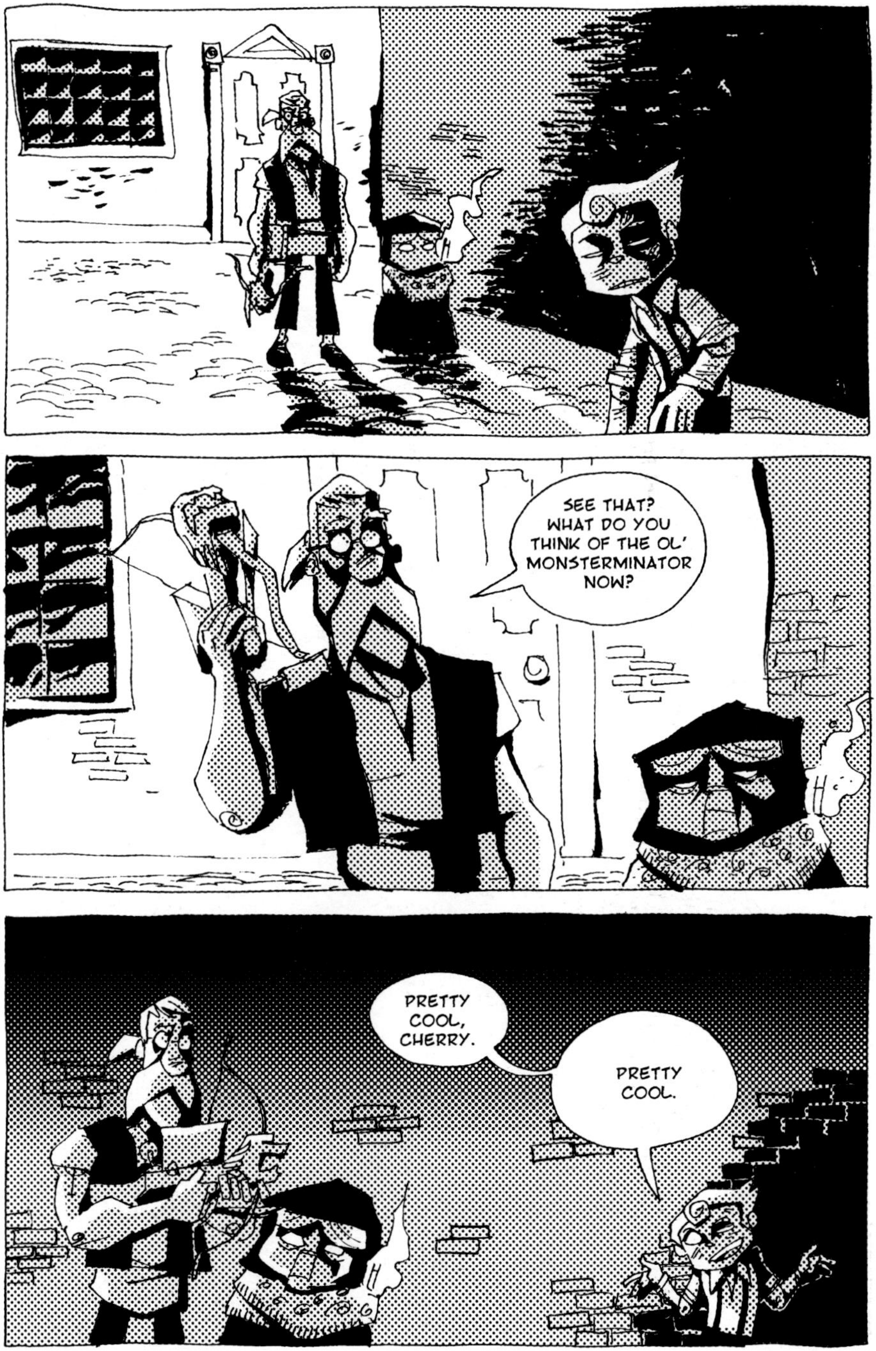
SEE THAT? WHAT DO YOU THINK OF THE OL' MONSTERMINATOR NOW?
PRETTY COOL, CHERRY.
PRETTY COOL.

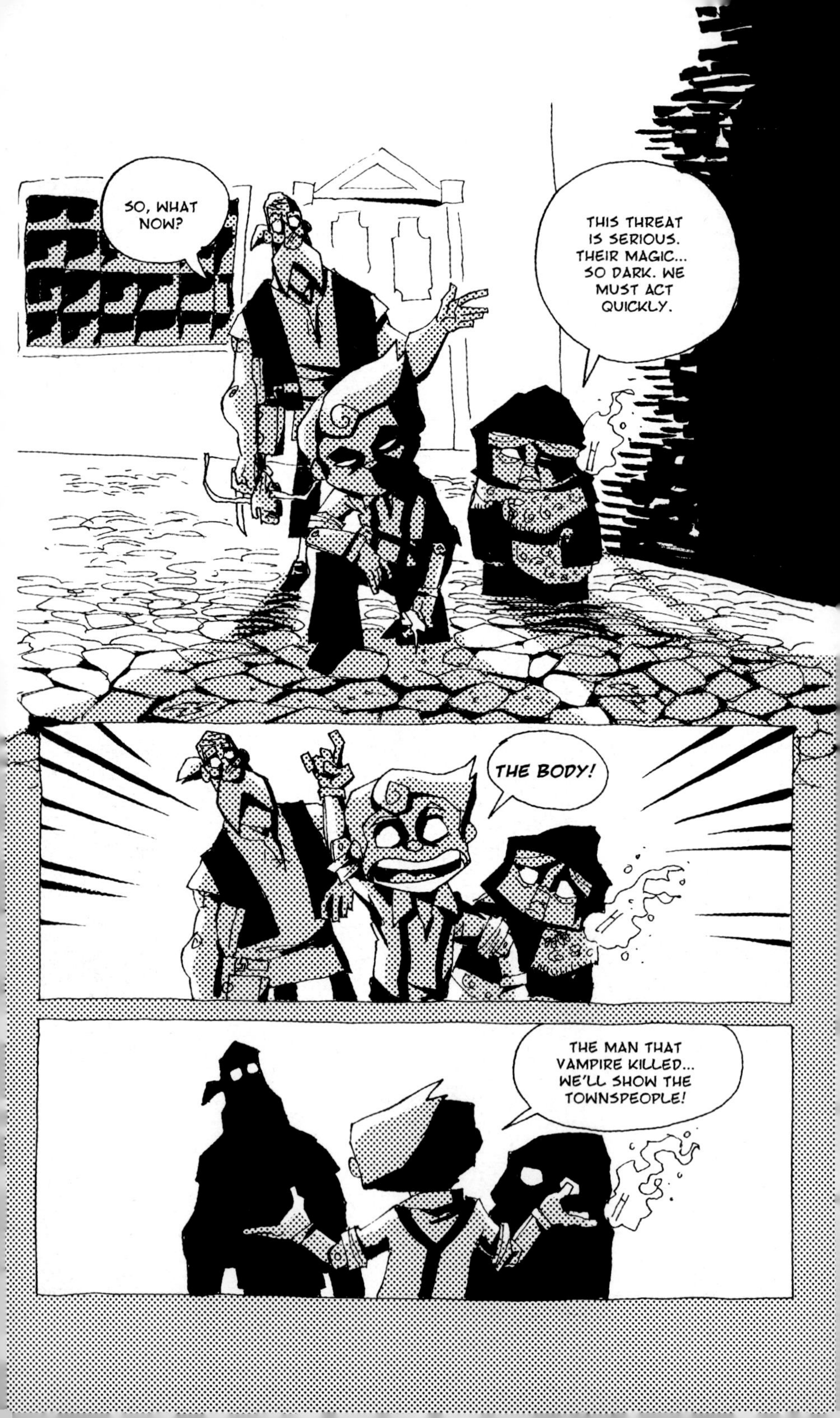
SO, WHAT NOW?
THIS THREAT IS SERIOUS. THEIR MAGIC... SO DARK. WE MUST ACT QUICKLY.
THE BODY!
THE MAN THAT VAMPIRE KILLED... WE'LL SHOW THE TOWNSPEOPLE!

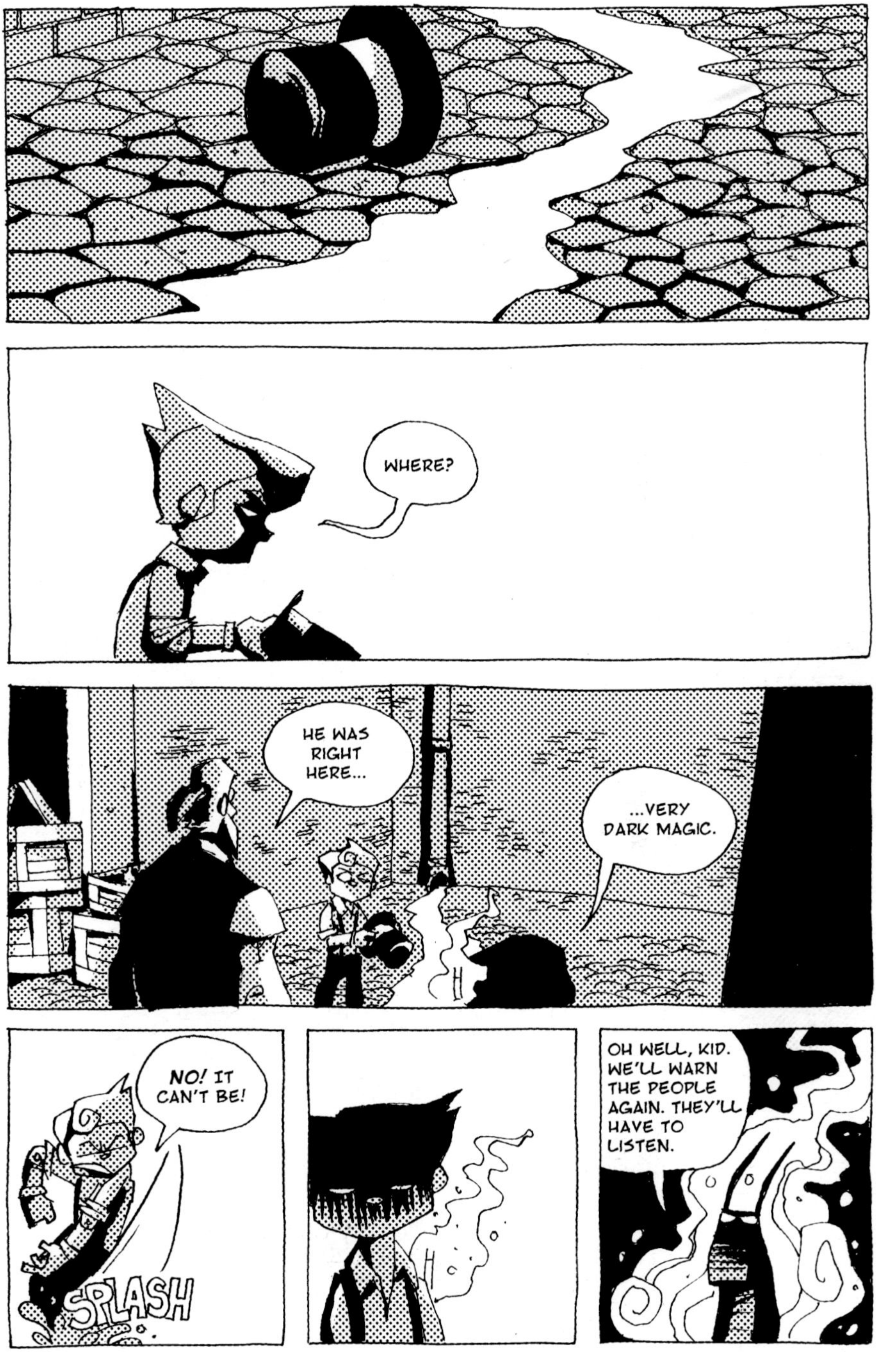
WHERE?
HE WAS RIGHT HERE...
...VERY DARK MAGIC.
NO! IT CAN'T BE!
SPLASH
OH WELL, KID. WE'LL WARN THE PEOPLE AGAIN. THEY'LL HAVE TO LISTEN.

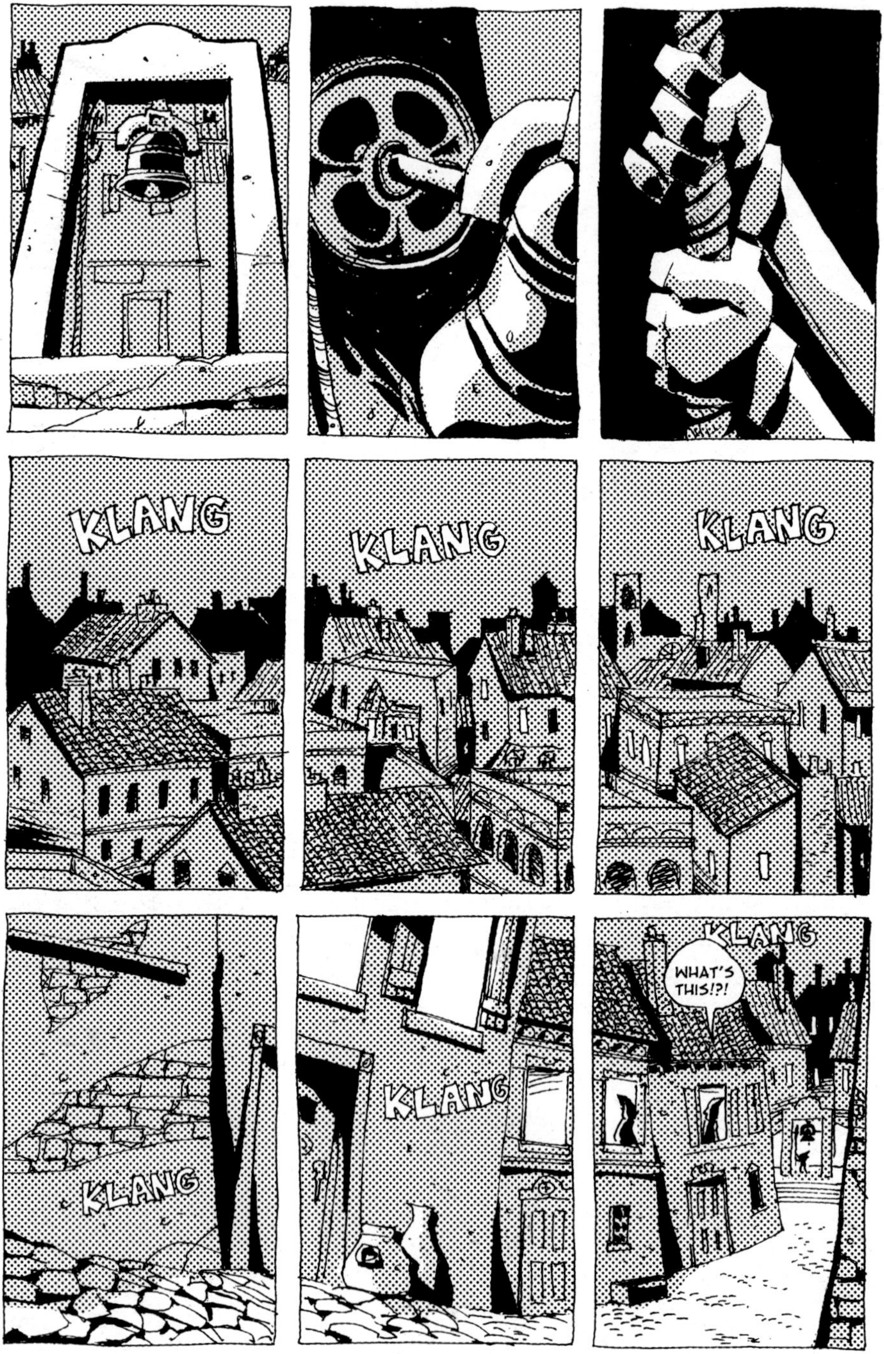
KLANG
KLANG
KLANG
KLANG
KLANG
KLANG
WHAT'S THIS!?!

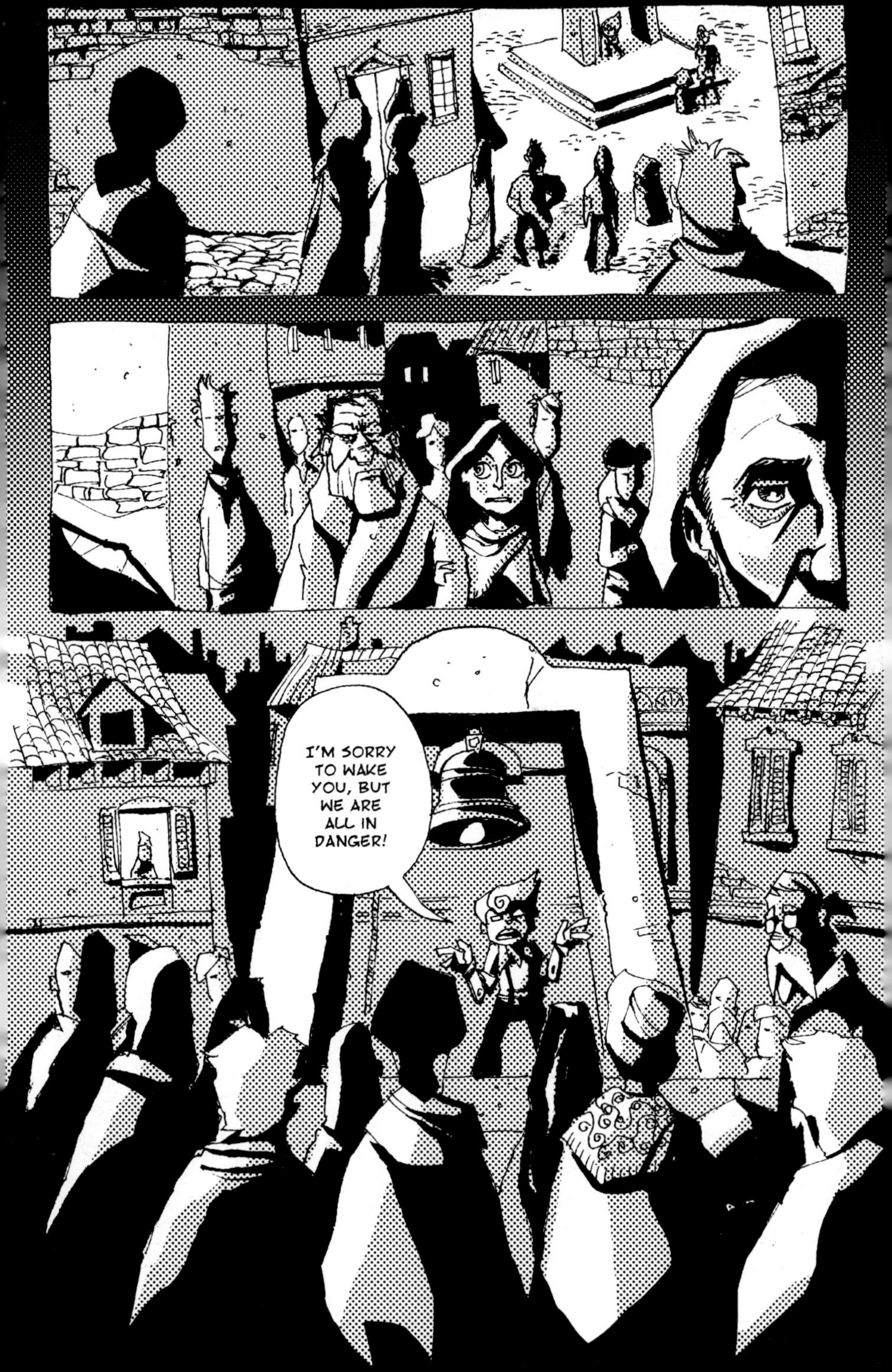
I'M SORRY TO WAKE YOU, BUT WE ARE ALL IN DANGER!

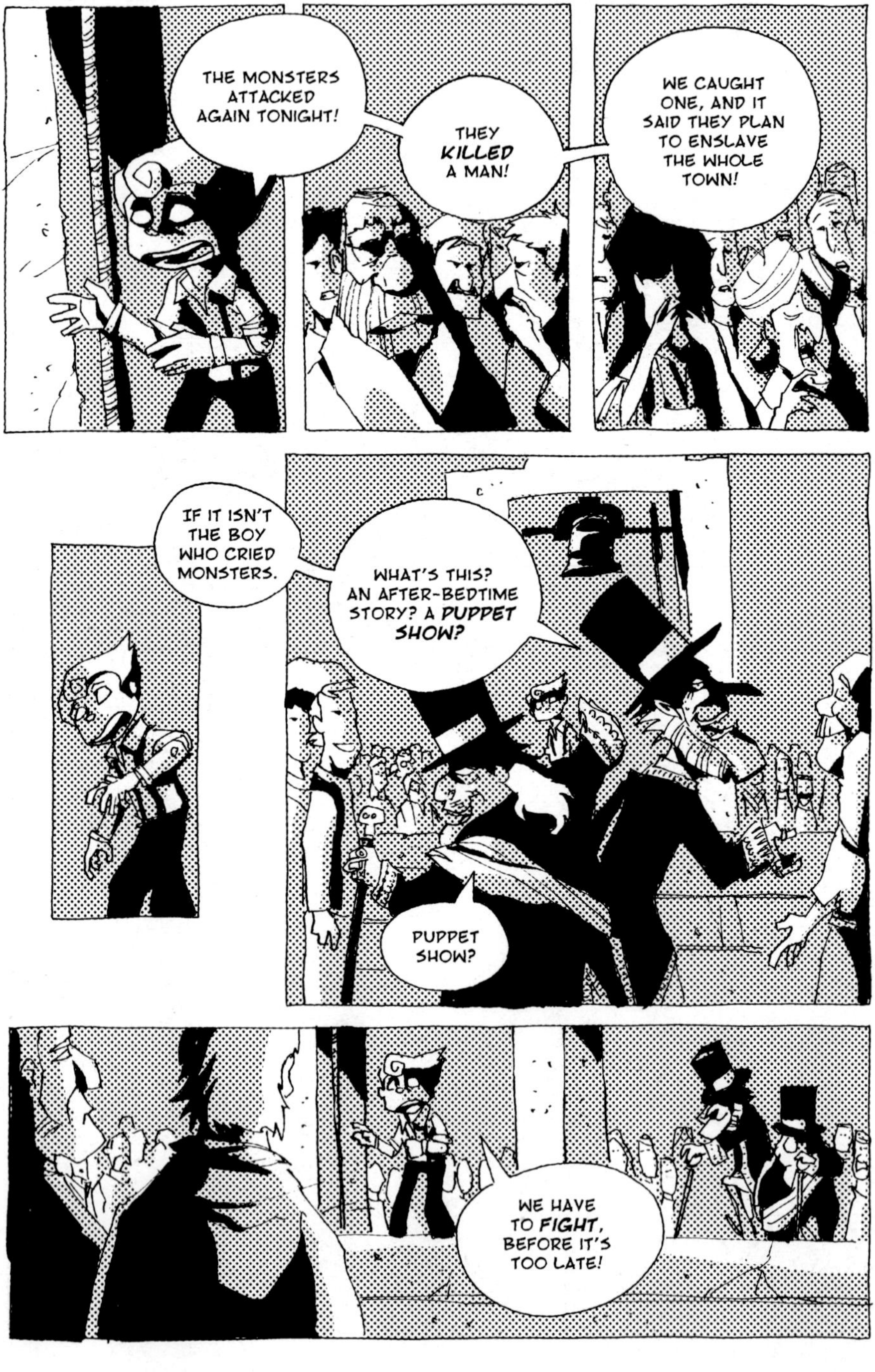
THE MONSTERS ATTACKED AGAIN TONIGHT!
THEY KILLED A MAN!
WE CAUGHT ONE, AND IT SAID THEY PLAN TO ENSLAVE THE WHOLE TOWN!
IF IT ISN'T THE BOY WHO CRIED MONSTERS.
WHAT'S THIS? AN AFTER-BEDTIME STORY? A PUPPET SHOW?
PUPPET SHOW?
WE HAVE TO FIGHT, BEFORE IT'S TOO LATE!

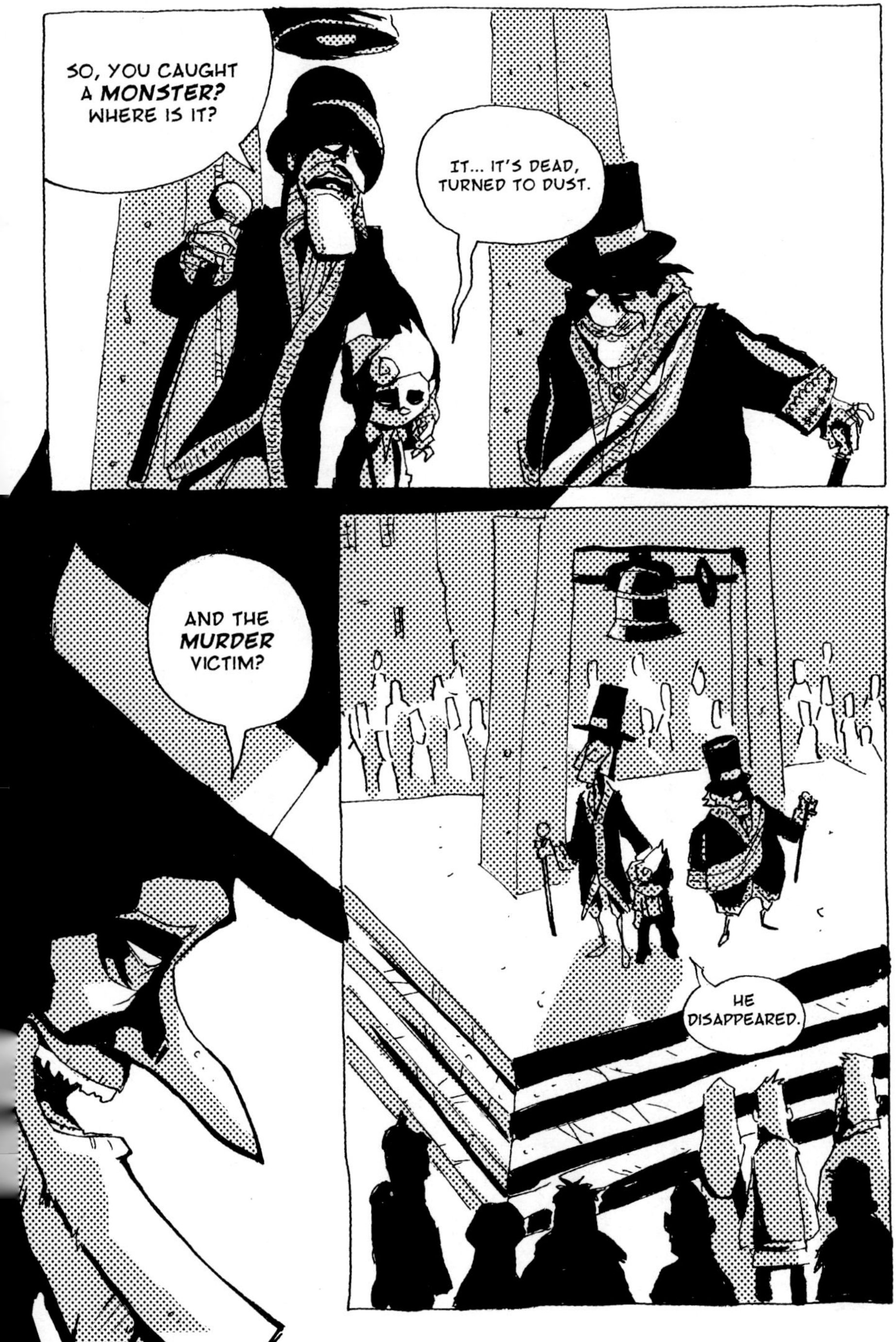
SO, YOU CAUGHT A MONSTER? WHERE IS IT?
IT... IT'S DEAD, TURNED TO DUST.
AND THE MURDER VICTIM?
HE DISAPPEARED.

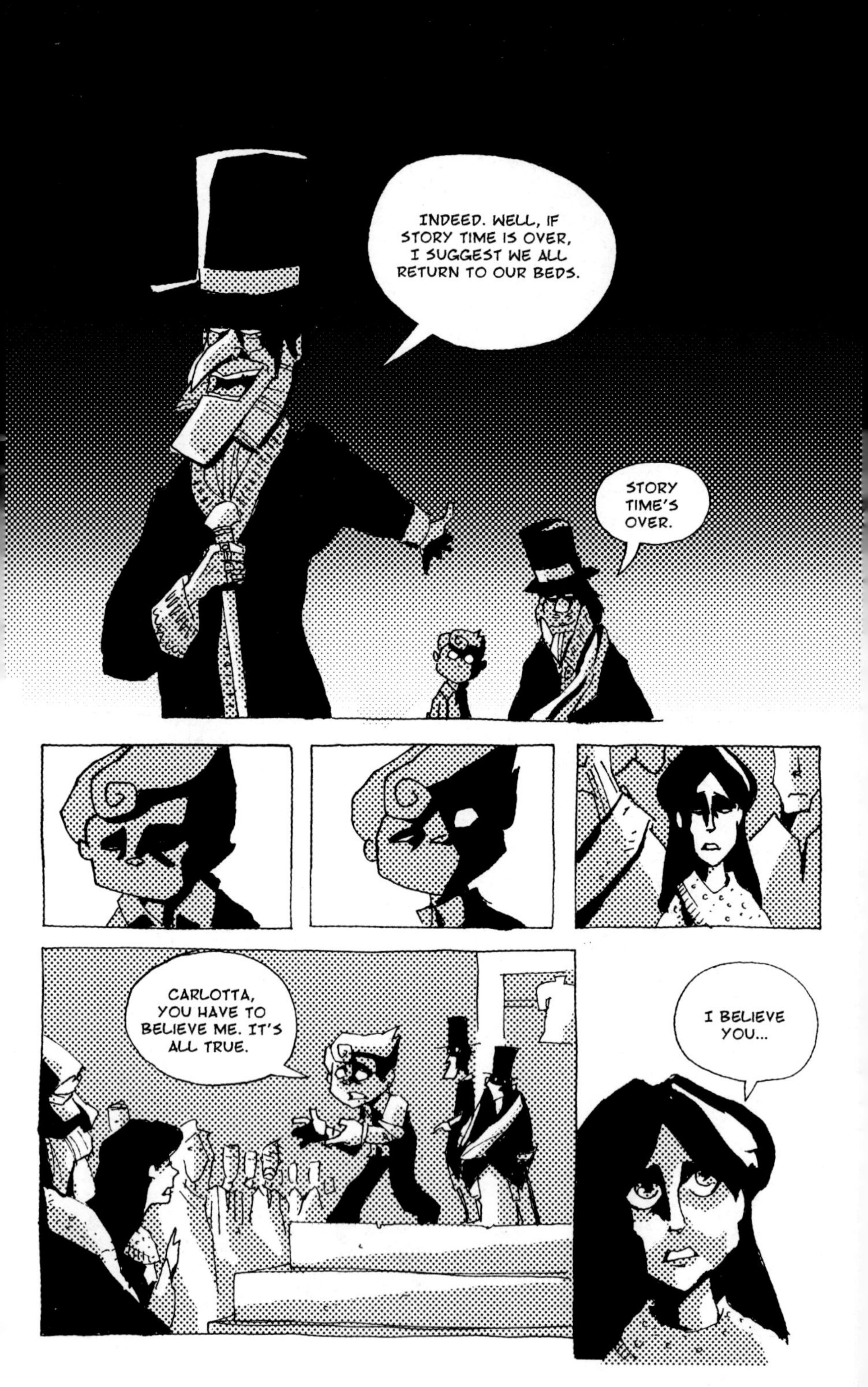
INDEED. WELL, IF STORY TIME IS OVER, I SUGGEST WE ALL RETURN TO OUR BEDS.
STORY TIME'S OVER.
CARLOTTA, YOU HAVE TO BELIEVE ME. IT'S ALL TRUE.
I BELIEVE YOU...

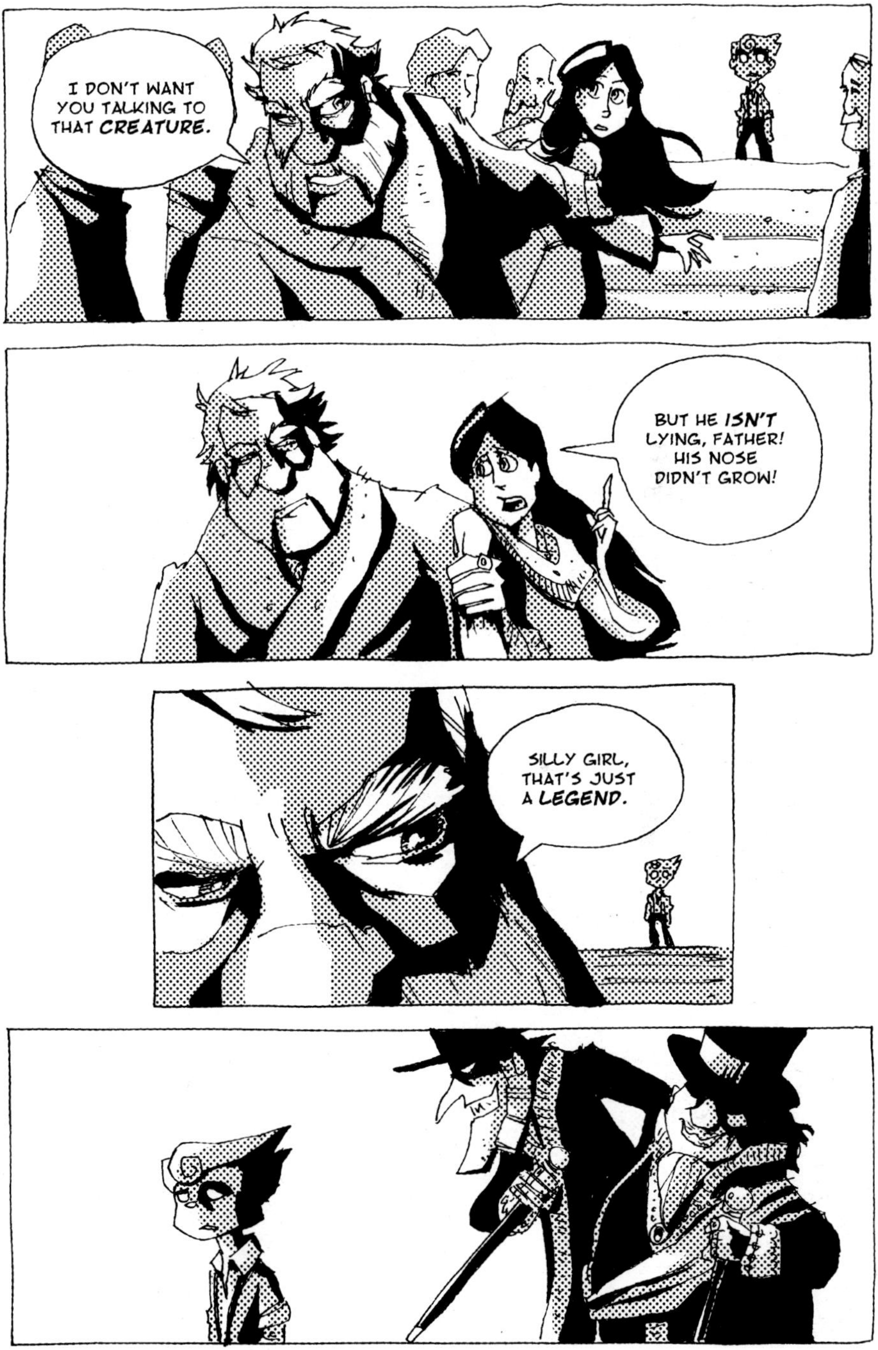
I DON'T WANT YOU TALKING TO THAT CREATURE.
BUT HE ISN'T LYING, FATHER! HIS NOSE DIDN'T GROW!
SILLY GIRL, THAT'S JUST A LEGEND.

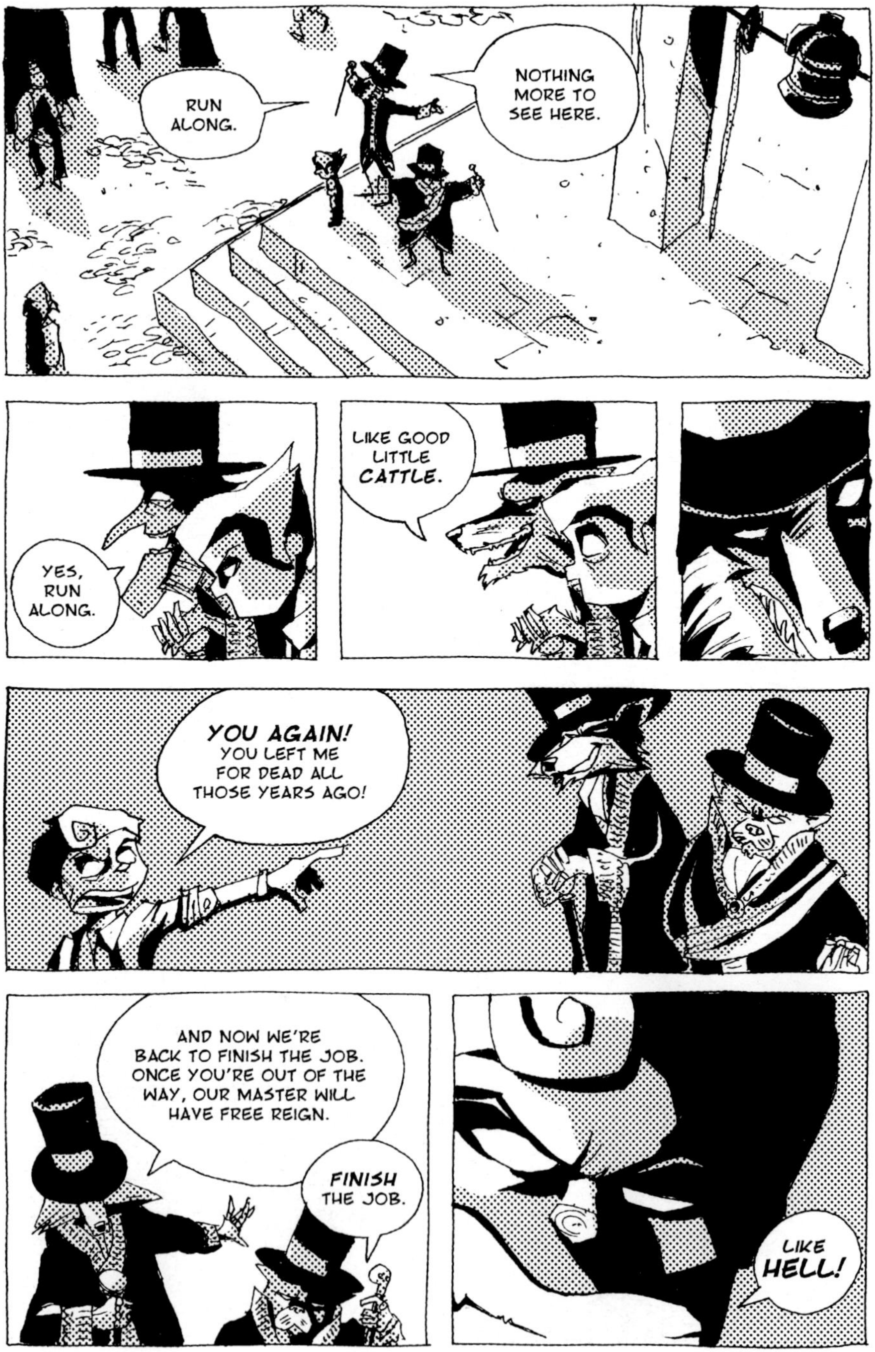
RUN ALONG.
NOTHING MORE TO SEE HERE.
YES, RUN ALONG.
LIKE GOOD LITTLE CATTLE.
YOU AGAIN! YOU LEFT ME FOR DEAD ALL THOSE YEARS AGO!
AND NOW WE'RE BACK TO FINISH THE JOB. ONCE YOU'RE OUT OF THE WAY, OUR MASTER WILL HAVE FREE REIGN.
FINISH THE JOB.
LIKE HELL!

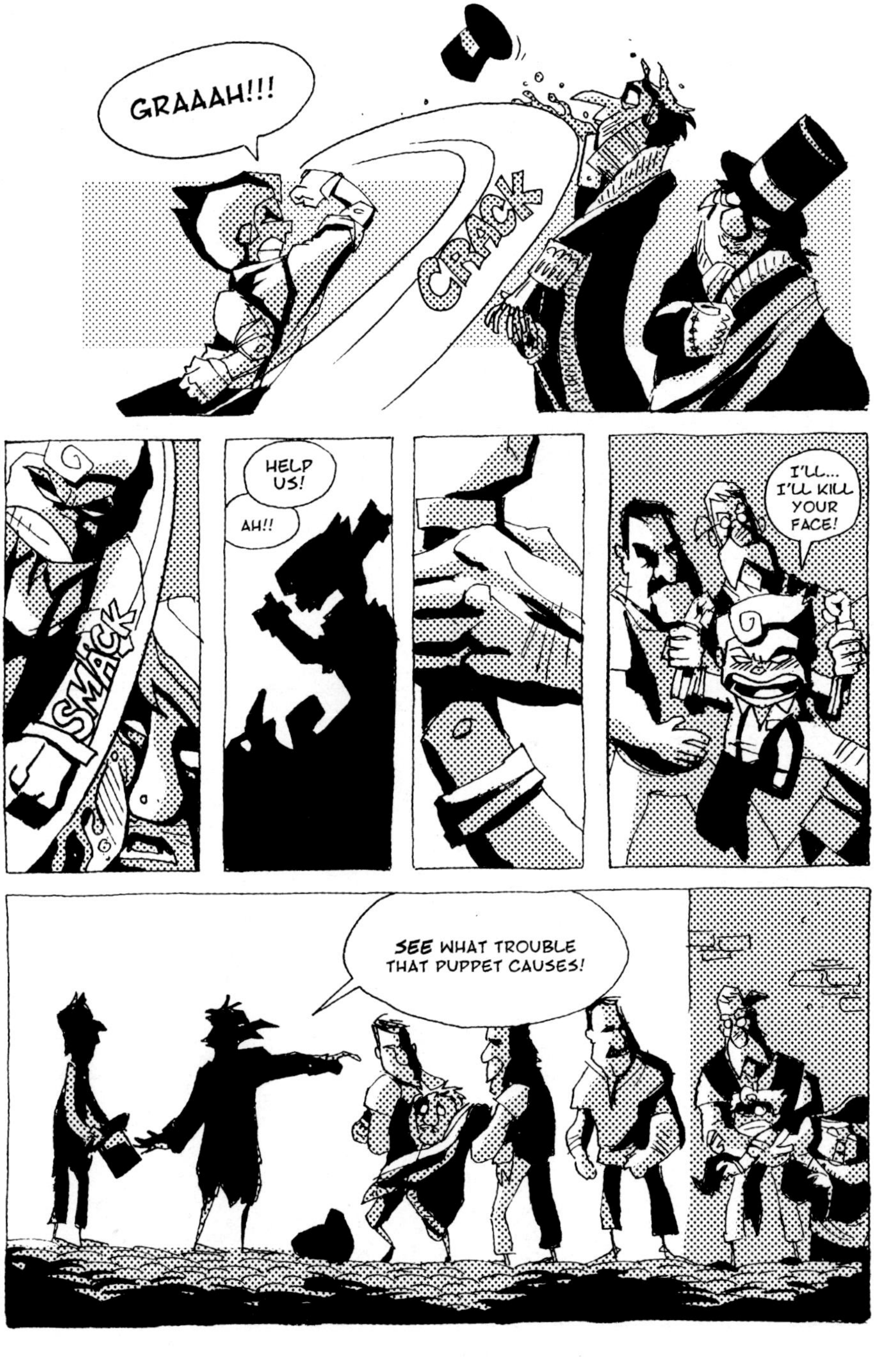
GRAAAH!!!
CRACK
SMACK
HELP US!
AH!!
I'LL... I'LL KILL YOUR FACE!
SEE WHAT TROUBLE THAT PUPPET CAUSES!

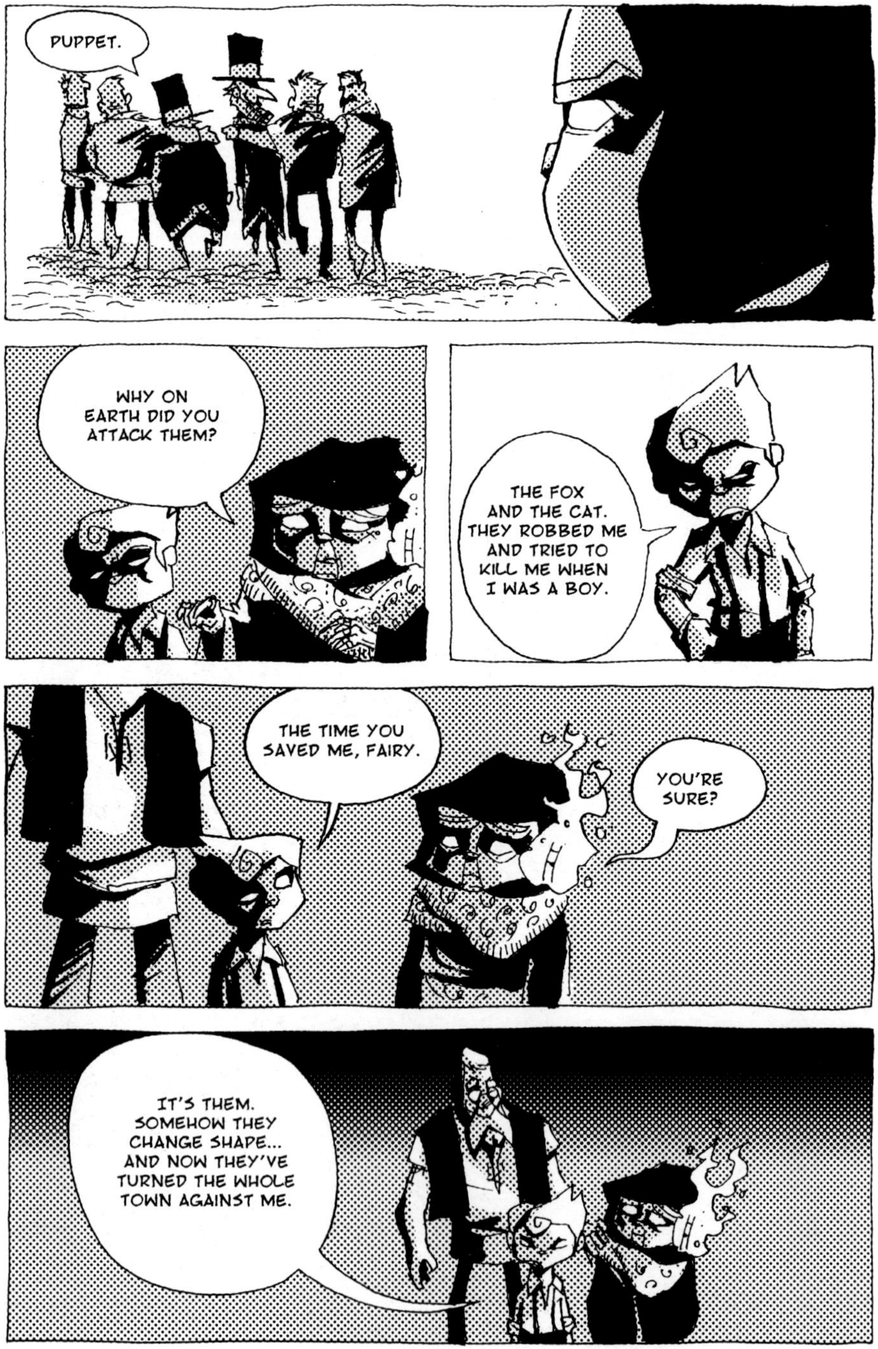
PUPPET.
WHY ON EARTH DID YOU ATTACK THEM?
THE FOX AND THE CAT. THEY ROBBED ME AND TRIED TO KILL ME WHEN I WAS A BOY.
THE TIME YOU SAVED ME, FAIRY.
YOU'RE SURE?
IT'S THEM. SOMEHOW THEY CHANGE SHAPE... AND NOW THEY'VE TURNED THE WHOLE TOWN AGAINST ME.

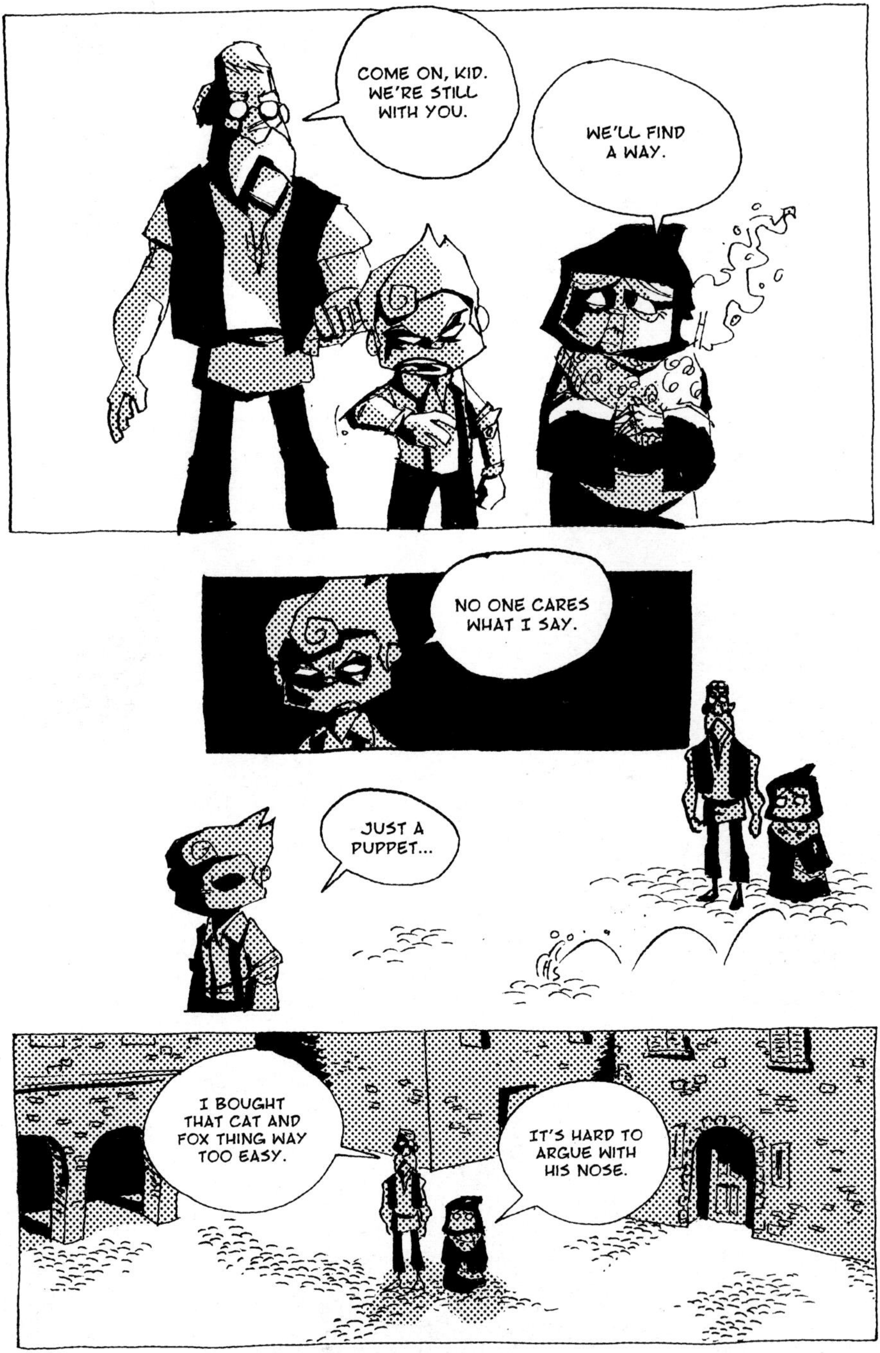
COME ON, KID. WE'RE STILL WITH YOU.
WE'LL FIND A WAY.
NO ONE CARES WHAT I SAY.
JUST A PUPPET...
I BOUGHT THAT CAT AND FOX THING WAY TOO EASY.
IT'S HARD TO ARGUE WITH HIS NOSE.

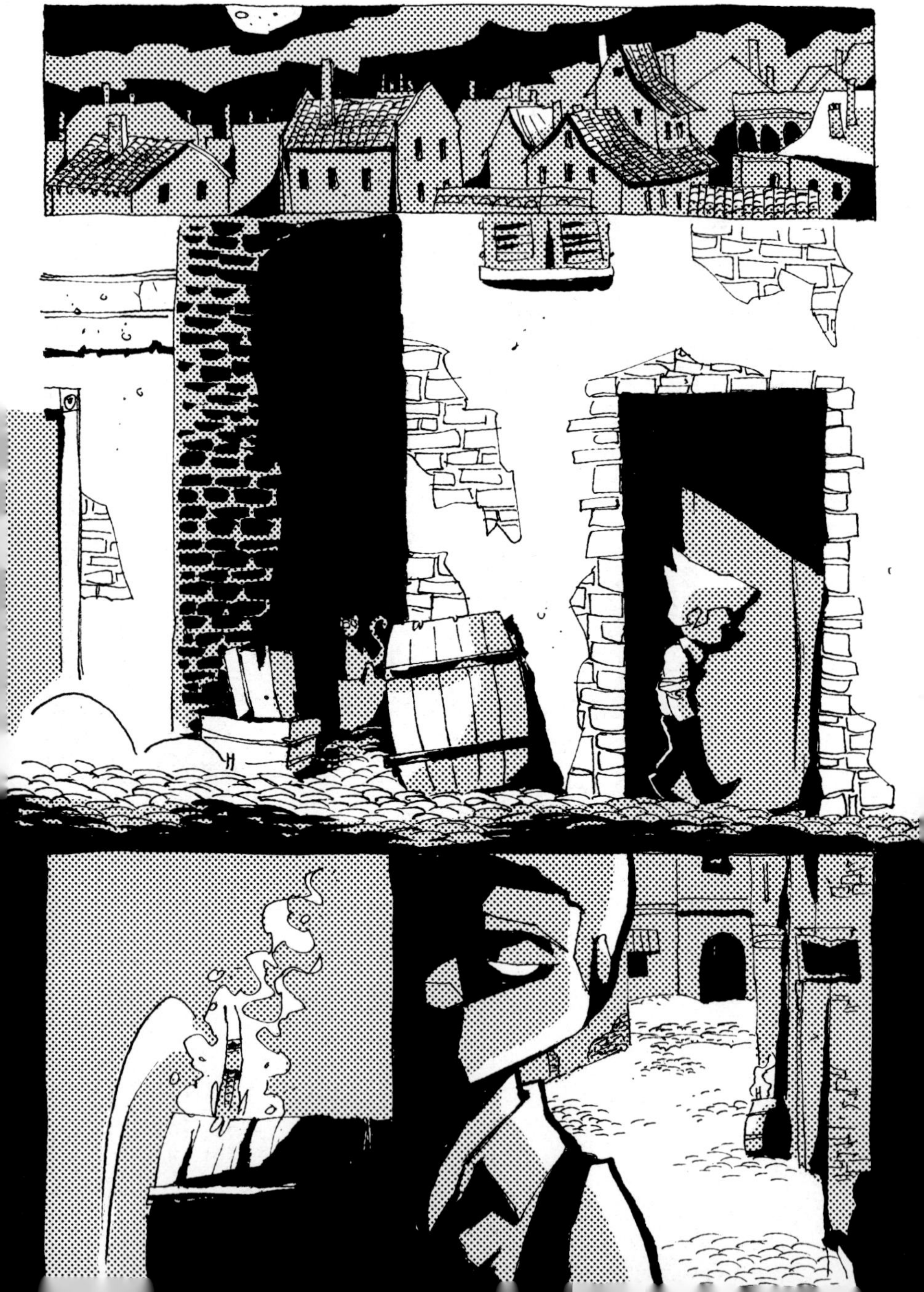

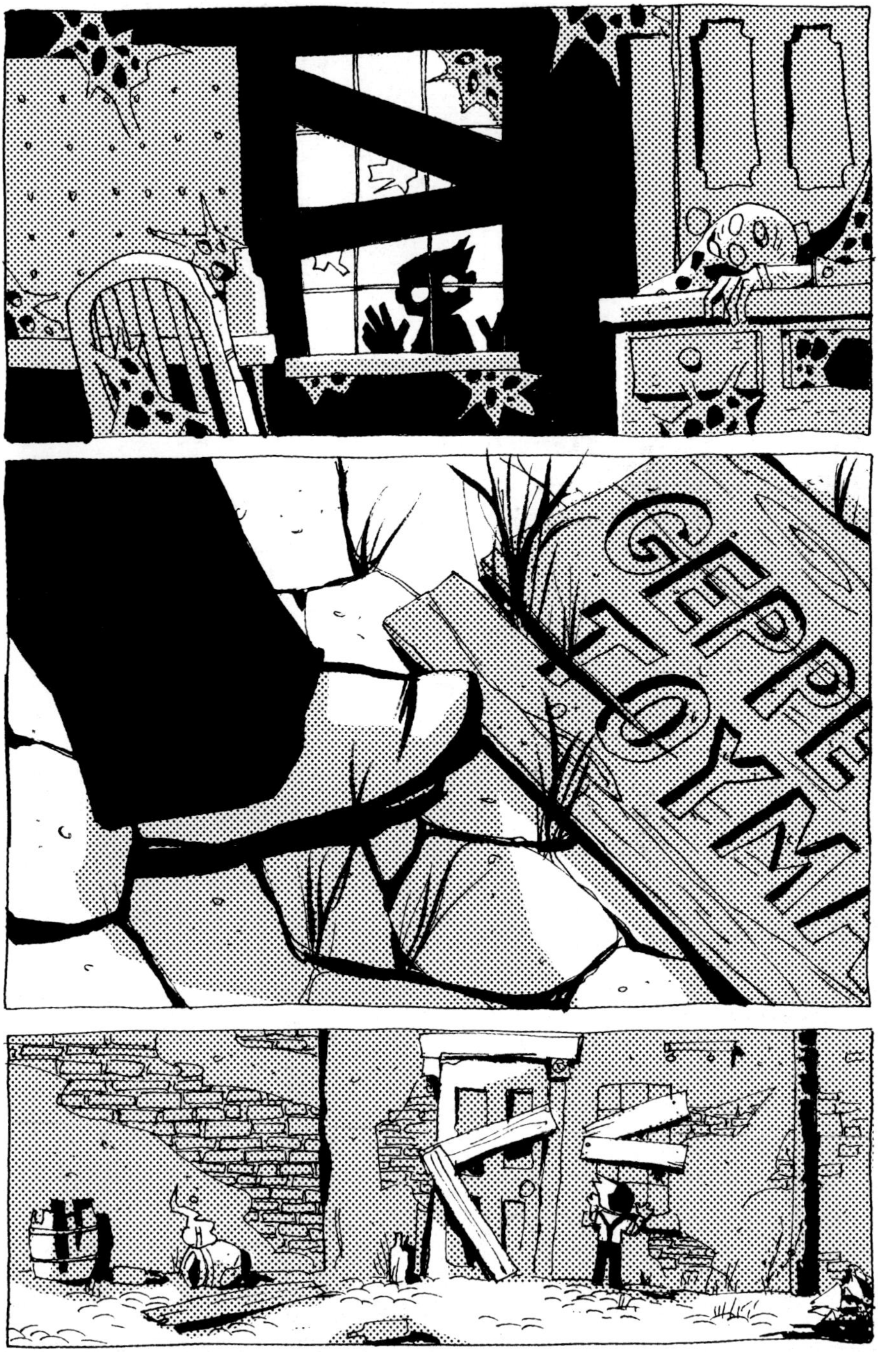
GEPPE

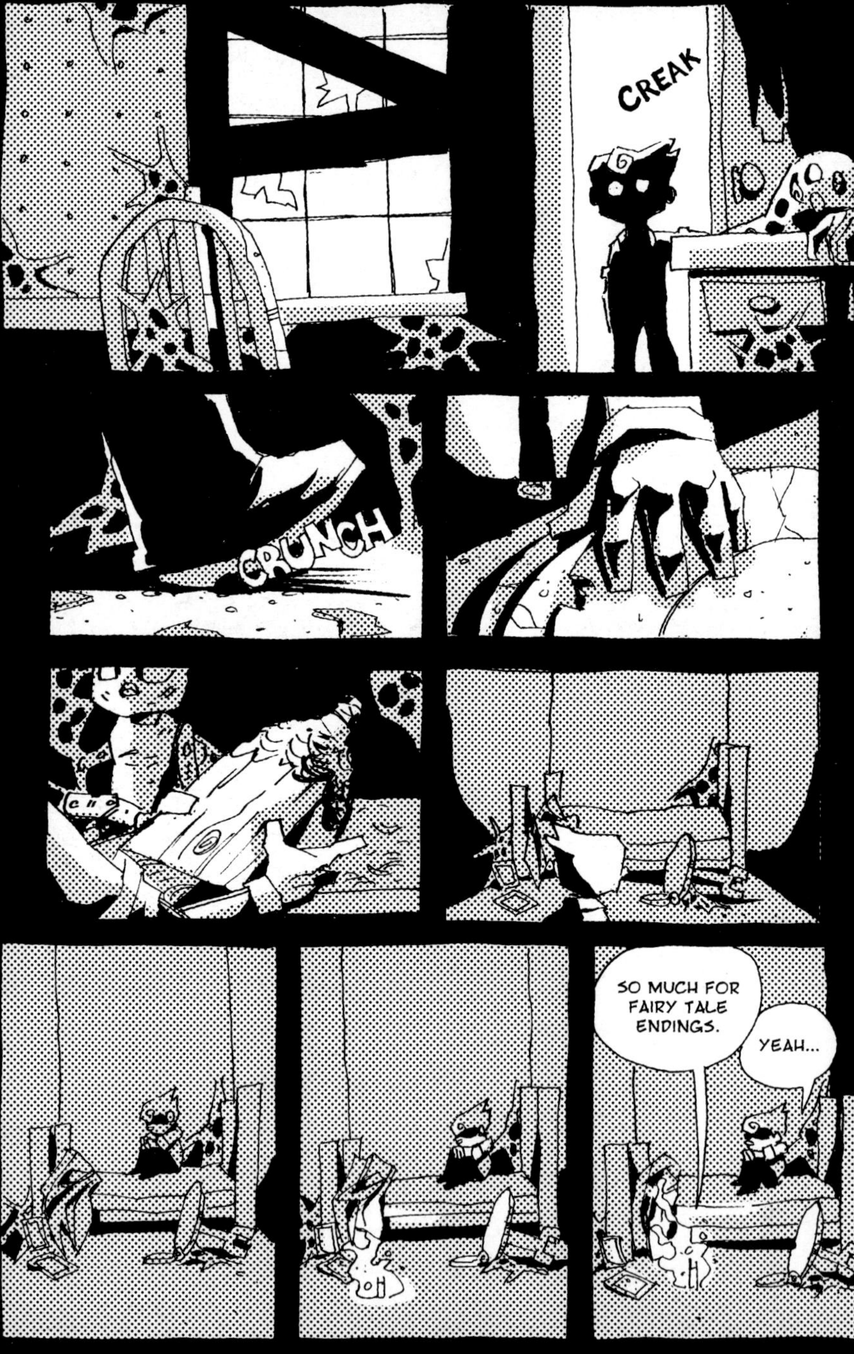
CREAK
CRUNCH
SO MUCH FOR FAIRY TALE ENDINGS.
YEAH...

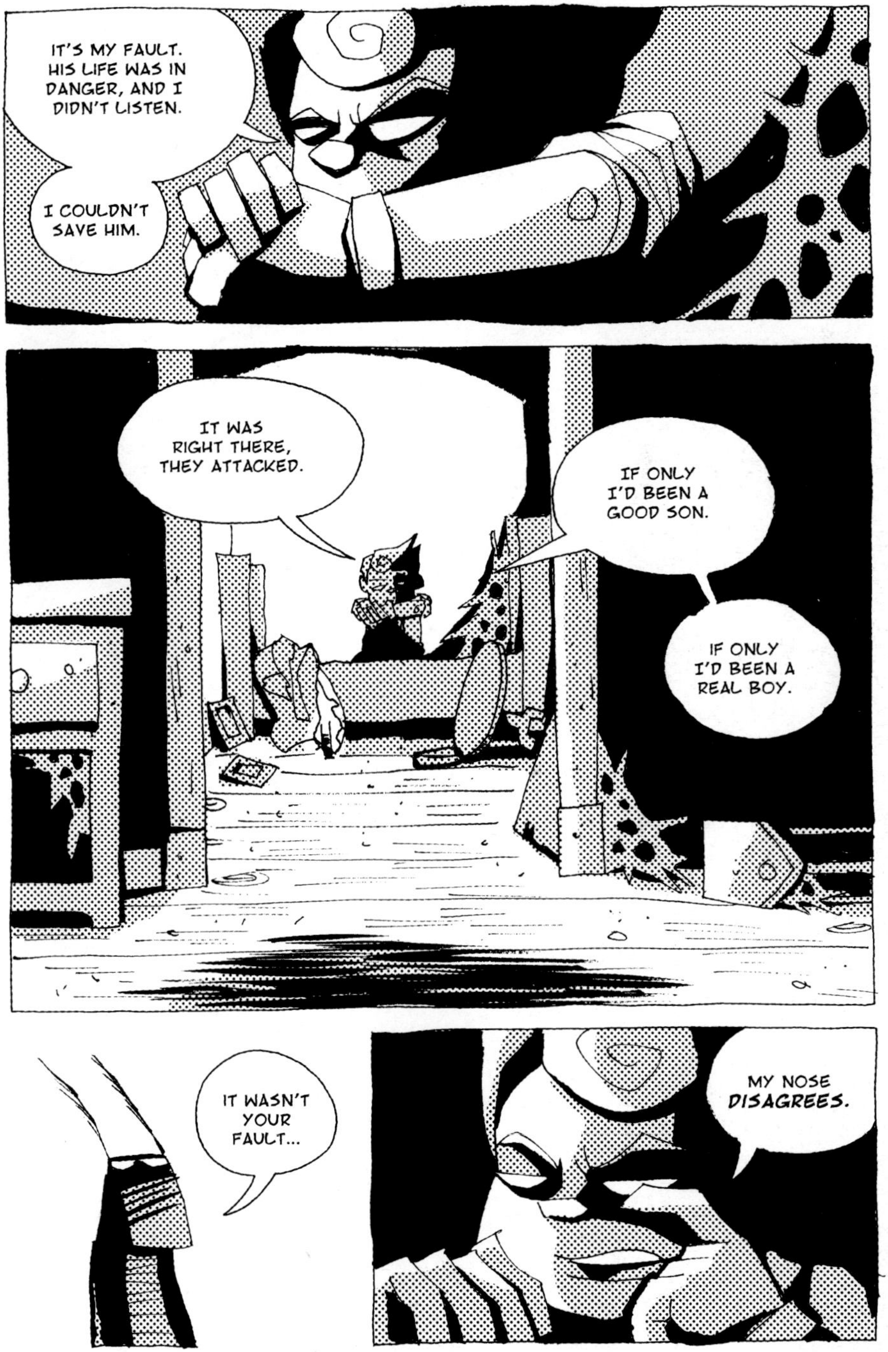
IT'S MY FAULT. HIS LIFE WAS IN DANGER, AND I DIDN'T LISTEN.
I COULDN'T SAVE HIM.
IT WAS RIGHT THERE, THEY ATTACKED.
IF ONLY I'D BEEN A GOOD SON.
IF ONLY I'D BEEN A REAL BOY.
IT WASN'T YOUR FAULT...
MY NOSE DISAGREES.

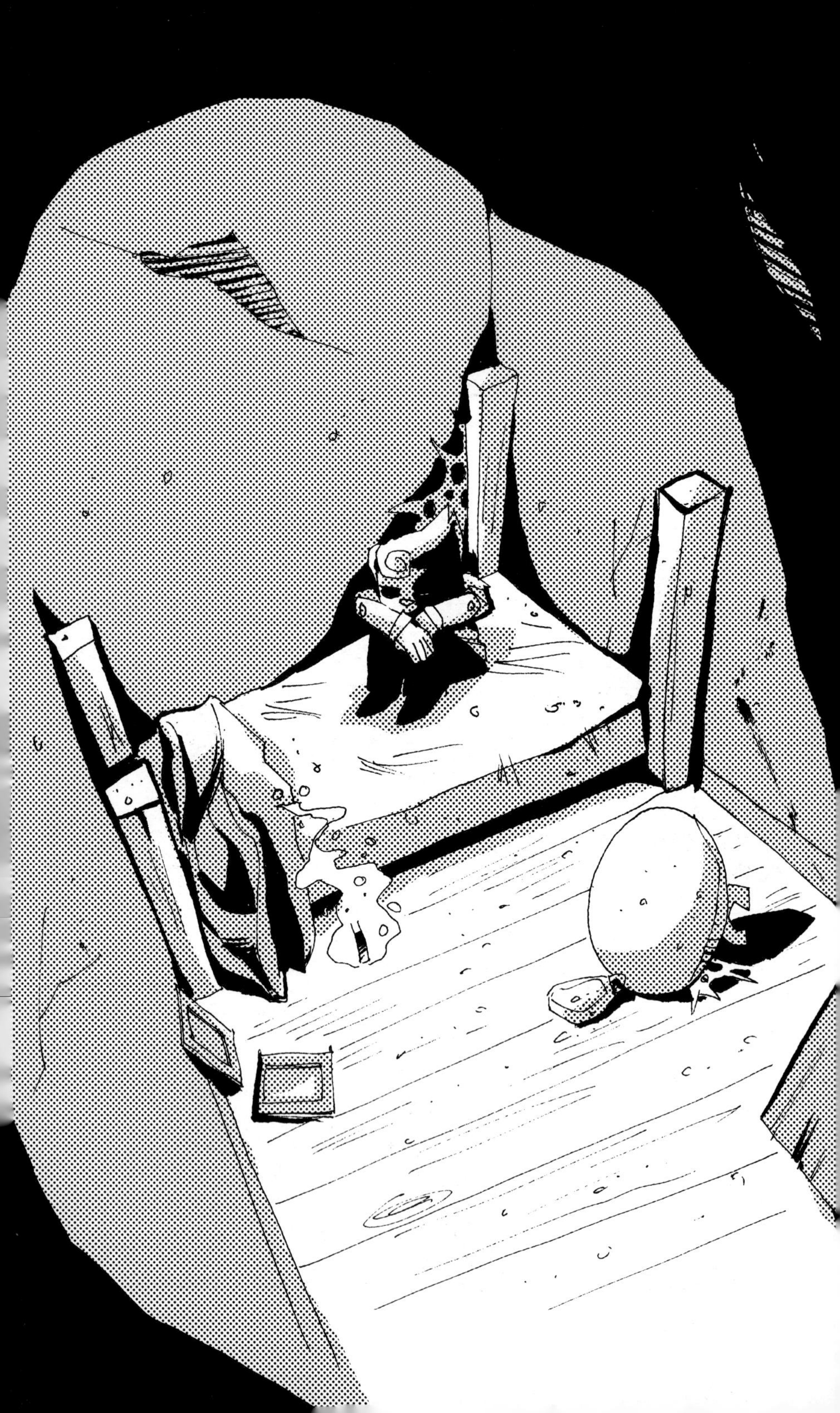

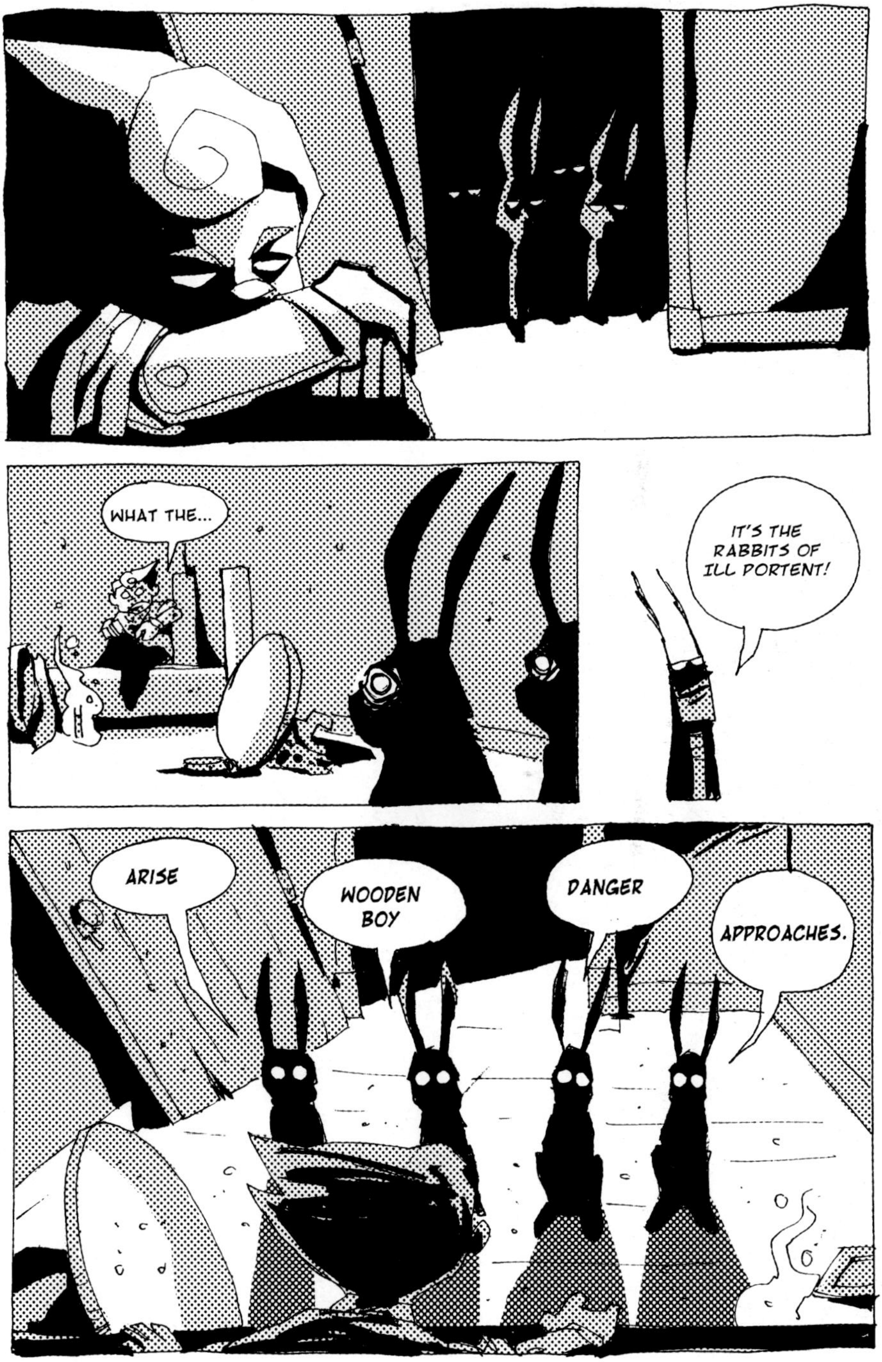
WHAT THE...
IT'S THE RABBITS OF ILL PORTENT!
ARISE
WOODEN BOY
DANGER
APPROACHES.

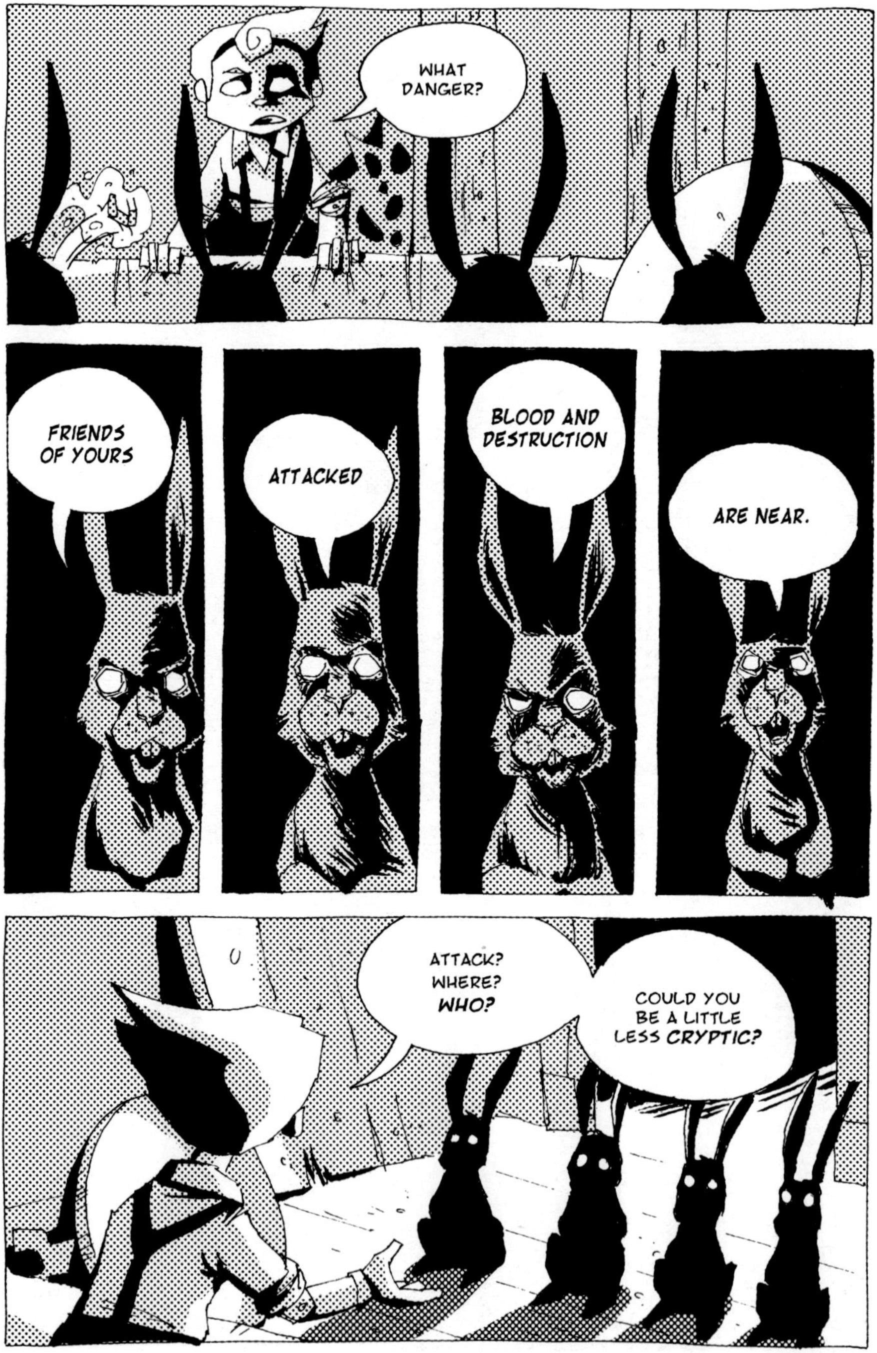
WHAT DANGER?
FRIENDS OF YOURS
ATTACKED
BLOOD AND DESTRUCTION
ARE NEAR.
ATTACK? WHERE? WHO?
COULD YOU BE A LITTLE LESS CRYPTIC?

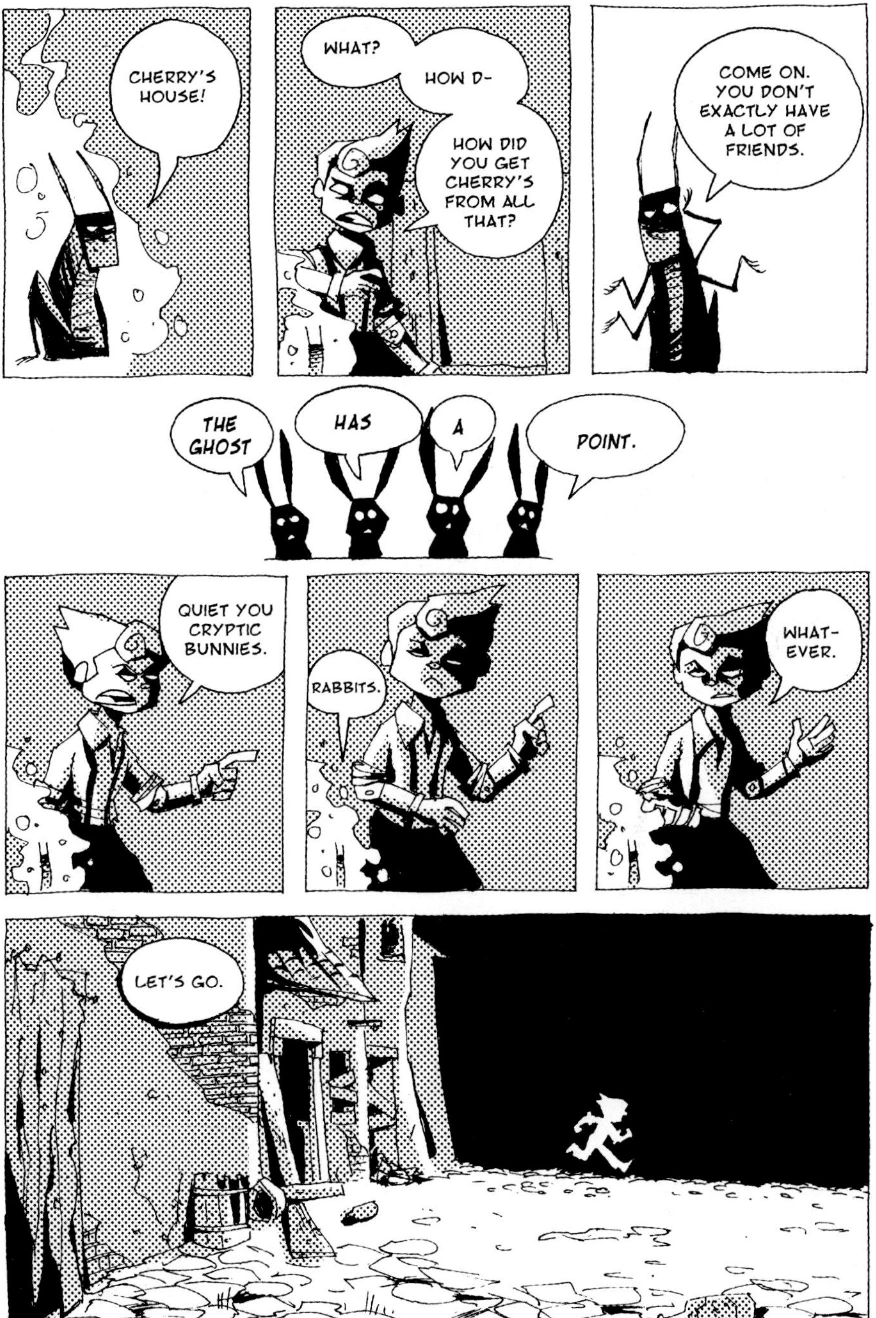
CHERRY'S HOUSE!
WHAT?
HOW D-
HOW DID YOU GET CHERRY'S FROM ALL THAT?
COME ON. YOU DON'T EXACTLY HAVE A LOT OF FRIENDS.
THE GHOST
HAS
A
POINT.
QUIET YOU CRYPTIC BUNNIES.
RABBITS.
WHAT-EVER.
LET'S GO.

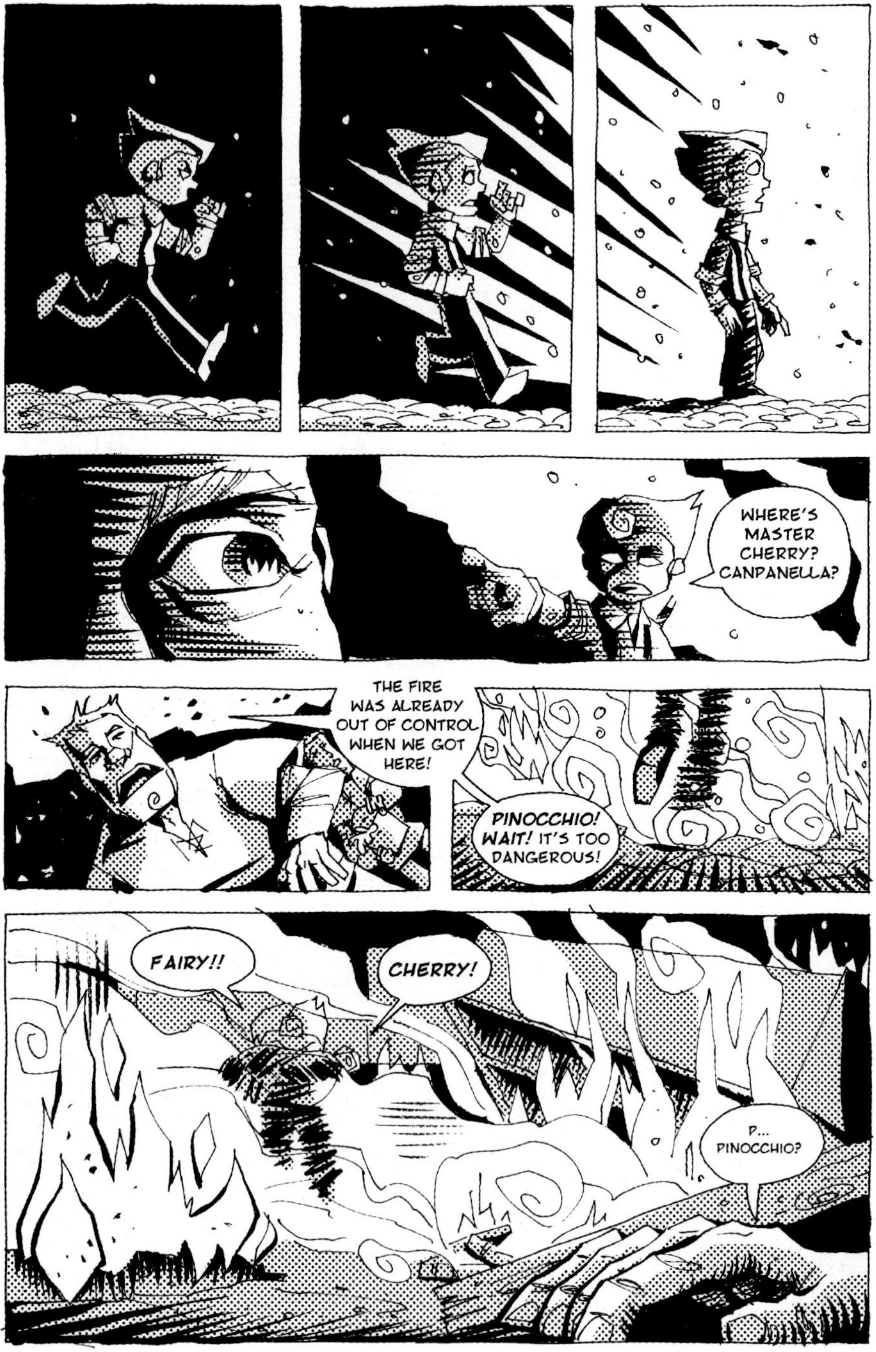
WHERE'S MASTER CHERRY? CANPANELLA?
THE FIRE WAS ALREADY OUT OF CONTROL WHEN WE GOT HERE!
PINOCCHIO! WAIT! IT'S TOO DANGEROUS!
FAIRY!!
CHERRY!
P... PINOCCHIO?

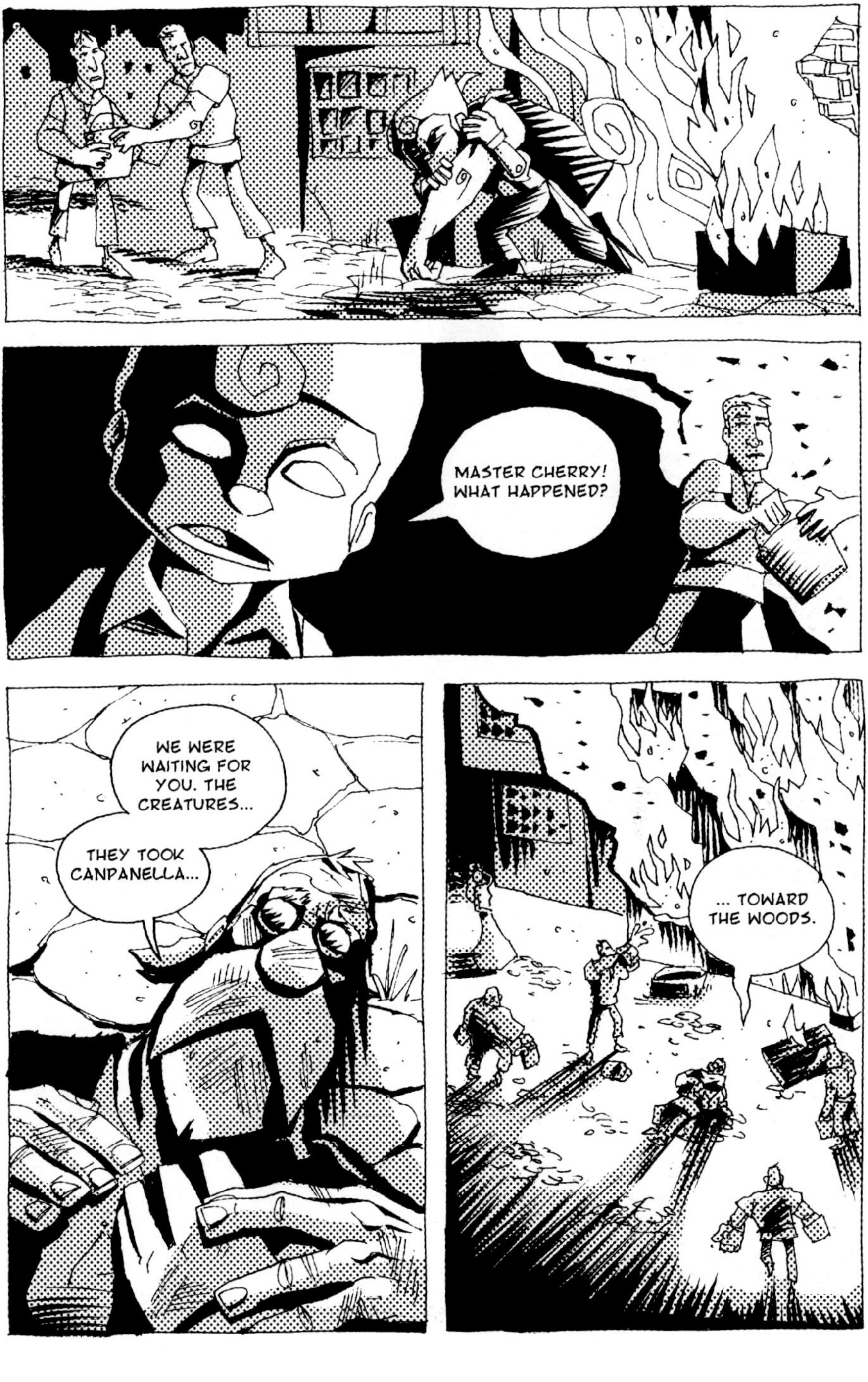
MASTER CHERRY! WHAT HAPPENED?
WE WERE WAITING FOR YOU. THE CREATURES...
THEY TOOK CANPANELLA...
... TOWARD THE WOODS.

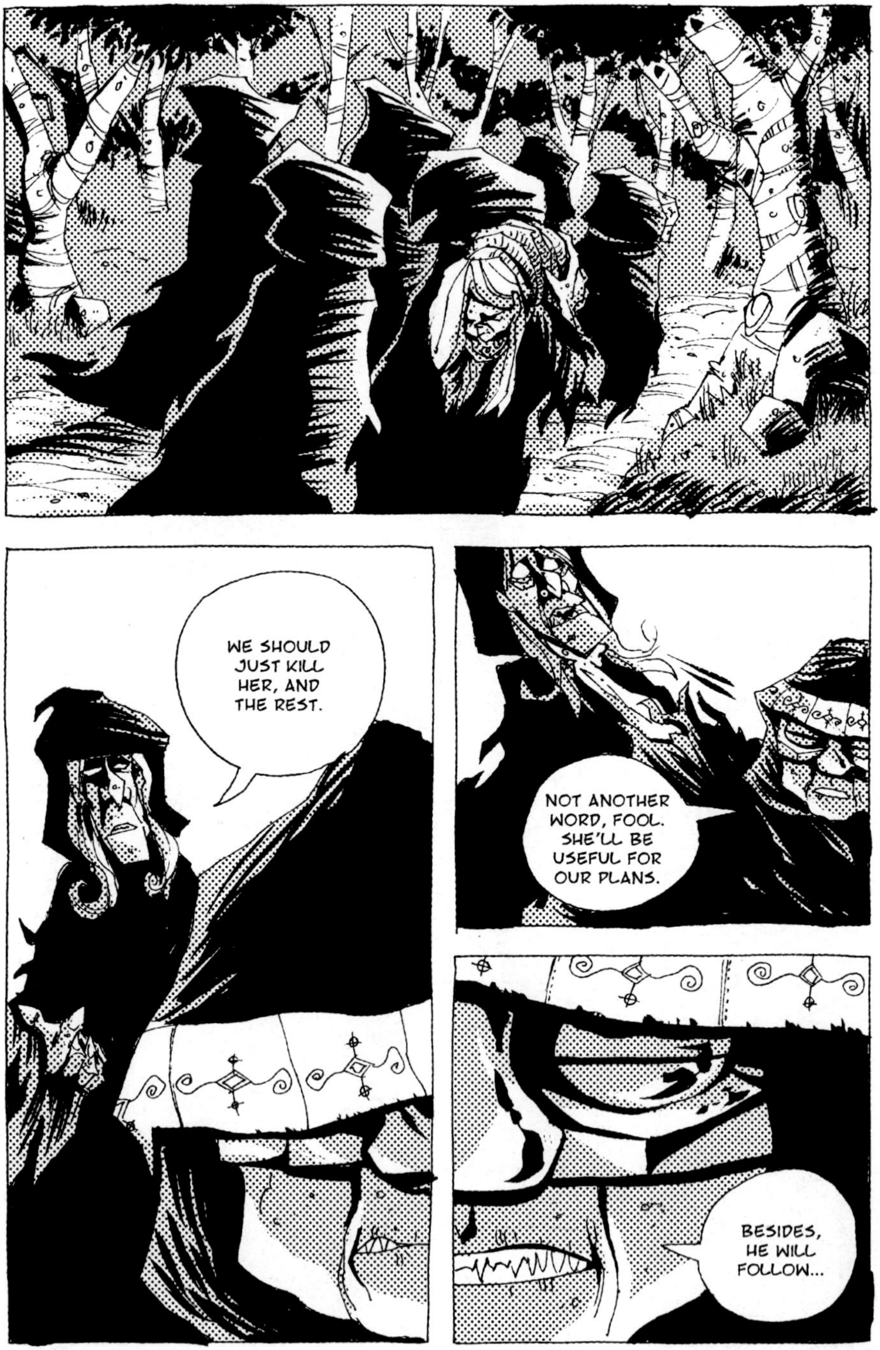
WE SHOULD JUST KILL HER, AND THE REST.
NOT ANOTHER WORD, FOOL. SHE'LL BE USEFUL FOR OUR PLANS.
BESIDES, HE WILL FOLLOW...

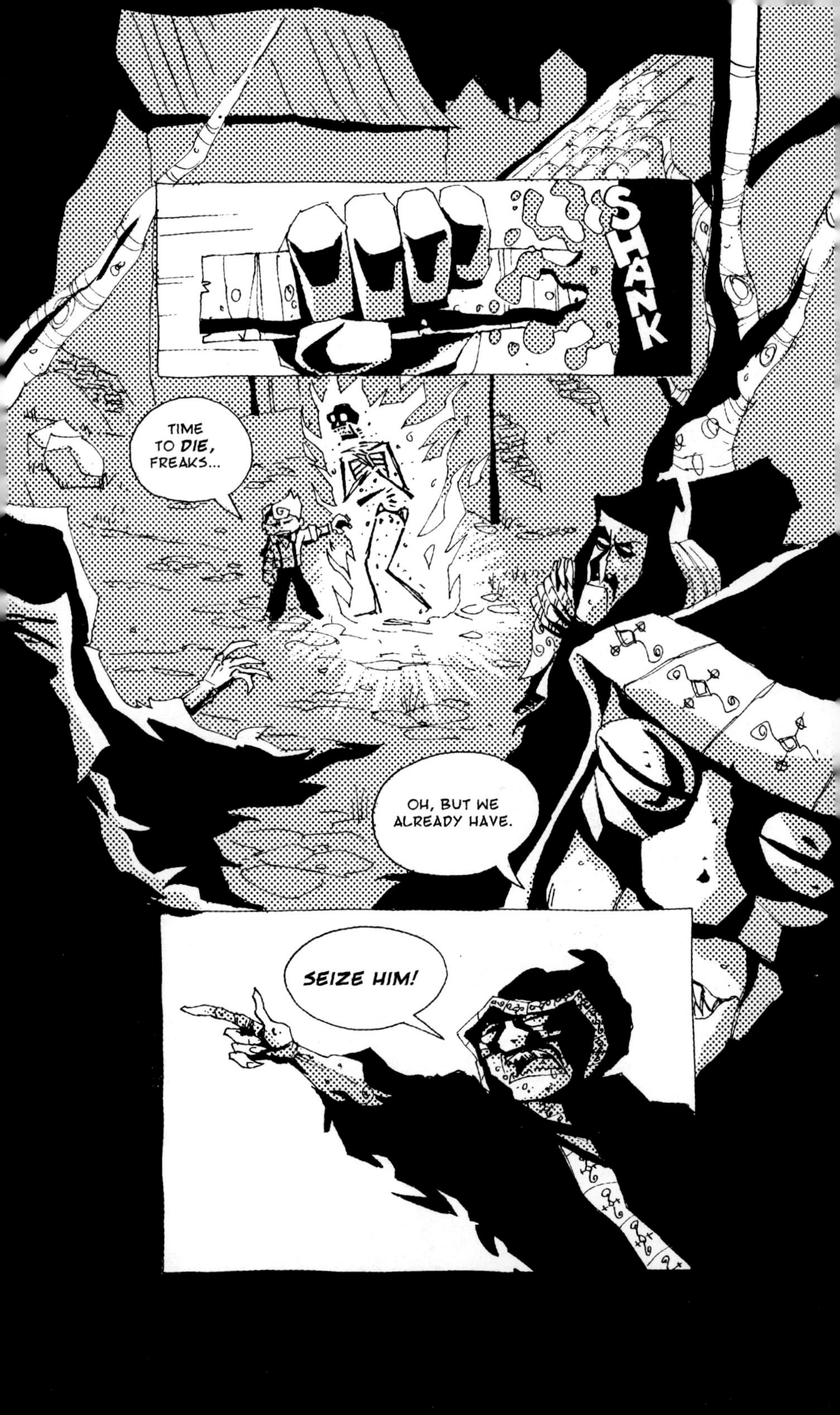
SHANK
TIME TO DIE, FREAKS...
OH, BUT WE ALREADY HAVE.
SEIZE HIM!

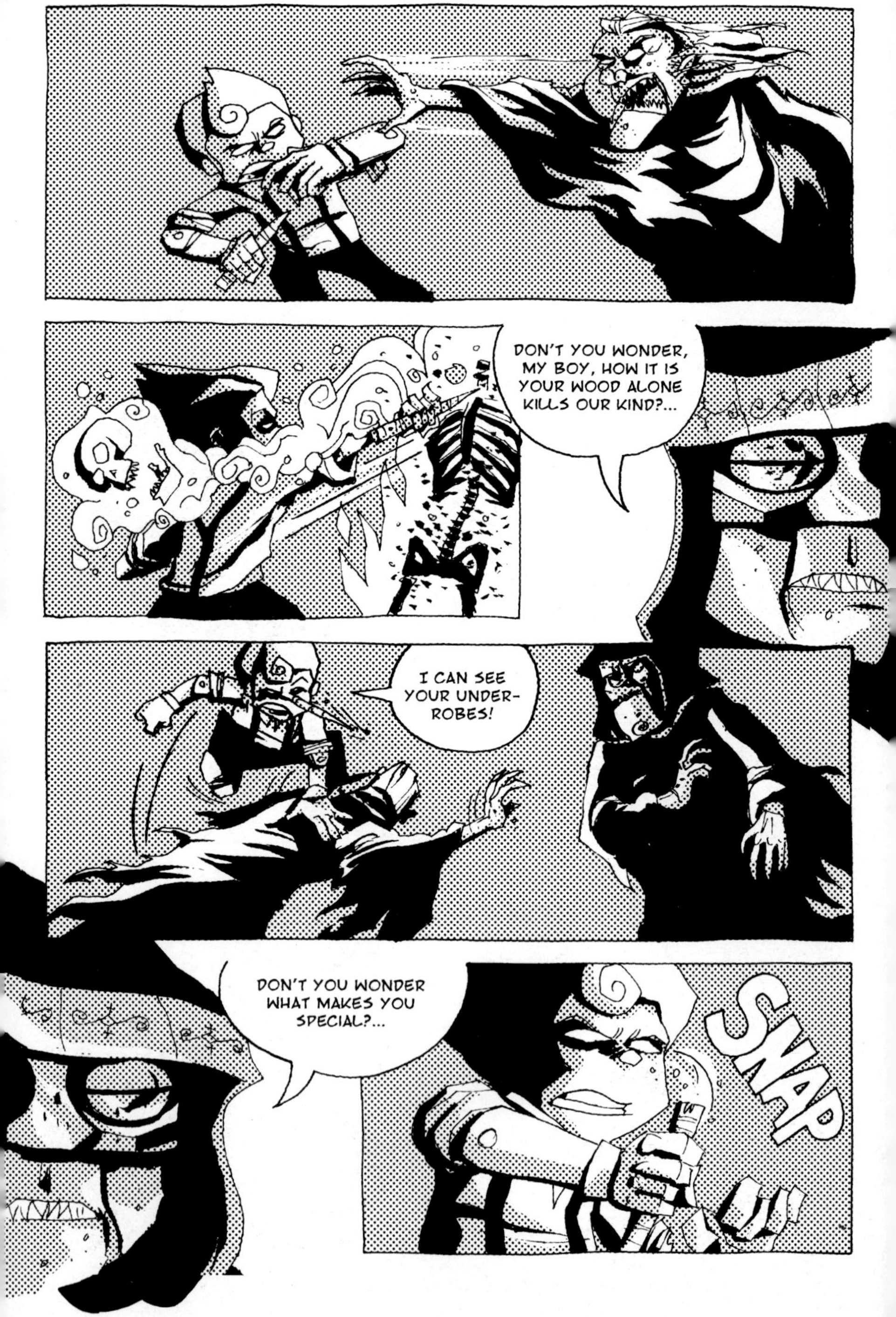
DON'T YOU WONDER, MY BOY, HOW IT IS YOUR WOOD ALONE KILLS OUR KIND?...
I CAN SEE YOUR UNDER-ROBES!
DON'T YOU WONDER WHAT MAKES YOU SPECIAL?...
SNAP

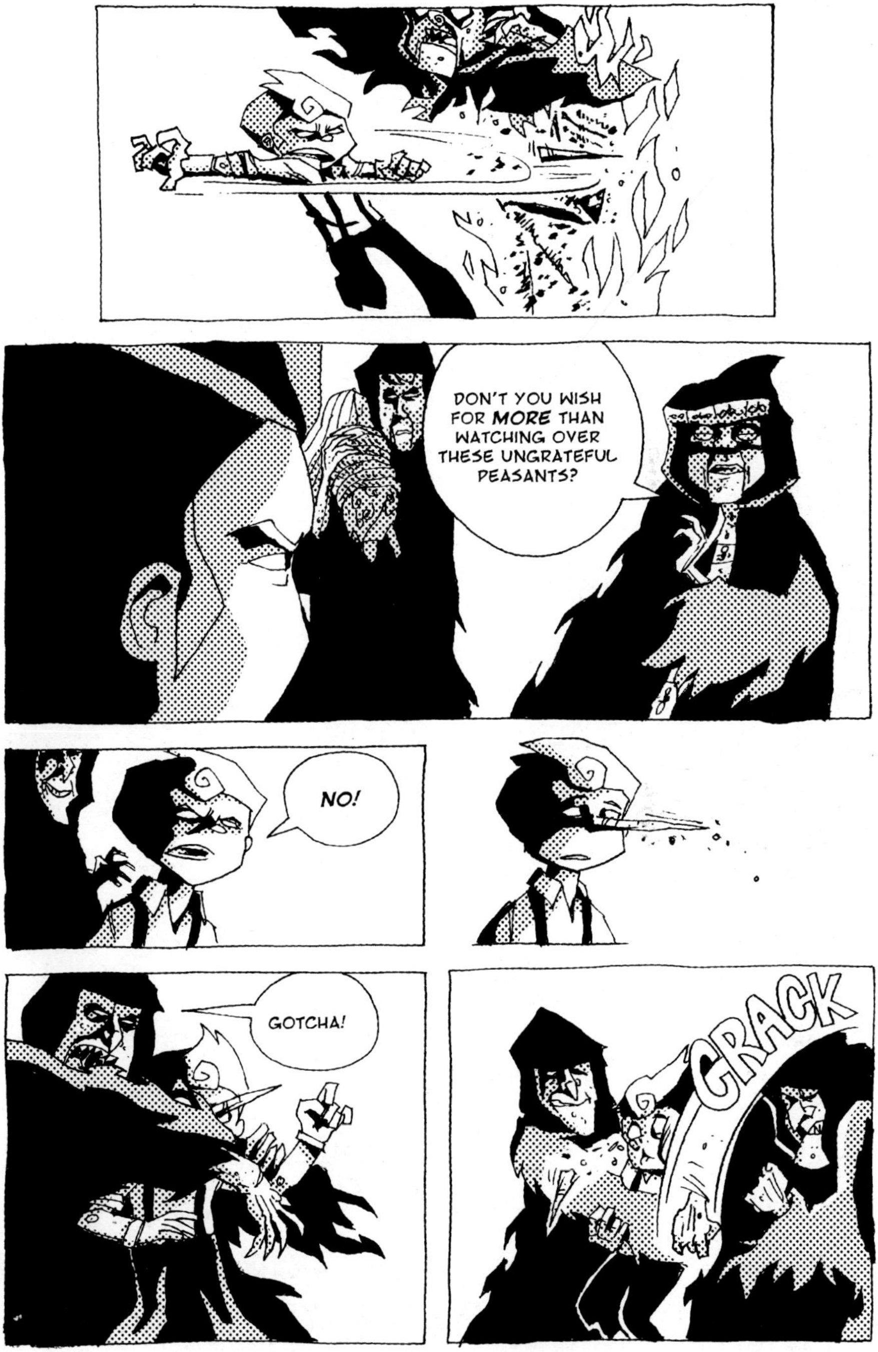
DON'T YOU WISH FOR **MORE** THAN WATCHING OVER THESE UNGRATEFUL PEASANTS?
NO!
GOTCHA!
CRACK

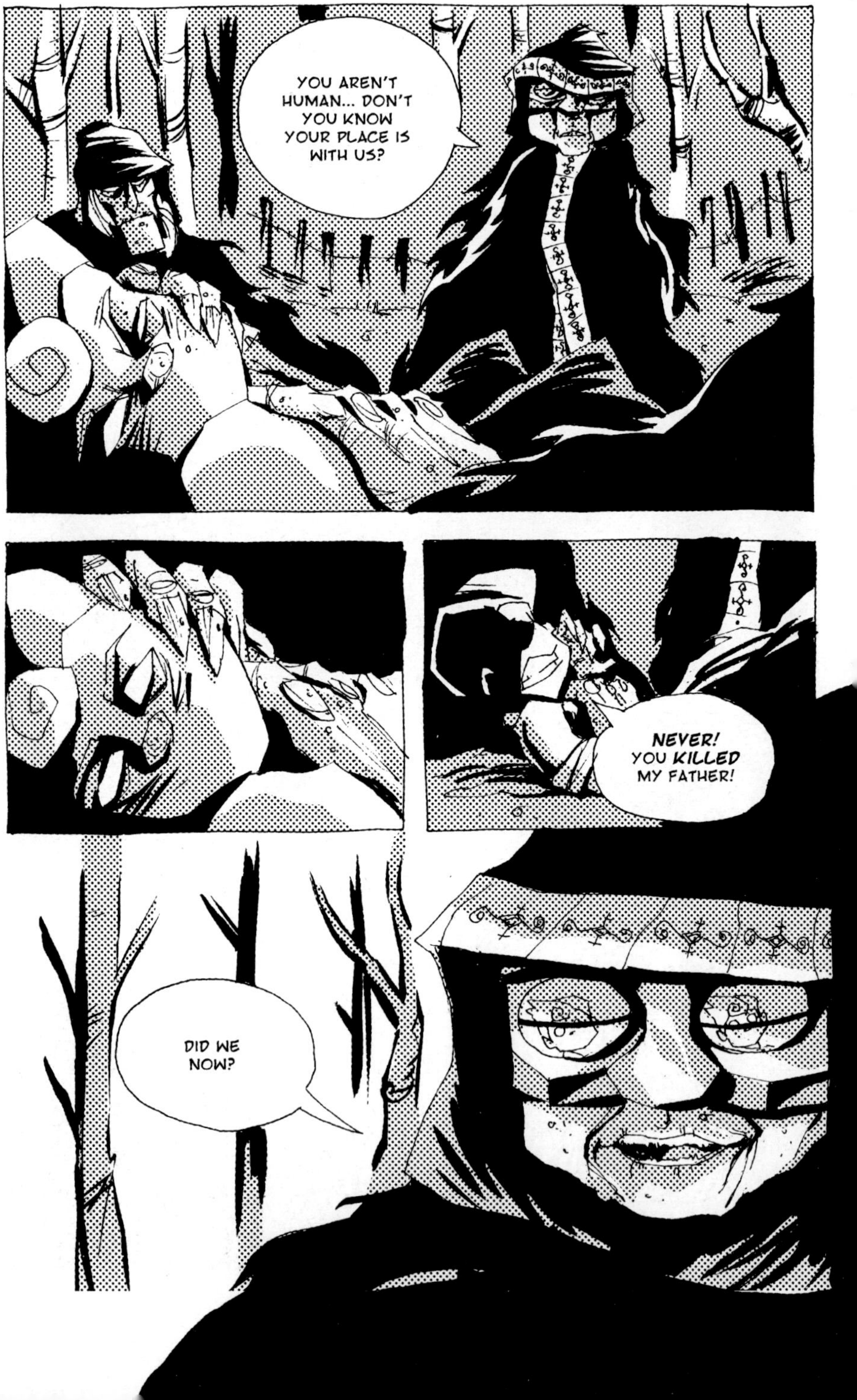
YOU AREN'T HUMAN... DON'T YOU KNOW YOUR PLACE IS WITH US?
NEVER! YOU KILLED MY FATHER!
DID WE NOW?

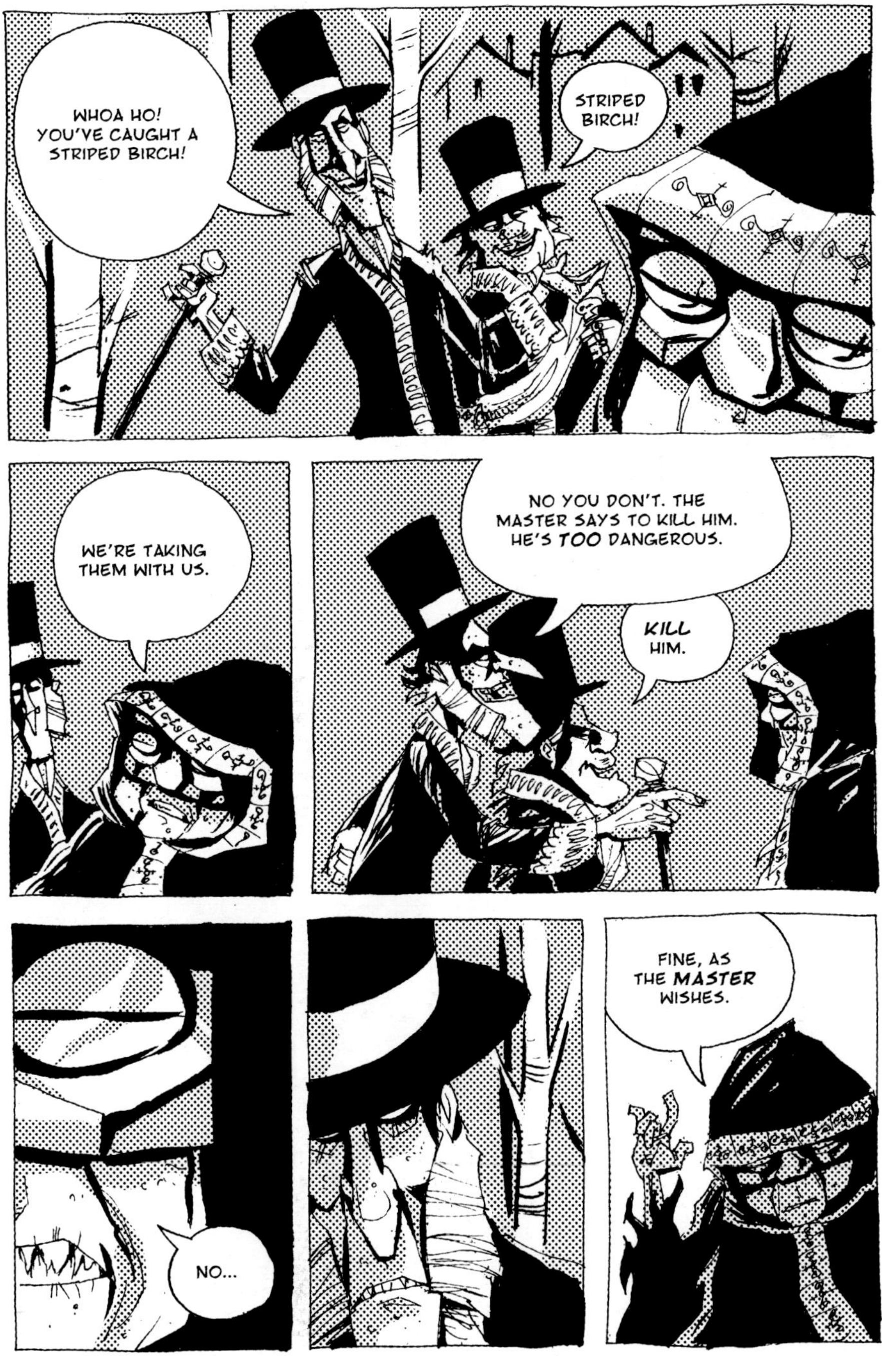
WHOA HO! YOU'VE CAUGHT A STRIPED BIRCH!
STRIPED BIRCH!
WE'RE TAKING THEM WITH US.
NO YOU DON'T. THE MASTER SAYS TO KILL HIM. HE'S TOO DANGEROUS.
KILL HIM.
NO...
FINE, AS THE MASTER WISHES.

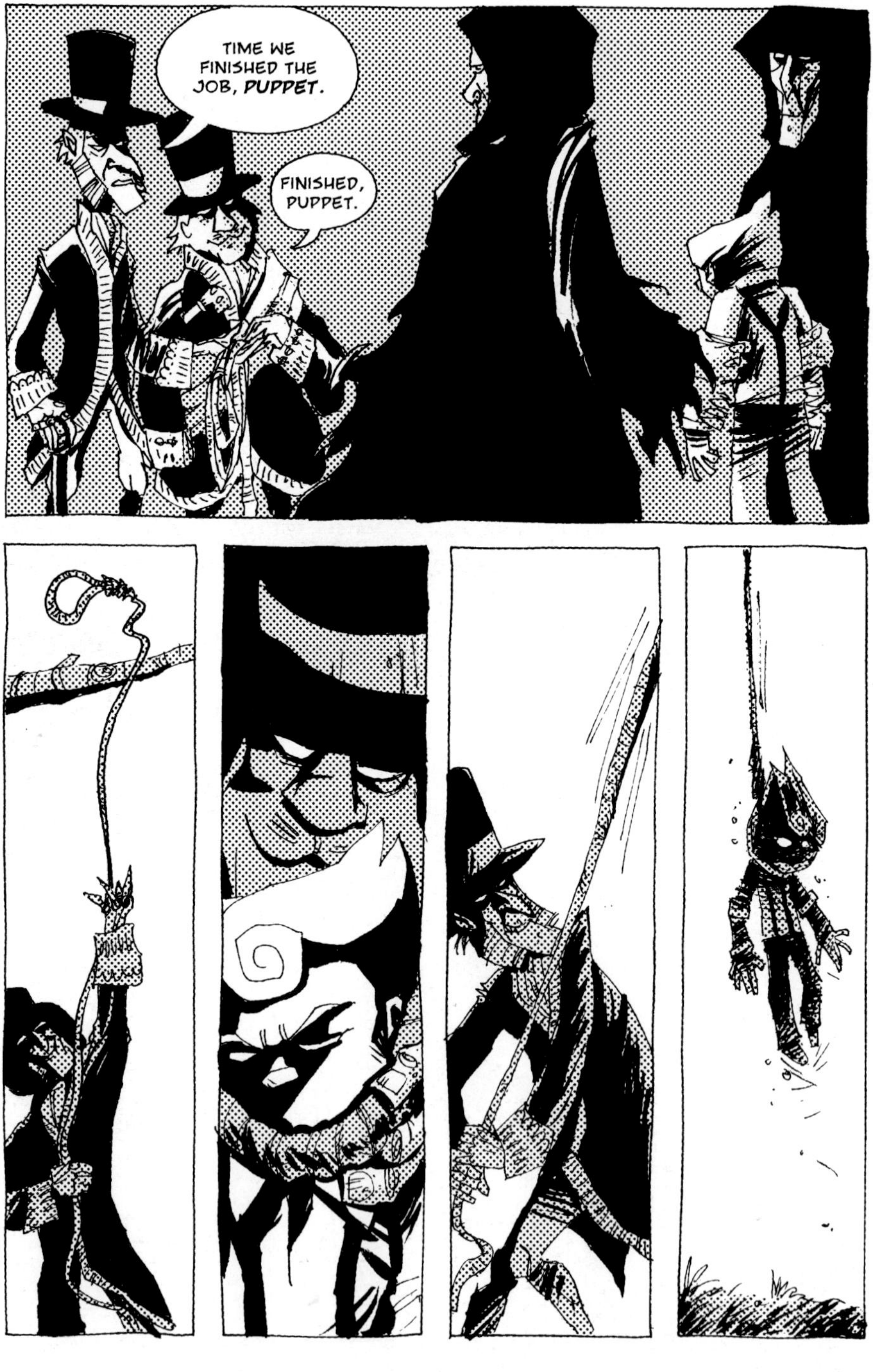
TIME WE FINISHED THE JOB, *PUPPET*.
FINISHED, PUPPET.

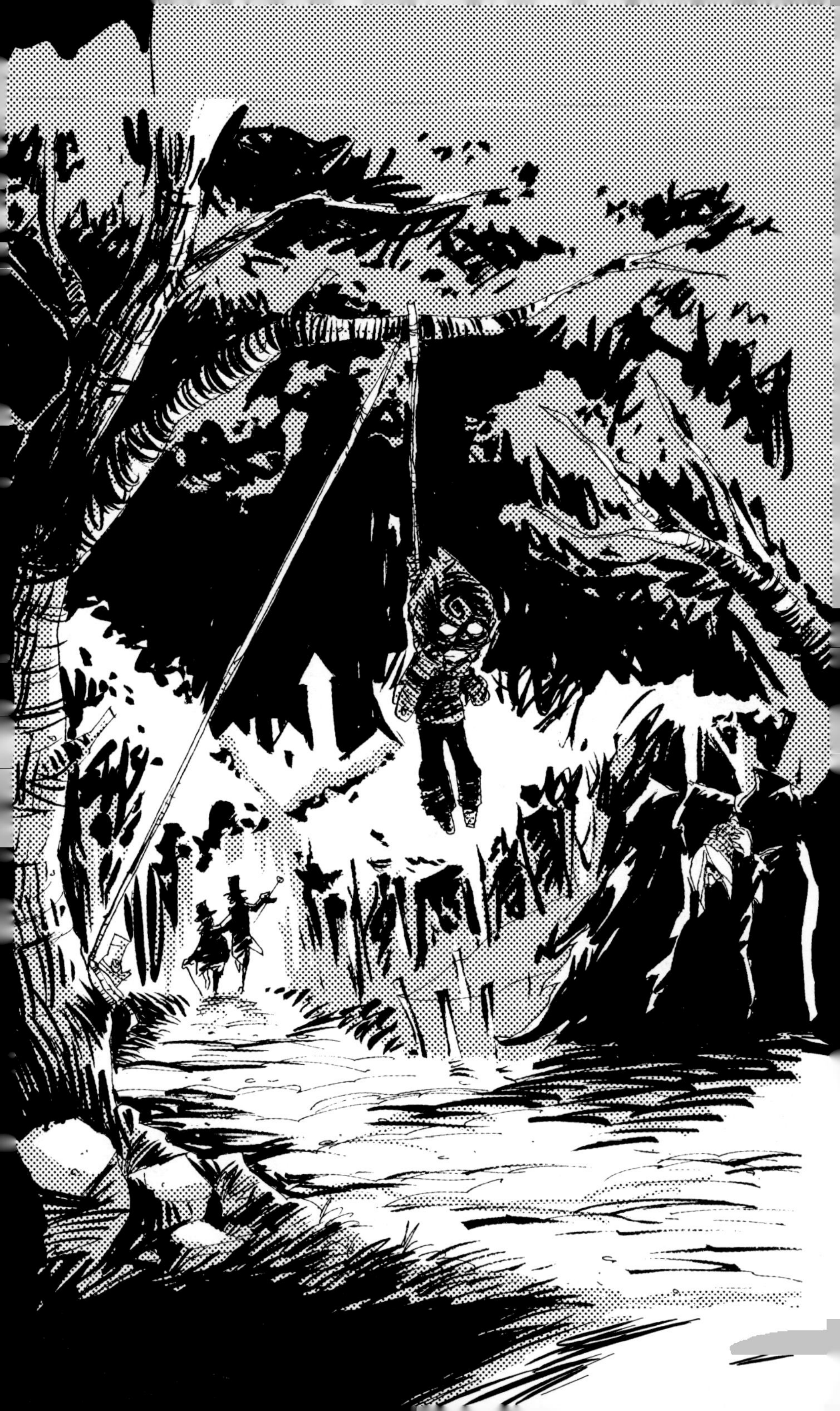

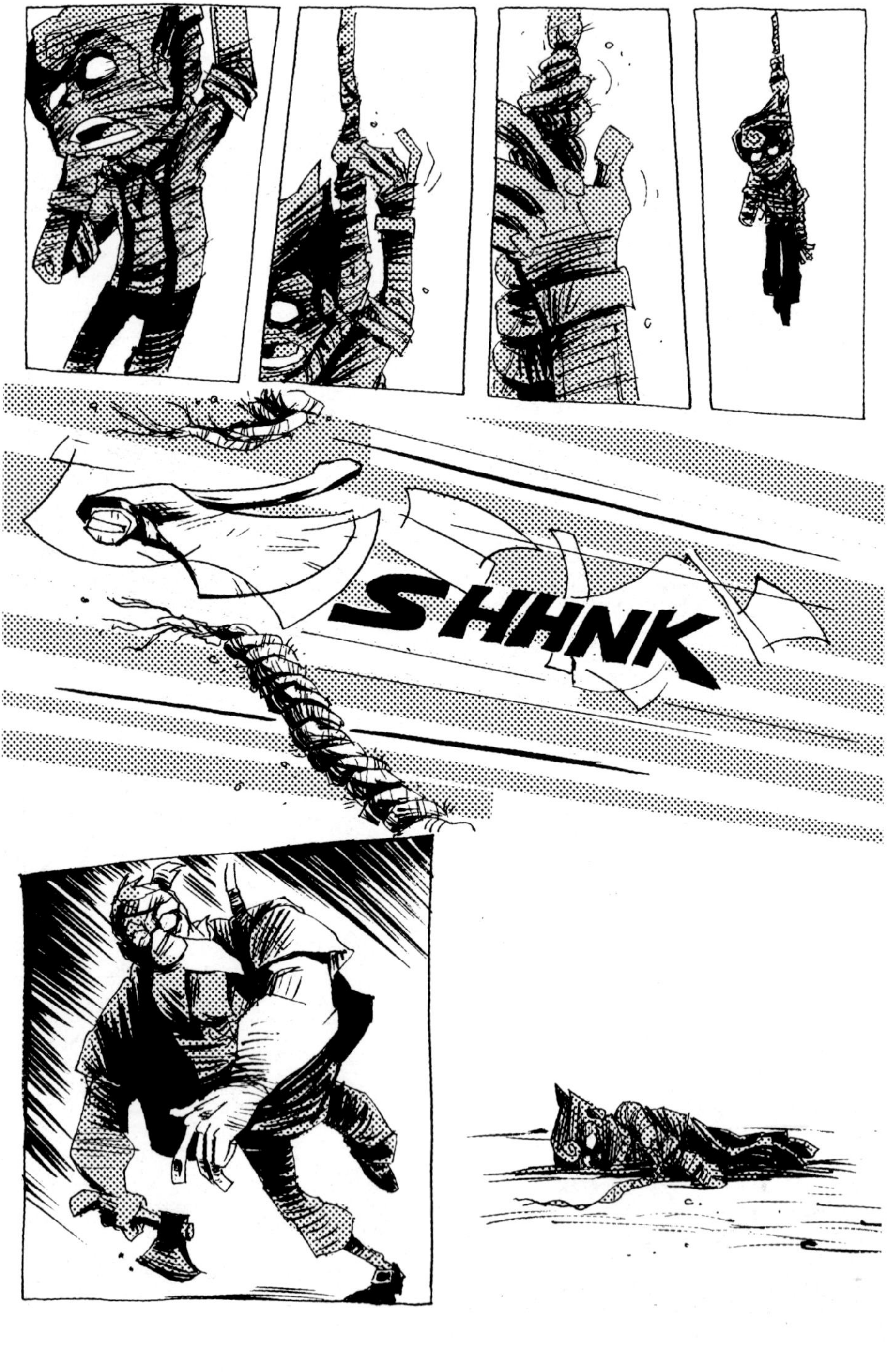
SHHNK

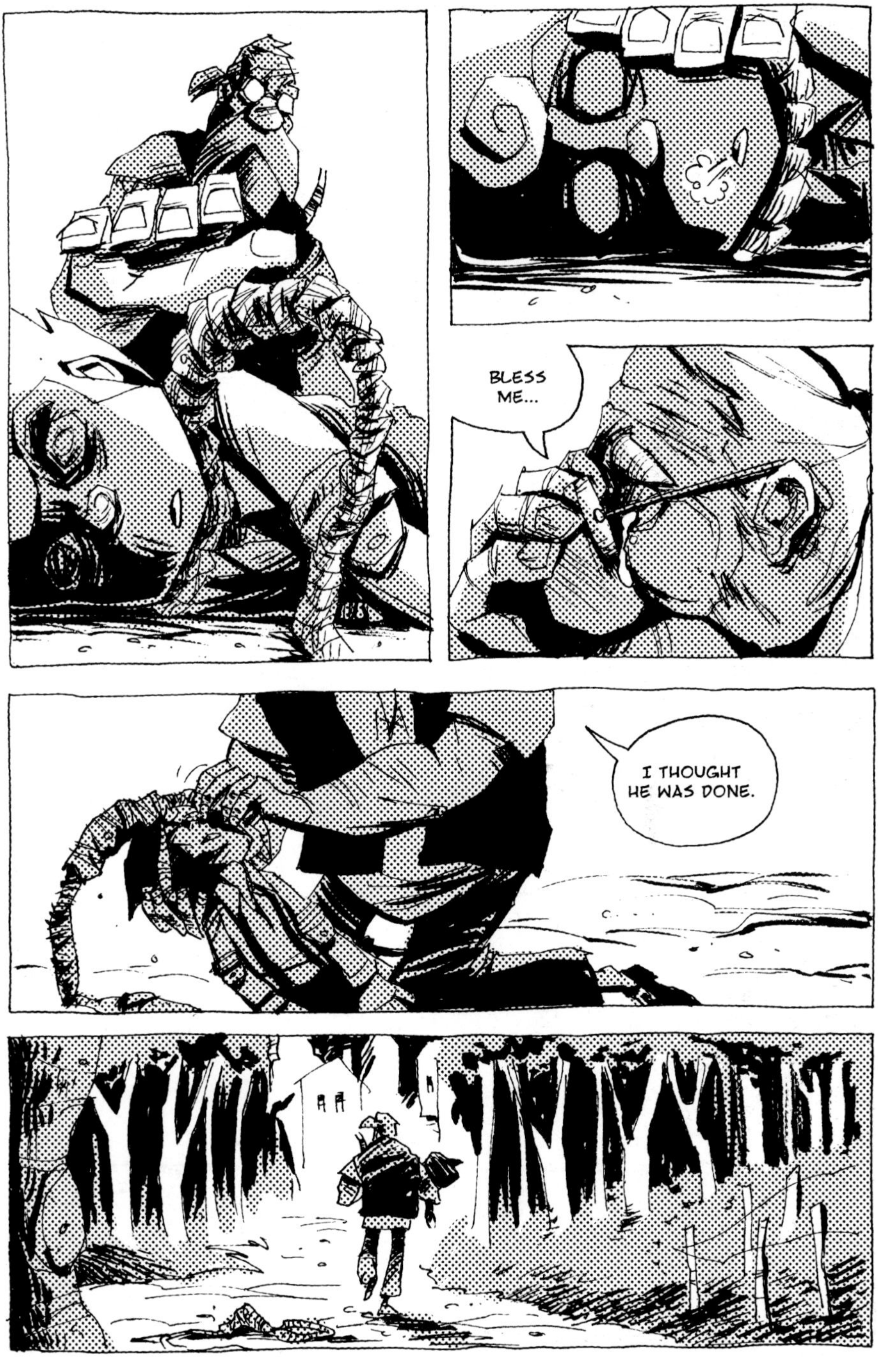
BLESS ME...
I THOUGHT HE WAS DONE.

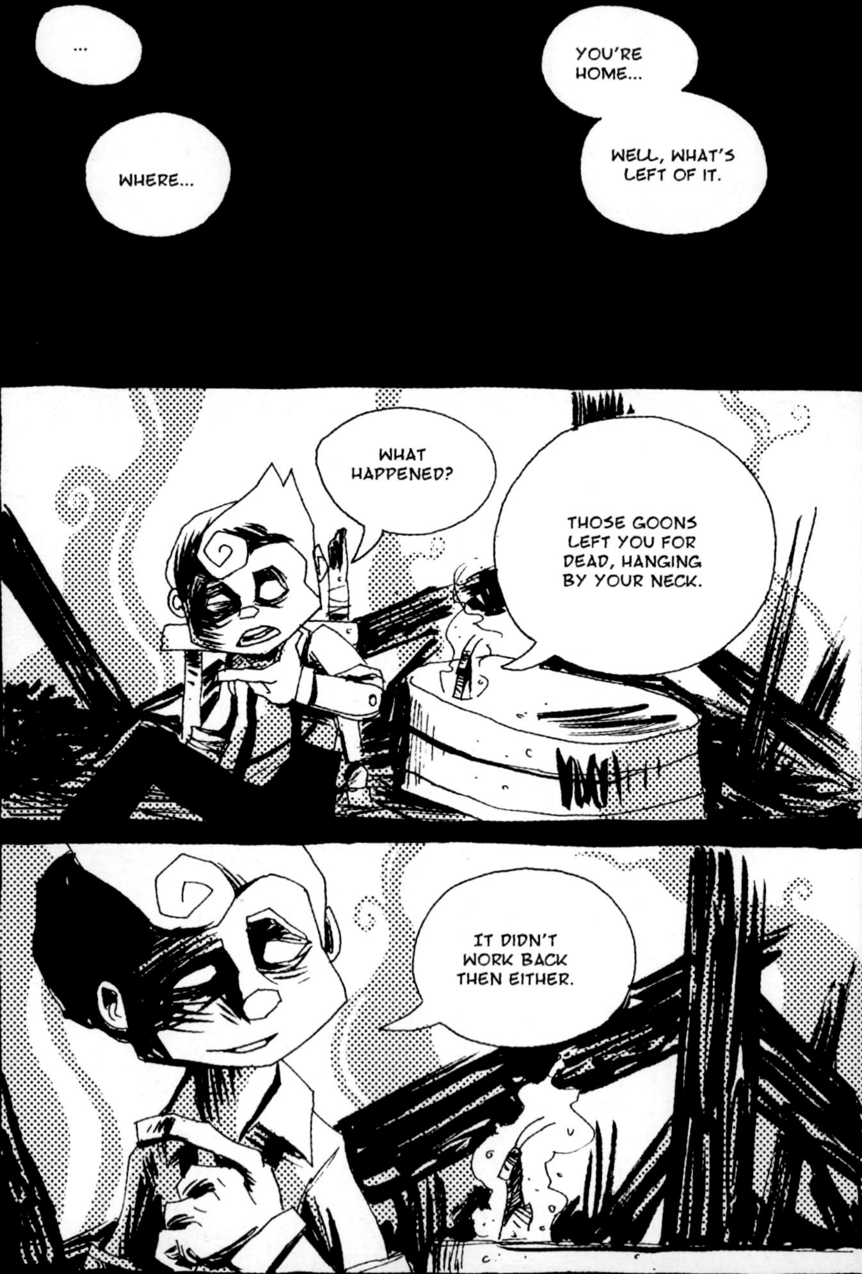
...
WHERE...
YOU'RE HOME...
WELL, WHAT'S LEFT OF IT.
WHAT HAPPENED?
THOSE GOONS LEFT YOU FOR DEAD, HANGING BY YOUR NECK.
IT DIDN'T WORK BACK THEN EITHER.

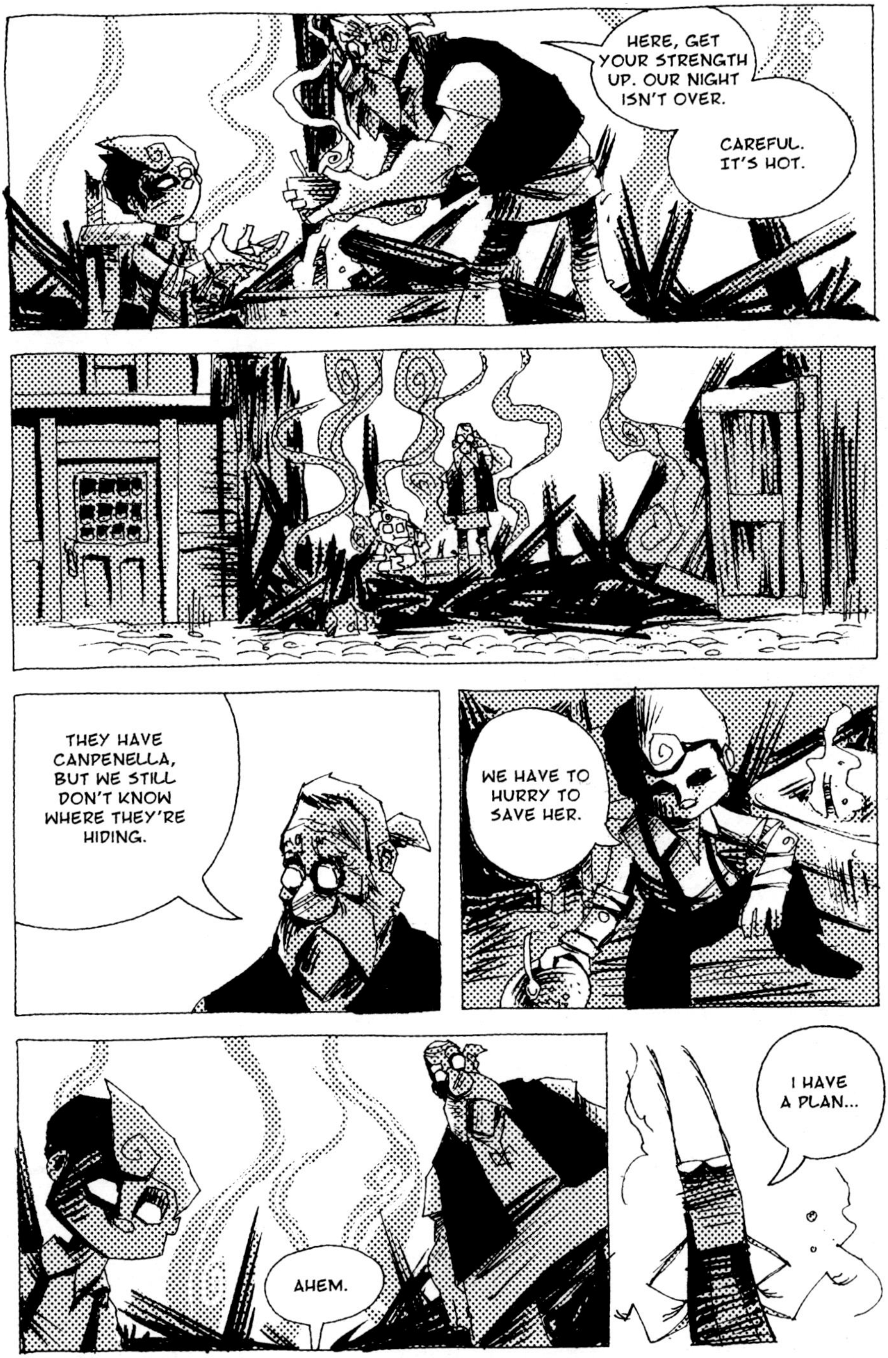
HERE, GET YOUR STRENGTH UP. OUR NIGHT ISN'T OVER.
CAREFUL. IT'S HOT.
THEY HAVE CANPENELLA, BUT WE STILL DON'T KNOW WHERE THEY'RE HIDING.
WE HAVE TO HURRY TO SAVE HER.
AHEM.
I HAVE A PLAN...

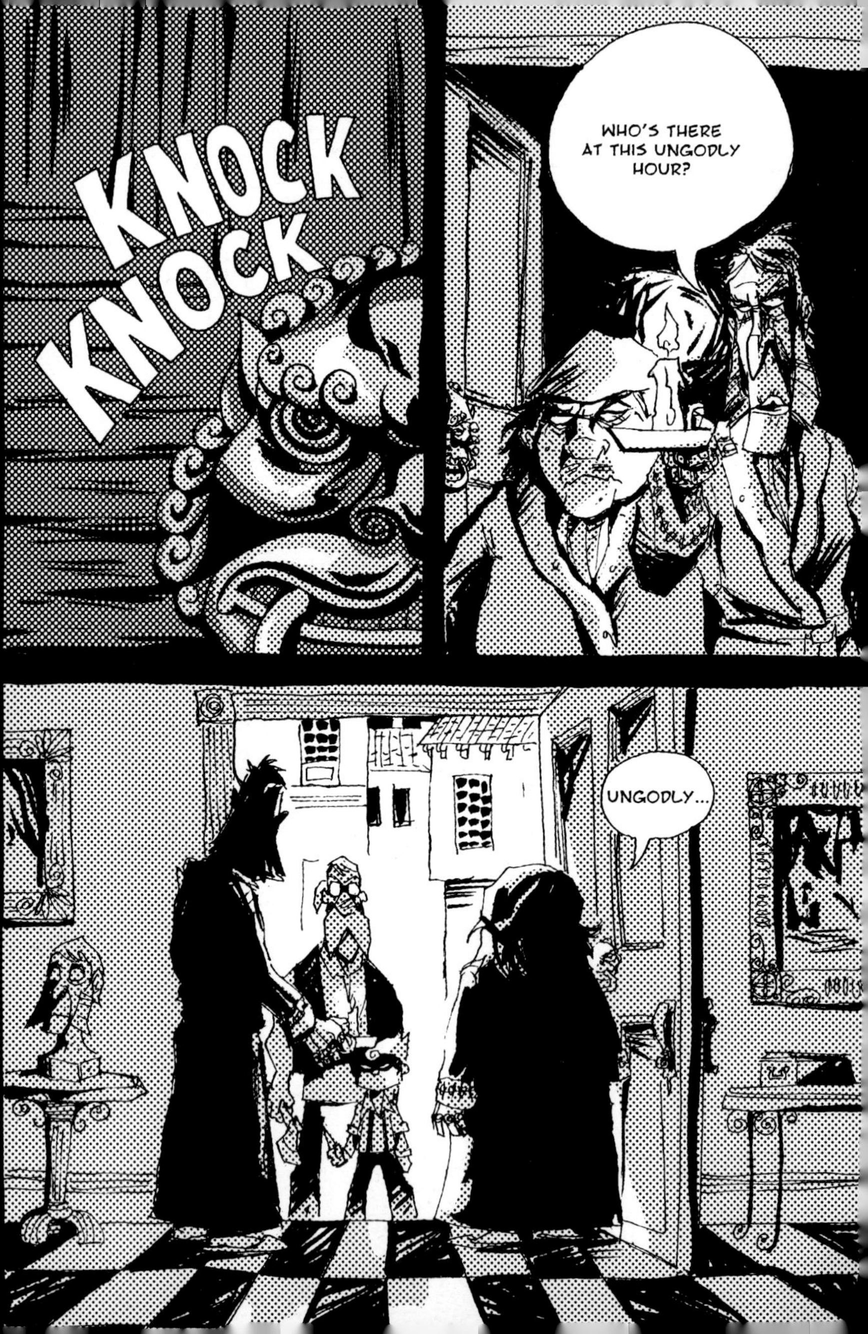
KNOCK KNOCK
WHO'S THERE AT THIS UNGODLY HOUR?
UNGODLY...

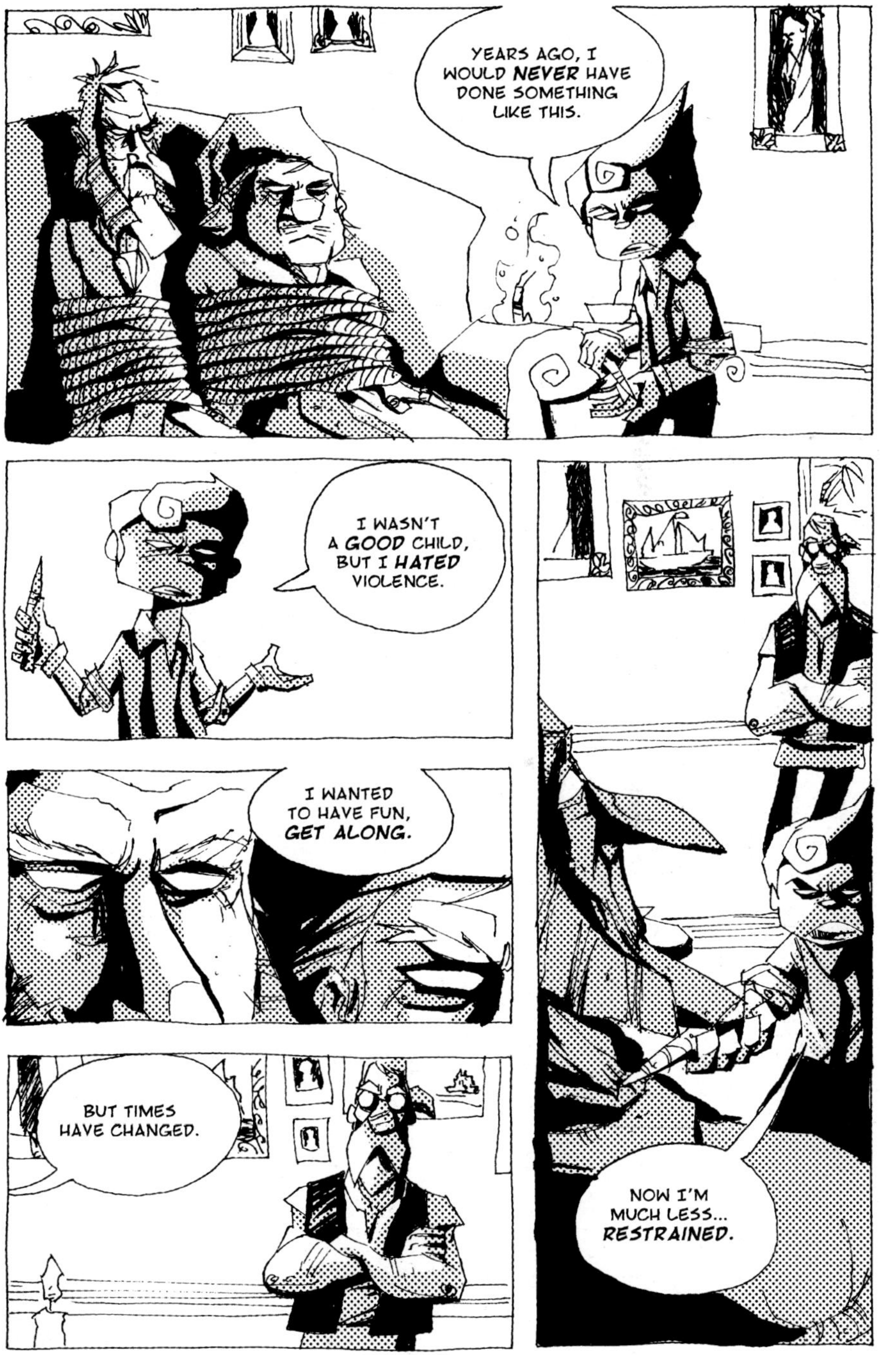
YEARS AGO, I WOULD **NEVER** HAVE DONE SOMETHING LIKE THIS.
I WASN'T A **GOOD** CHILD, BUT I **HATED** VIOLENCE.
I WANTED TO HAVE FUN, **GET ALONG.**
BUT TIMES HAVE CHANGED.
NOW I'M MUCH LESS... **RESTRAINED.**

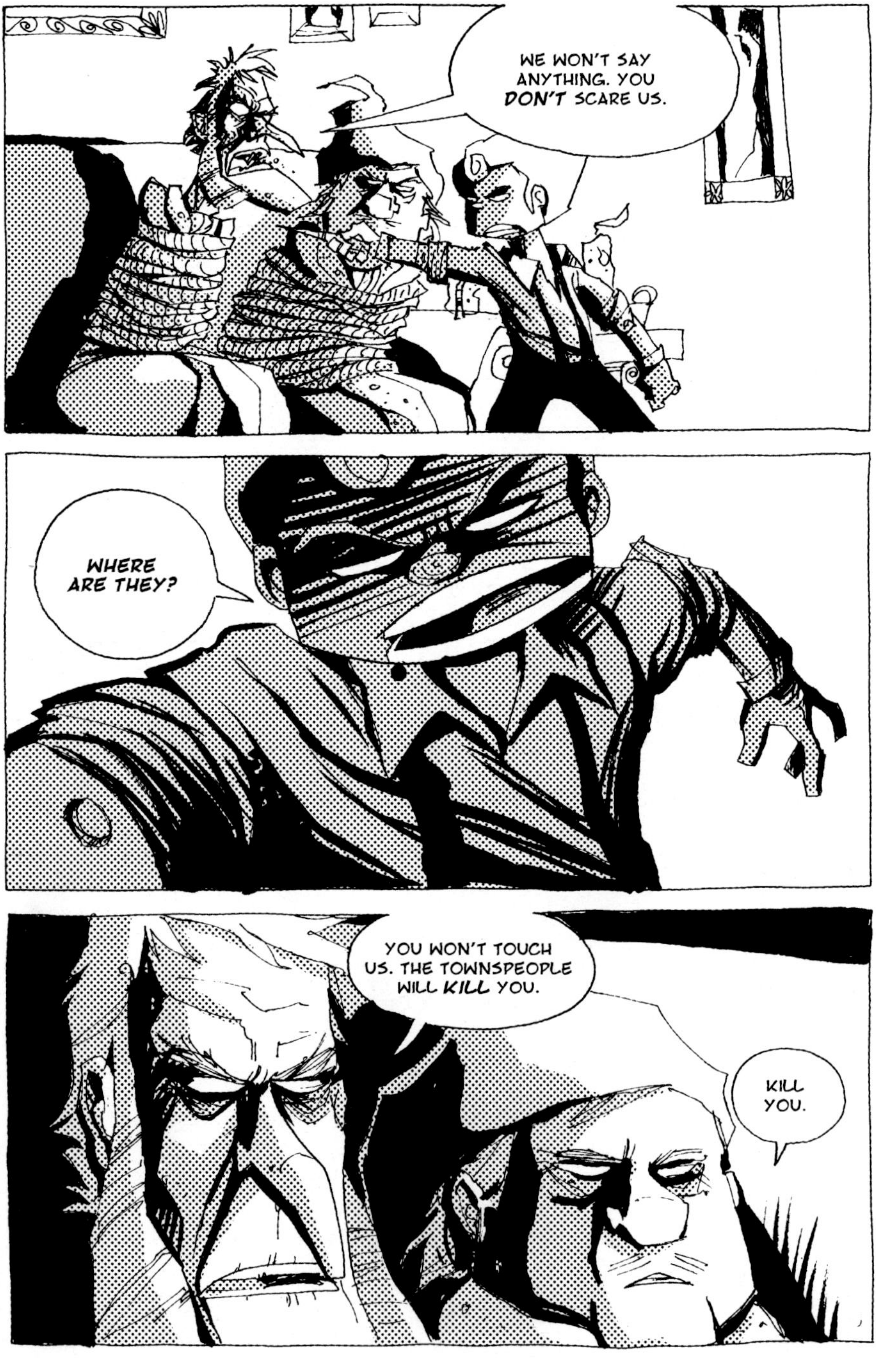
WE WON'T SAY ANYTHING. YOU DON'T SCARE US.
WHERE ARE THEY?
YOU WON'T TOUCH US. THE TOWNSPEOPLE WILL KILL YOU.
KILL YOU.

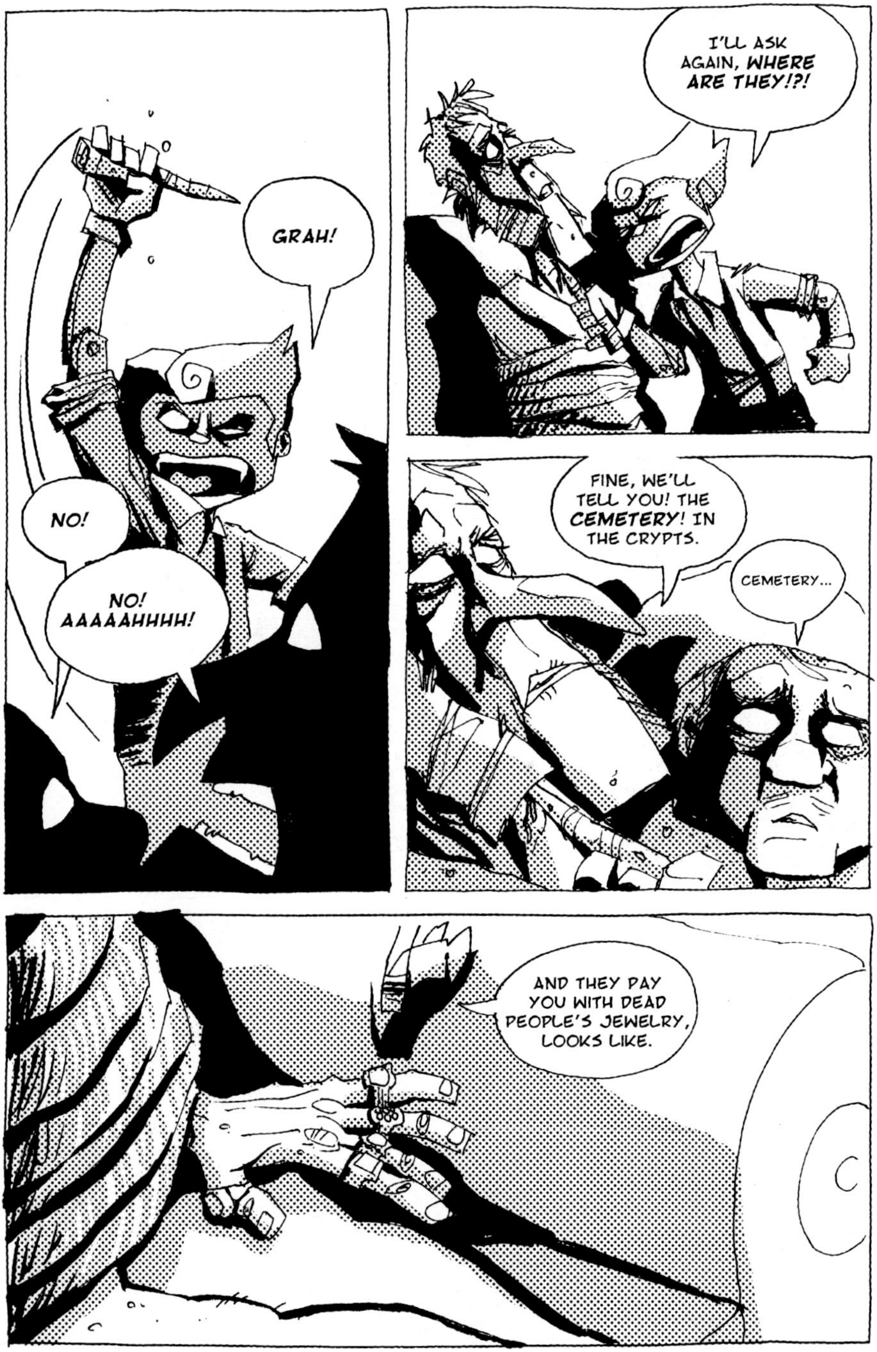
GRAH!
NO!
NO! AAAAAHHHH!
I'LL ASK AGAIN, WHERE ARE THEY!?!
FINE, WE'LL TELL YOU! THE CEMETERY! IN THE CRYPTS.
CEMETERY...
AND THEY PAY YOU WITH DEAD PEOPLE'S JEWELRY, LOOKS LIKE.

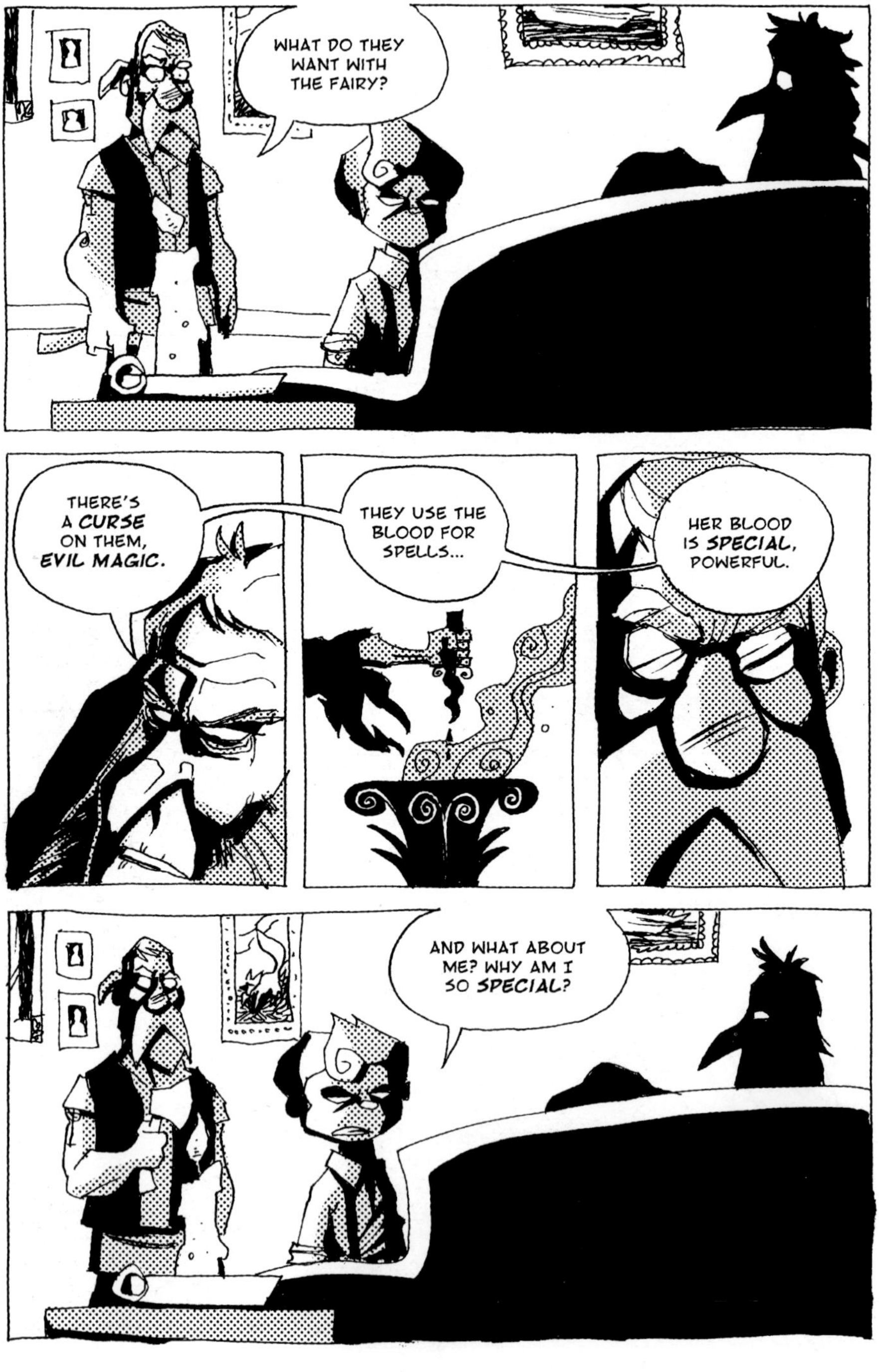
WHAT DO THEY WANT WITH THE FAIRY?
THERE'S A CURSE ON THEM, EVIL MAGIC.
THEY USE THE BLOOD FOR SPELLS...
HER BLOOD IS SPECIAL, POWERFUL.
AND WHAT ABOUT ME? WHY AM I SO SPECIAL?

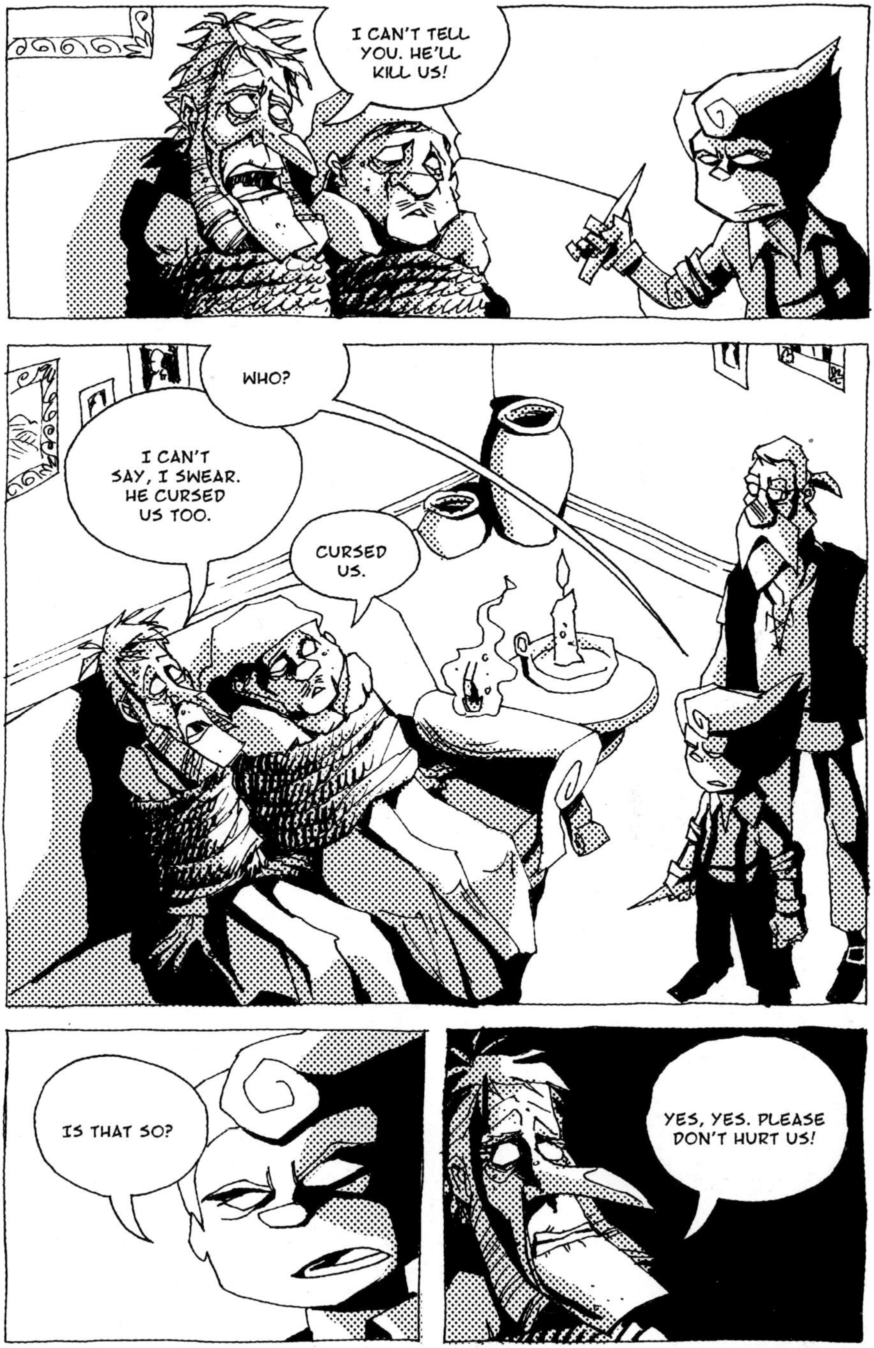
I CAN'T TELL YOU. HE'LL KILL US!
WHO?
I CAN'T SAY, I SWEAR. HE CURSED US TOO.
CURSED US.
IS THAT SO?
YES, YES. PLEASE DON'T HURT US!

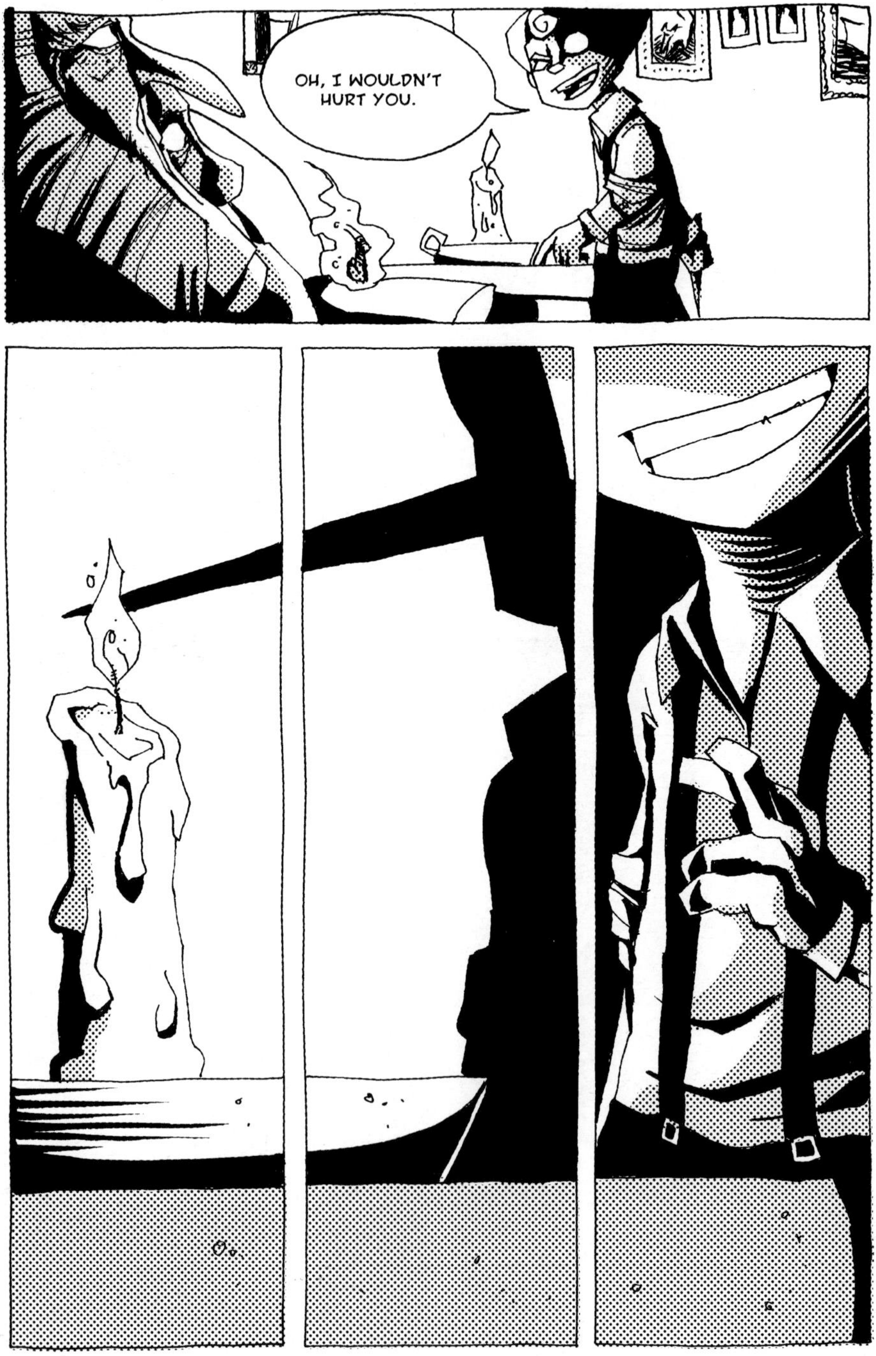
OH, I WOULDN'T HURT YOU.

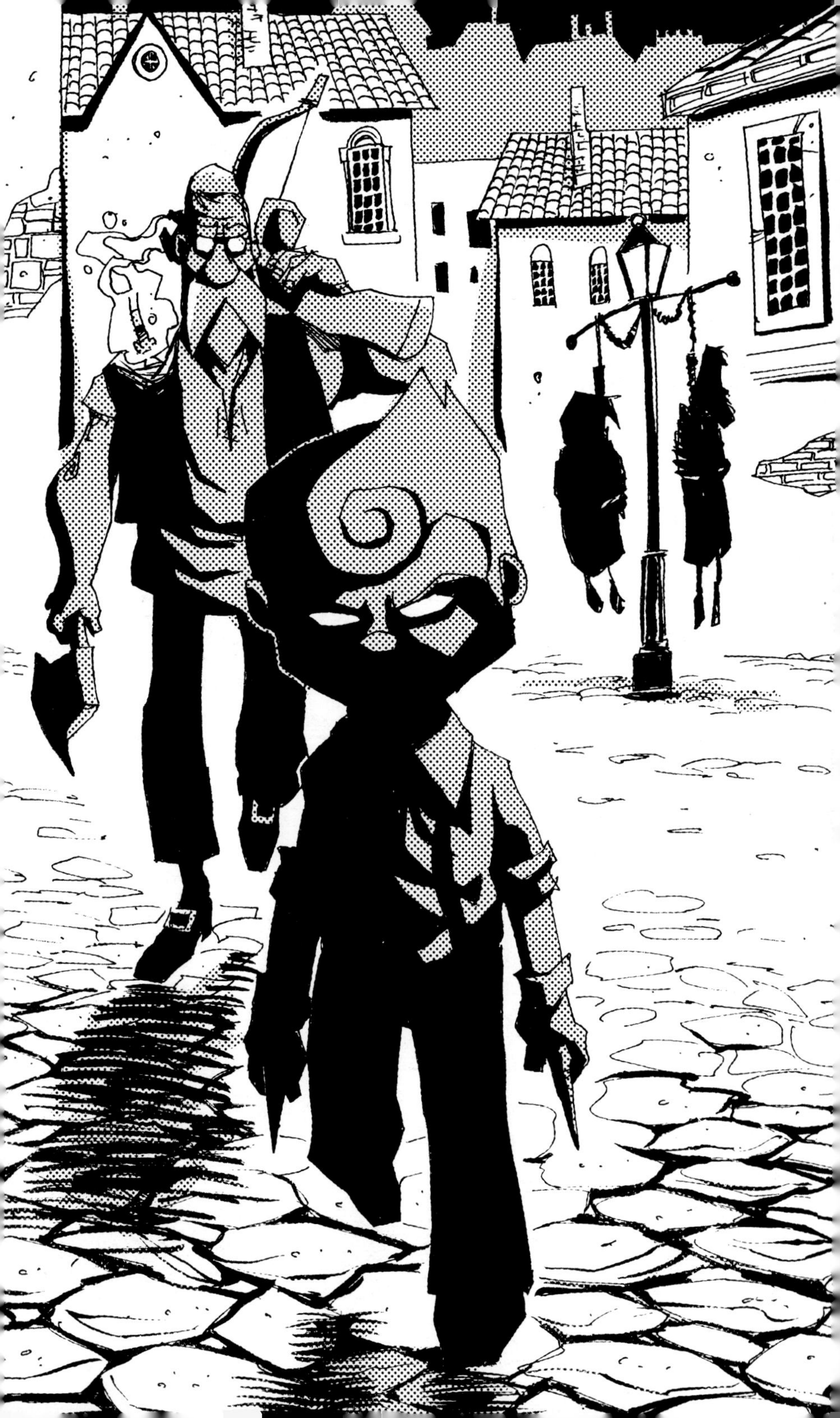

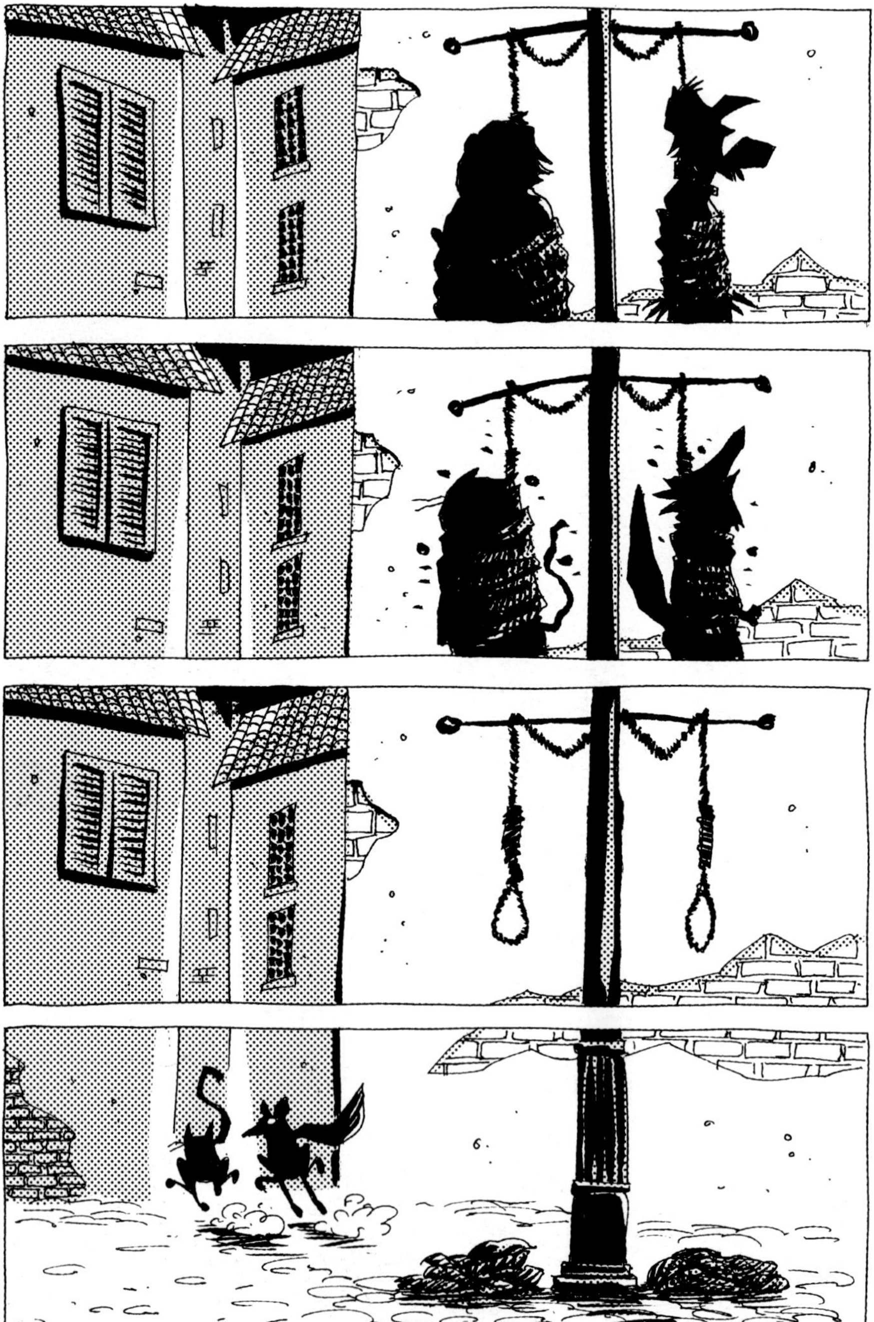

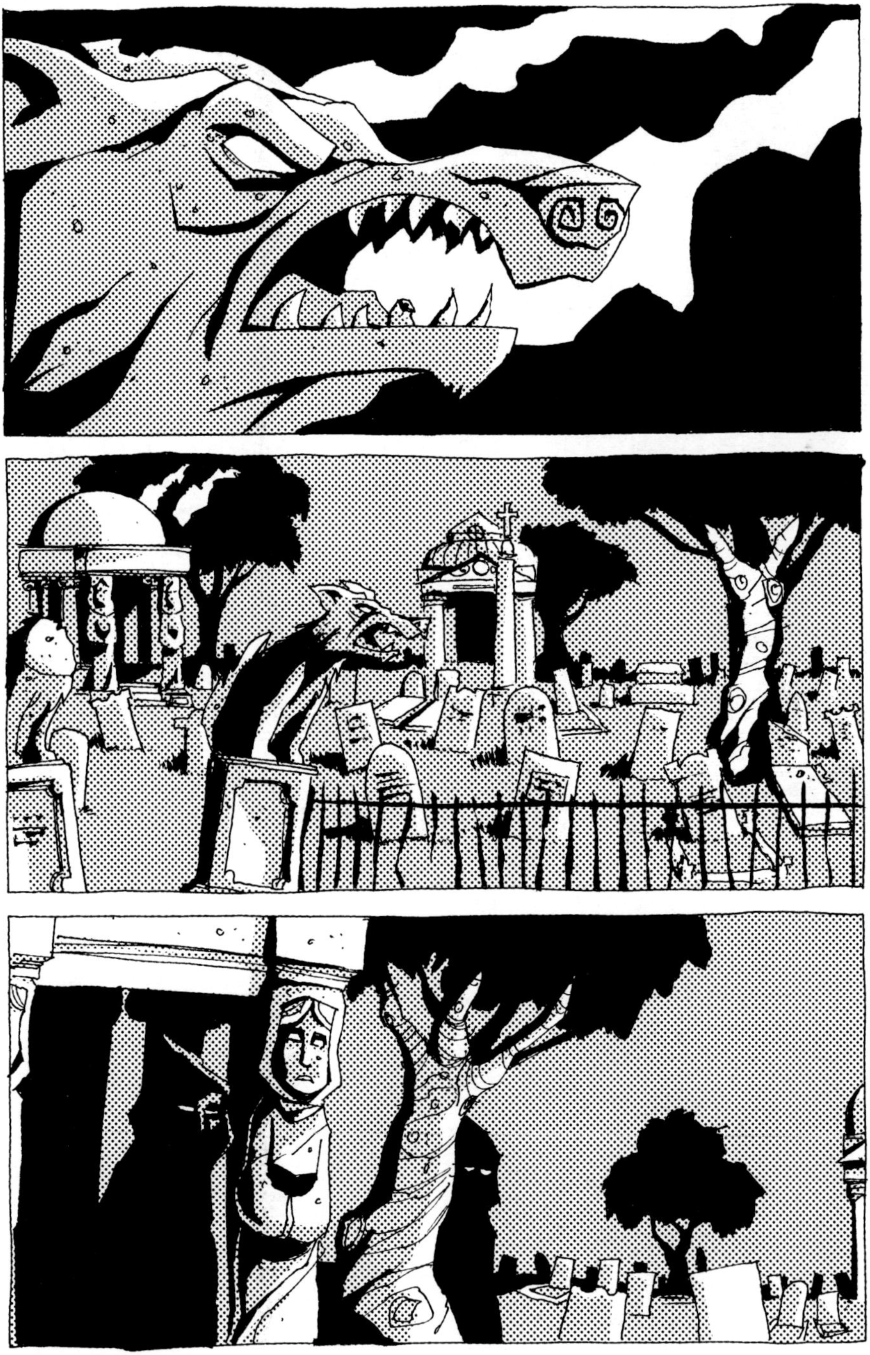

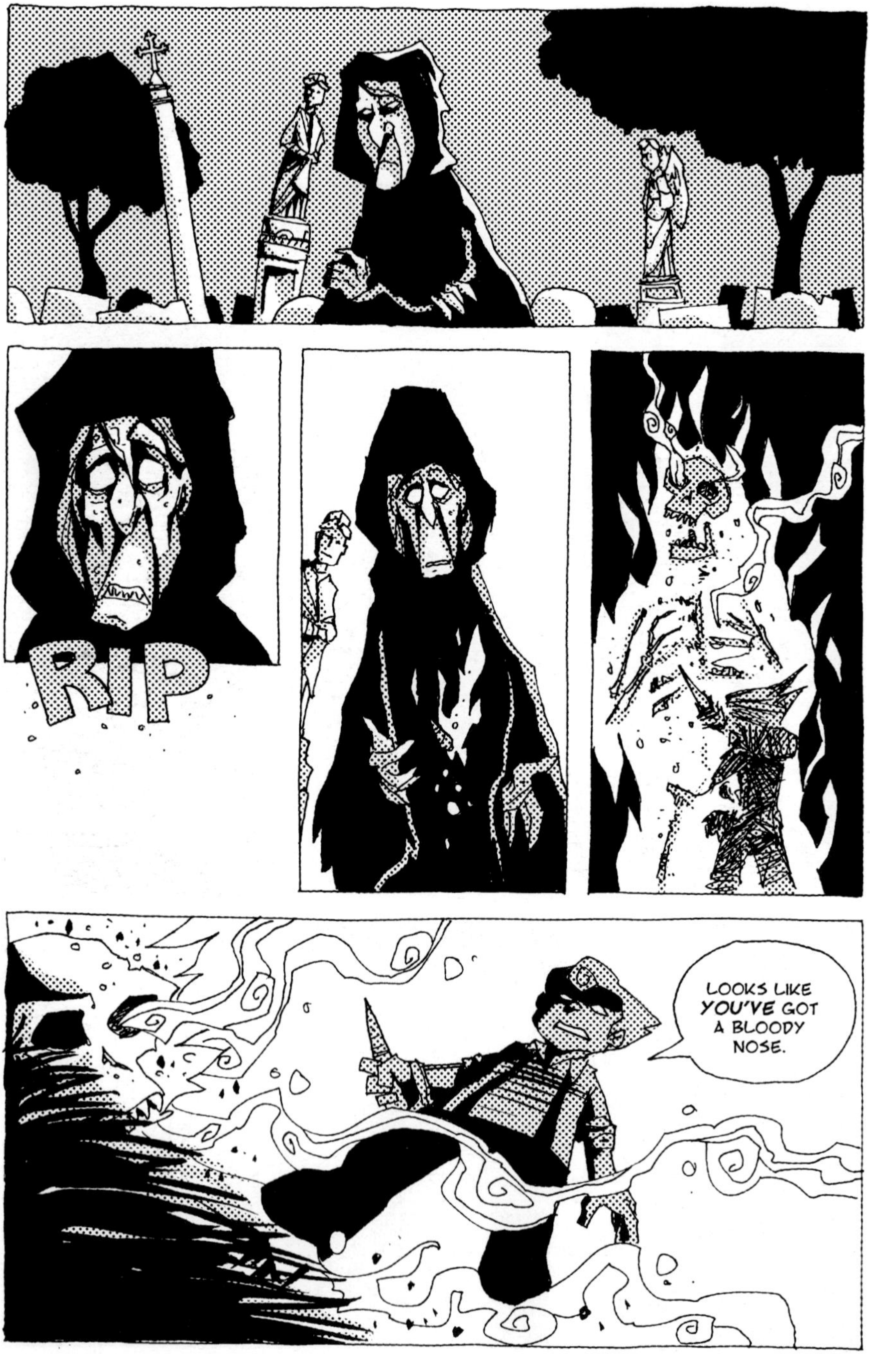
RIP
LOOKS LIKE YOU'VE GOT A BLOODY NOSE.

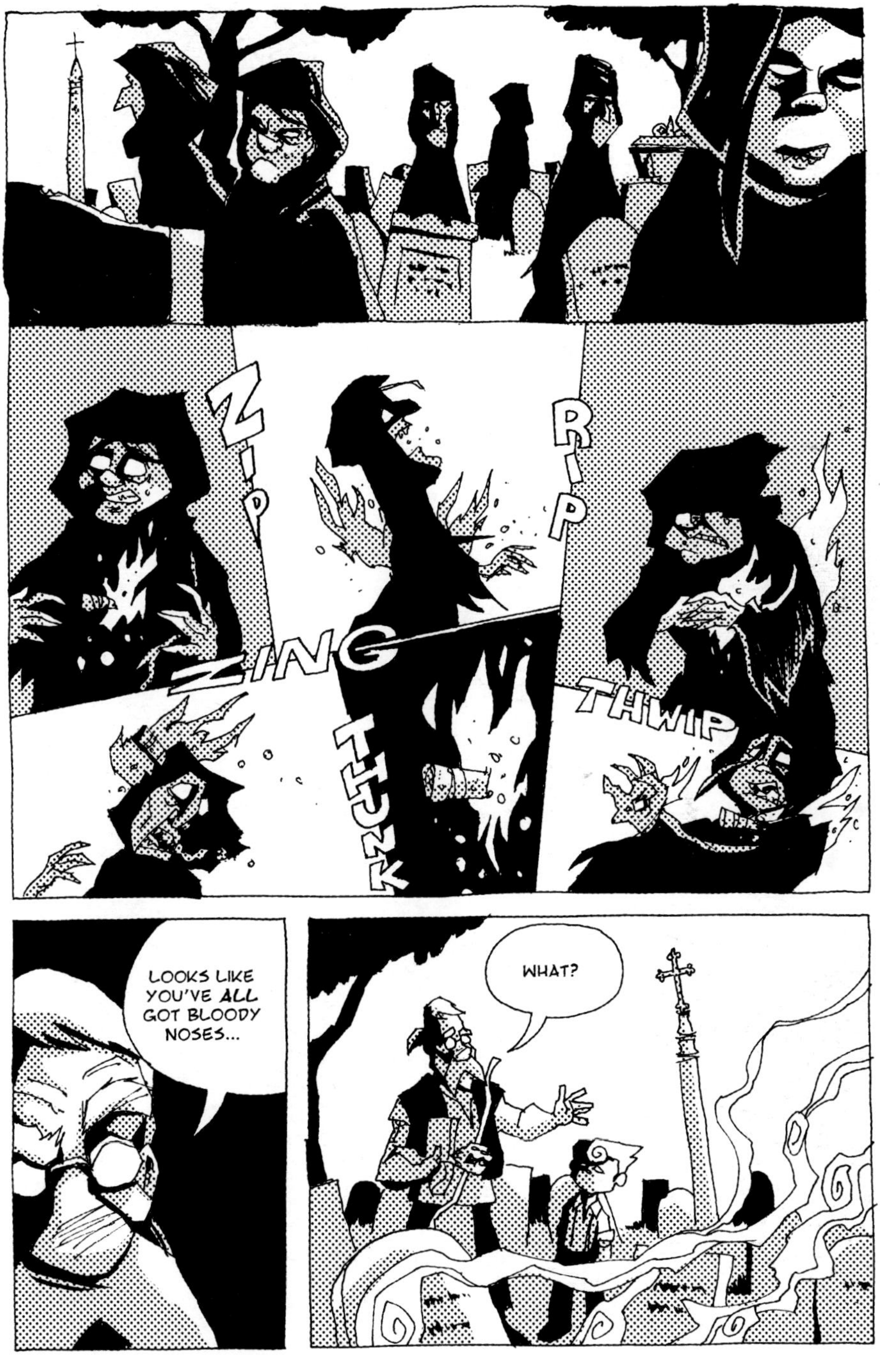
ZIP
RIP
ZING
THUNK
THWIP
LOOKS LIKE YOU'VE **ALL** GOT BLOODY NOSES...
WHAT?

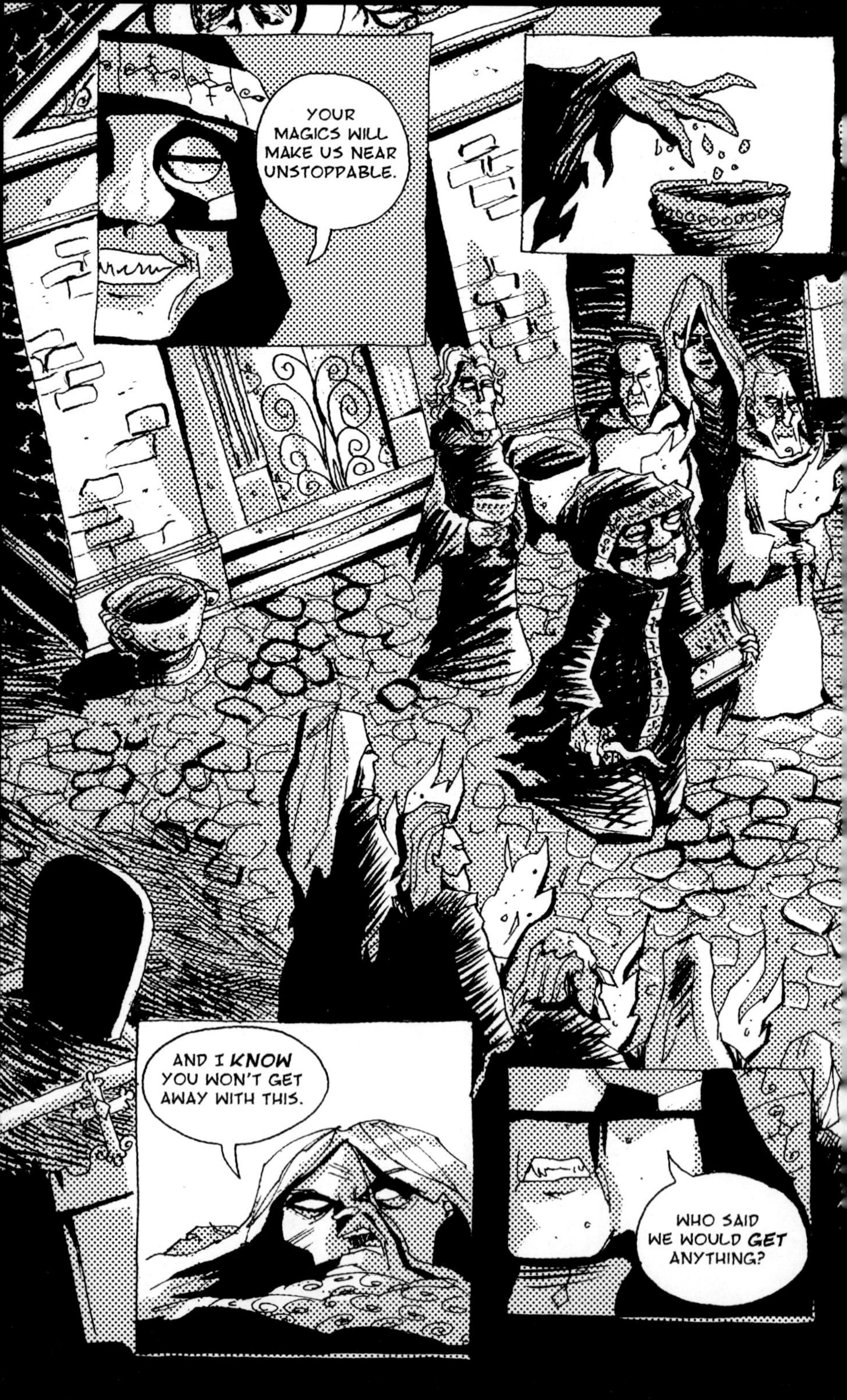
YOUR MAGICS WILL MAKE US NEAR UNSTOPPABLE.
AND I KNOW YOU WON'T GET AWAY WITH THIS.
WHO SAID WE WOULD GET ANYTHING?

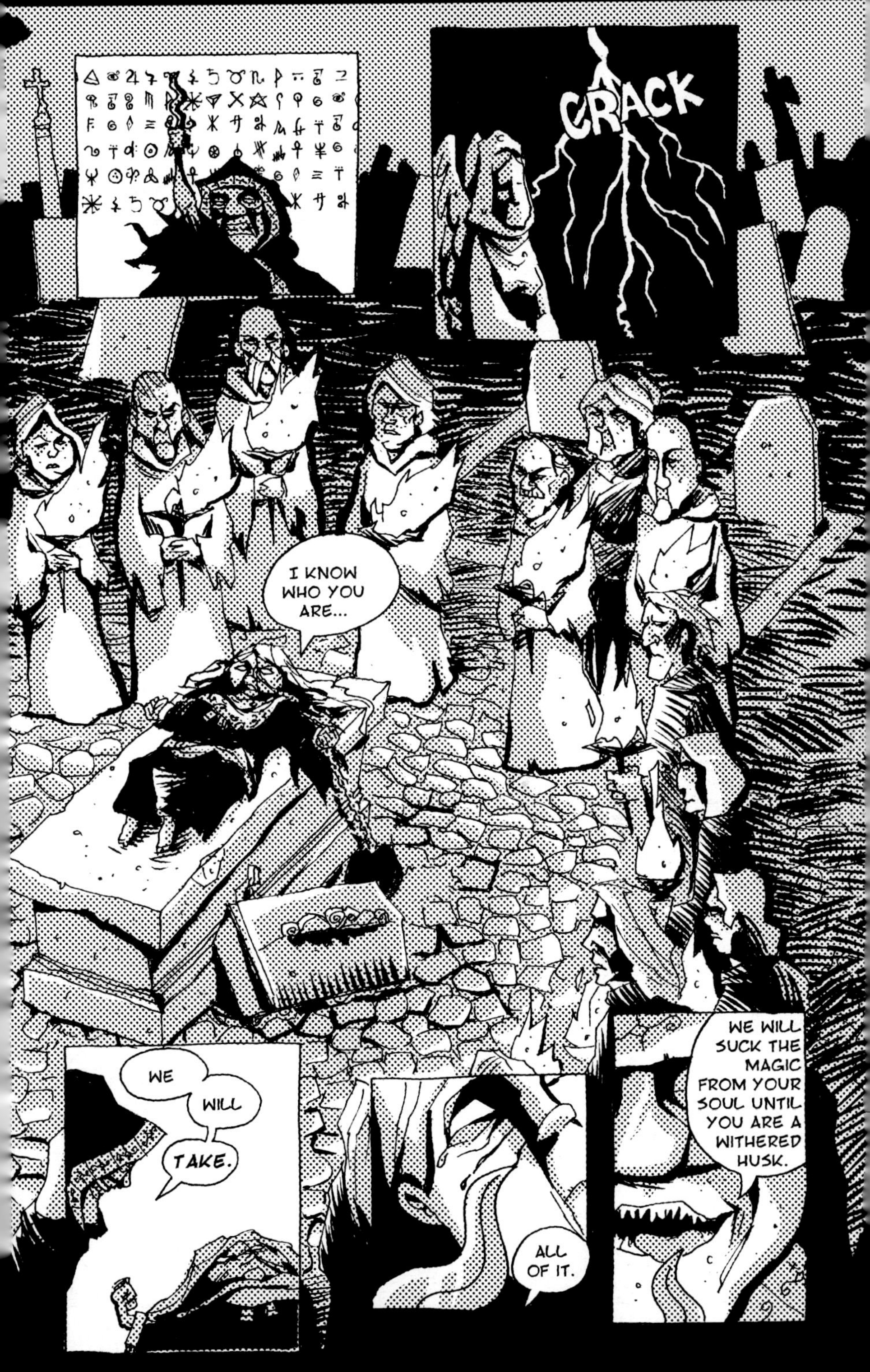
CRACK
I KNOW WHO YOU ARE...
WE
WILL
TAKE.
ALL OF IT.
WE WILL SUCK THE MAGIC FROM YOUR SOUL UNTIL YOU ARE A WITHERED HUSK.

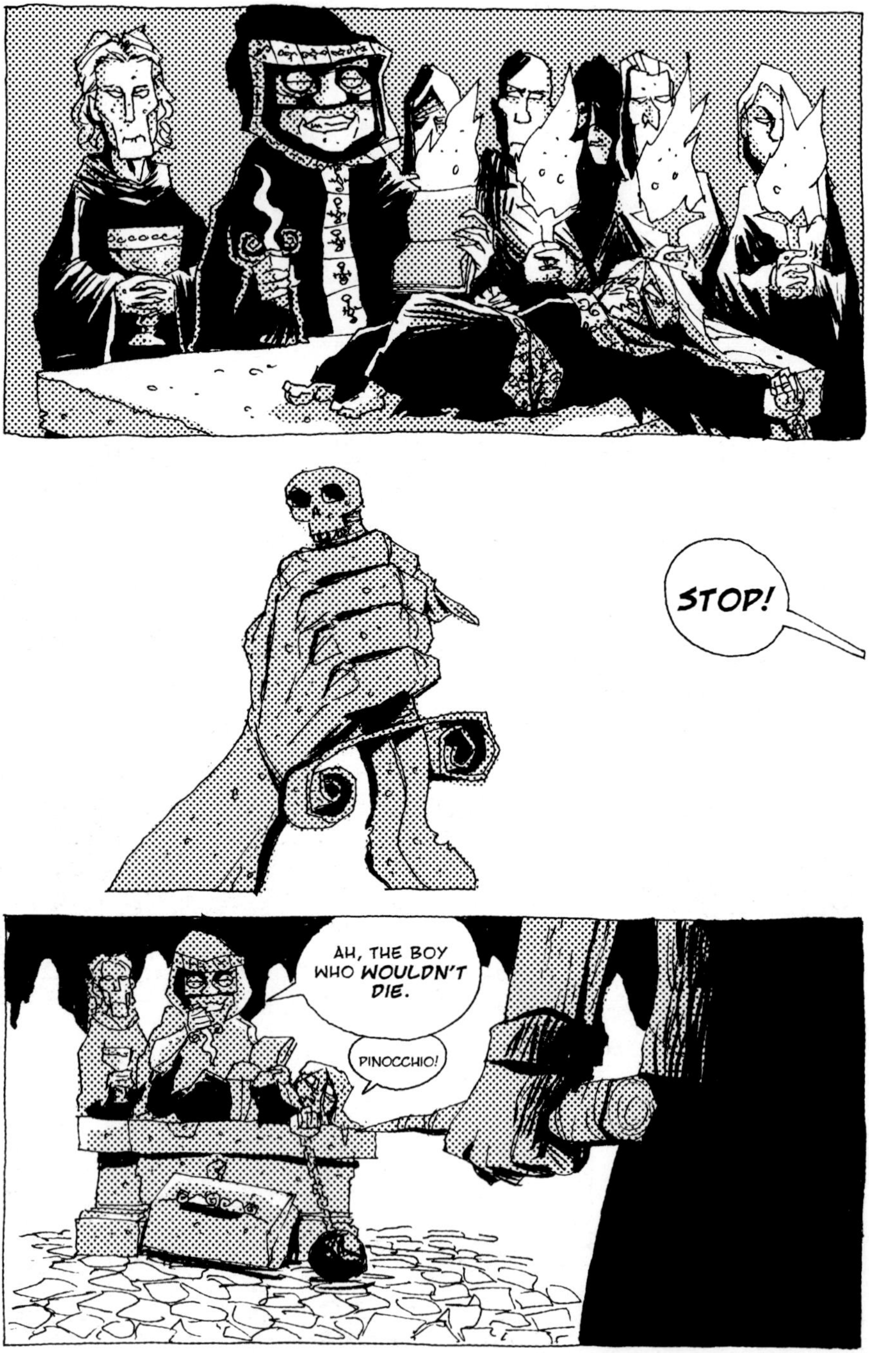
STOP!
AH, THE BOY WHO WOULDN'T DIE.
PINOCCHIO!

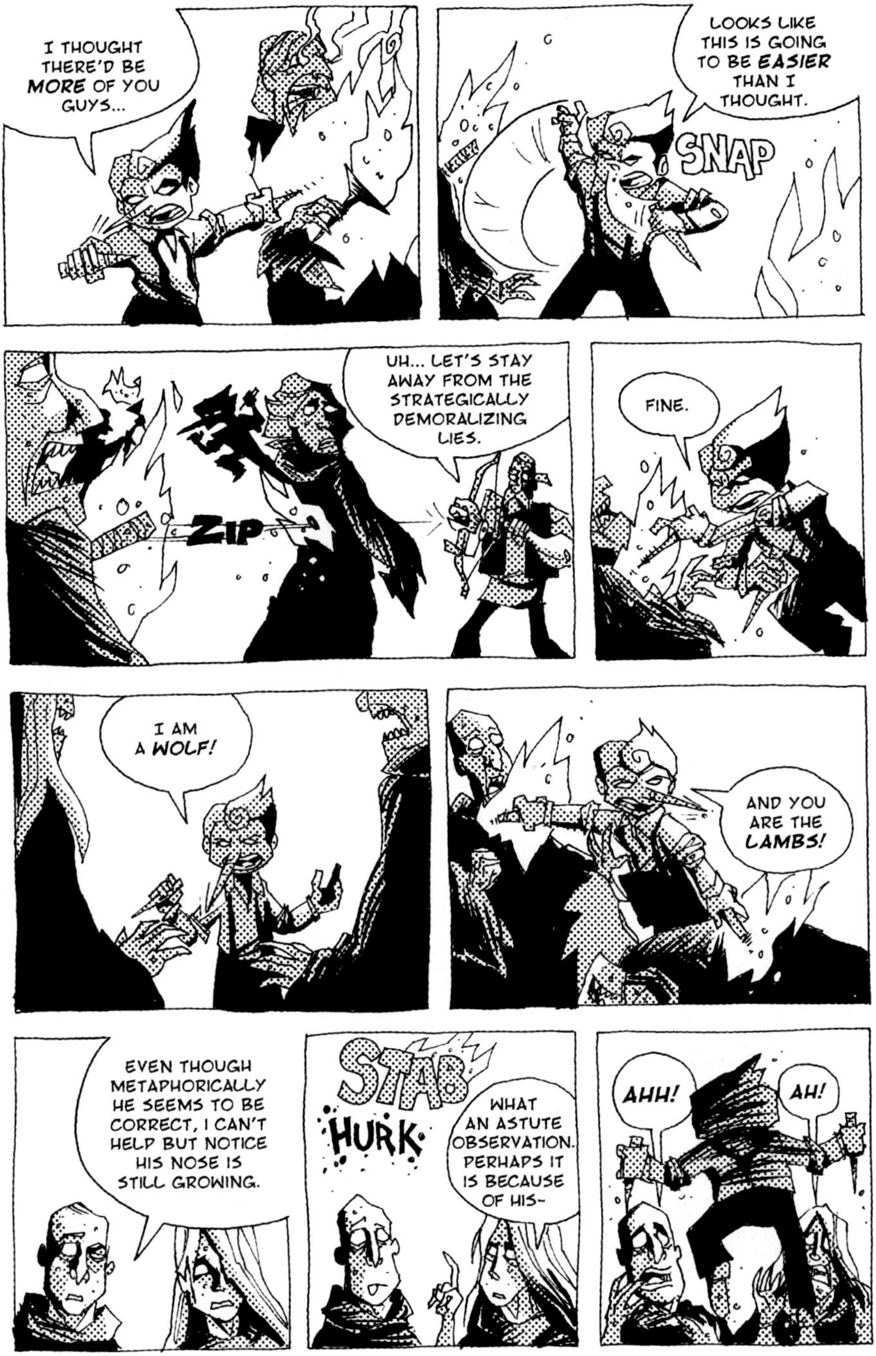
I THOUGHT THERE'D BE MORE OF YOU GUYS...
LOOKS LIKE THIS IS GOING TO BE EASIER THAN I THOUGHT.
SNAP
ZIP
UH... LET'S STAY AWAY FROM THE STRATEGICALLY DEMORALIZING LIES.
FINE.
I AM A WOLF!
AND YOU ARE THE LAMBS!
EVEN THOUGH METAPHORICALLY HE SEEMS TO BE CORRECT, I CAN'T HELP BUT NOTICE HIS NOSE IS STILL GROWING.
STAB
HURK
WHAT AN ASTUTE OBSERVATION. PERHAPS IT IS BECAUSE OF HIS-
AHH!
AH!

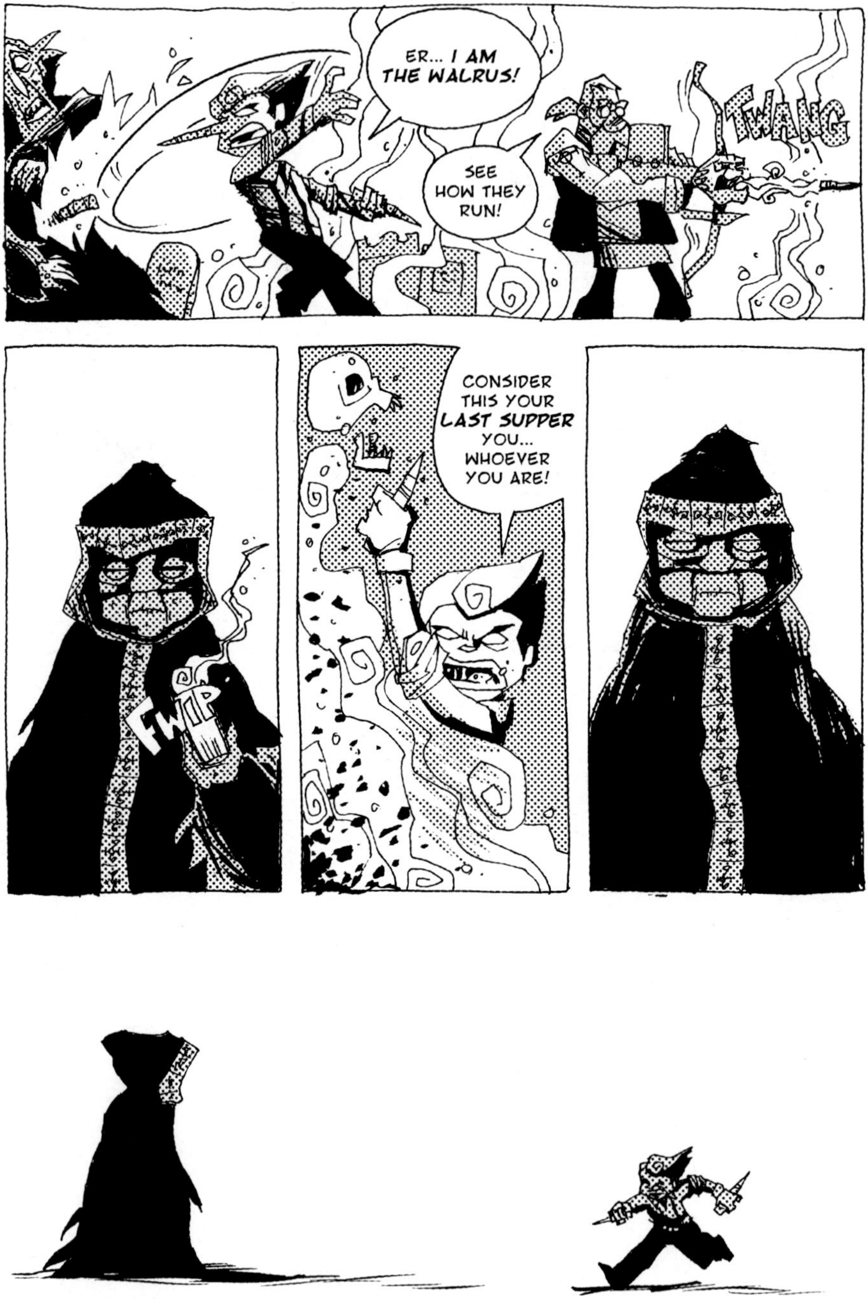
ER... I AM THE WALRUS!
SEE HOW THEY RUN!
TWANG
FWIP
CONSIDER THIS YOUR LAST SUPPER YOU... WHOEVER YOU ARE!

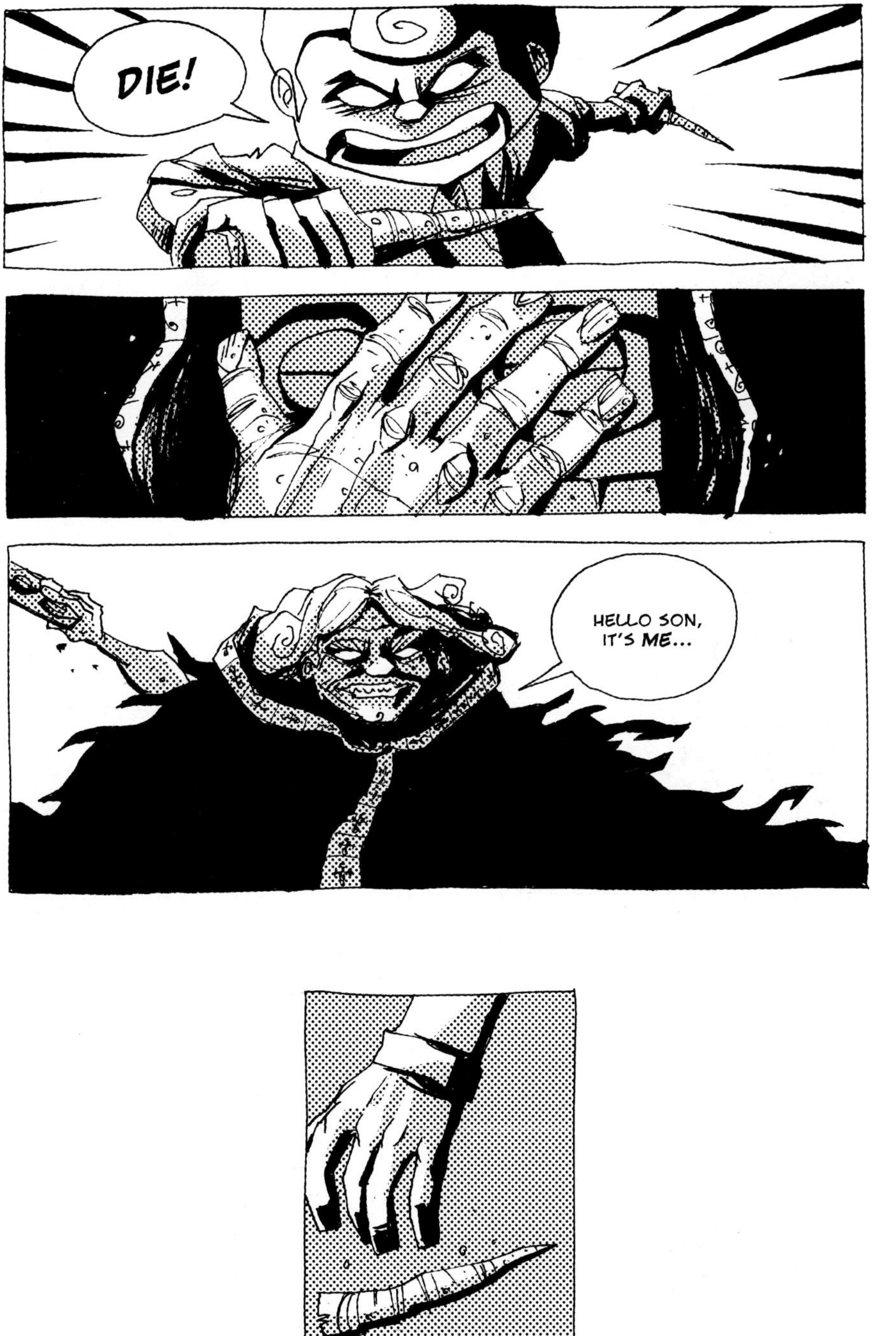
DIE!
HELLO SON, IT'S ME...

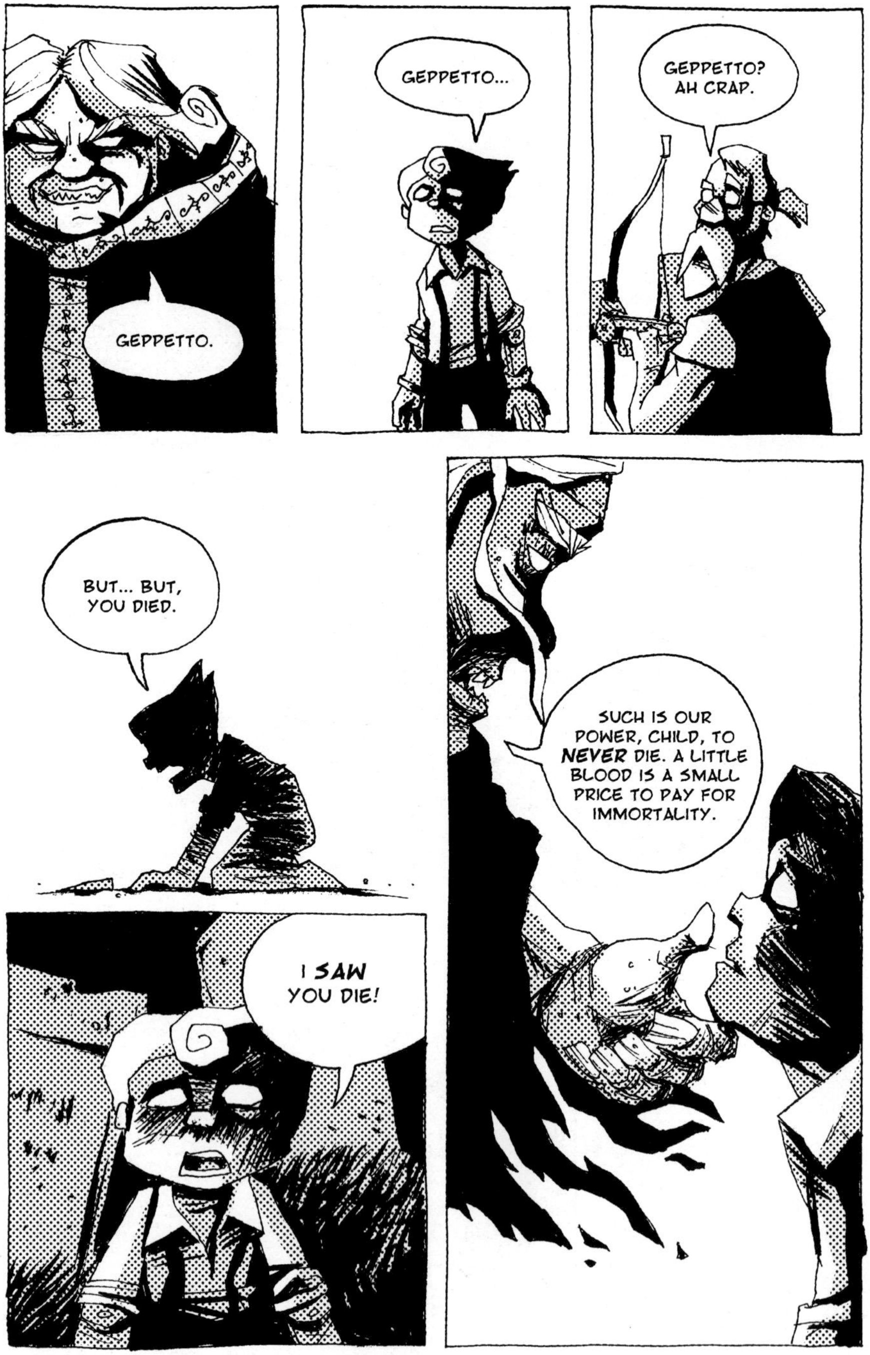
GEPPETTO.
GEPPETTO...
GEPPETTO?
AH CRAP.
BUT... BUT,
YOU DIED.
I SAW
YOU DIE!
SUCH IS OUR POWER, CHILD, TO NEVER DIE. A LITTLE BLOOD IS A SMALL PRICE TO PAY FOR IMMORTALITY.

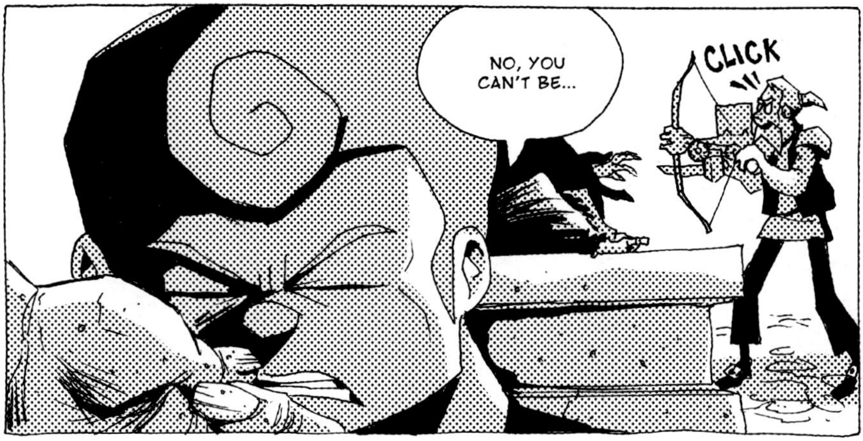
NO, YOU CAN'T BE...
CLICK

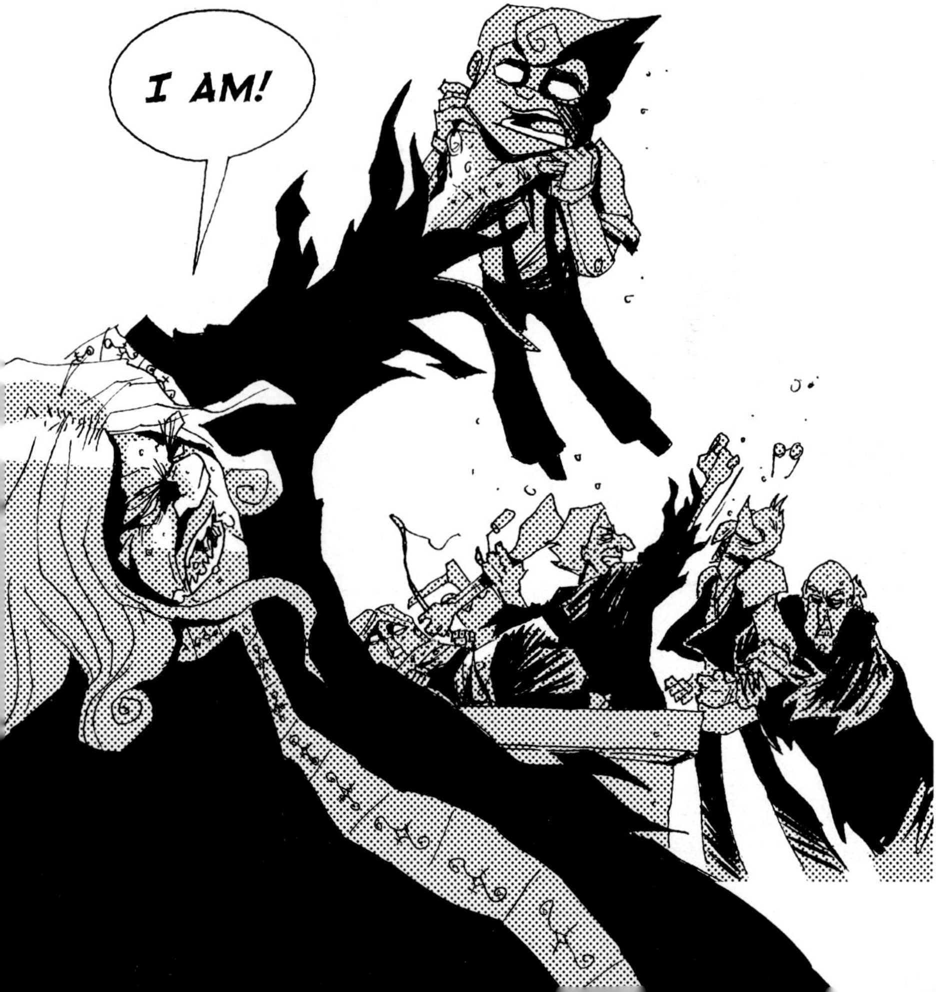
I AM!

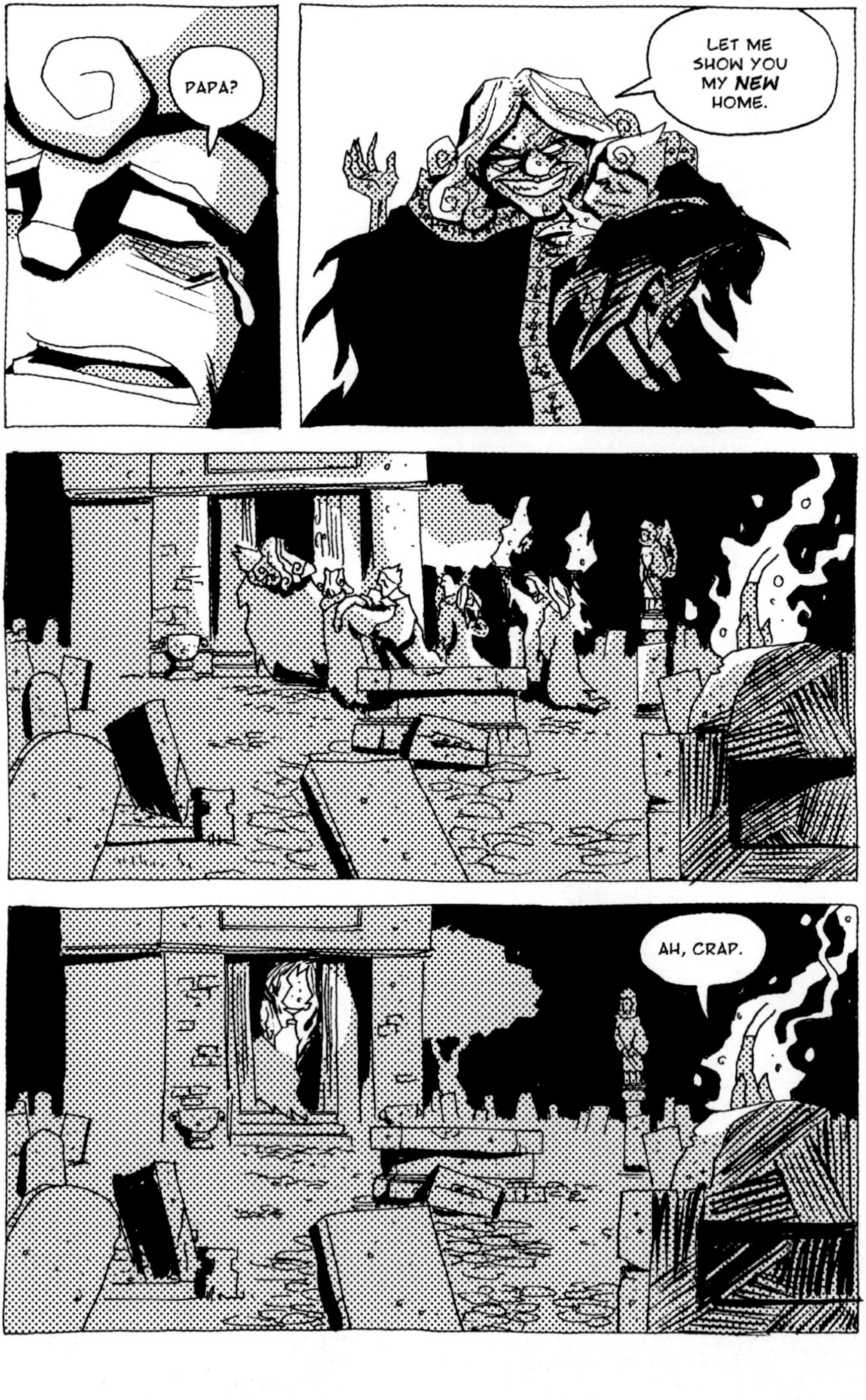
PAPA?
LET ME SHOW YOU MY **NEW** HOME.
AH, CRAP.

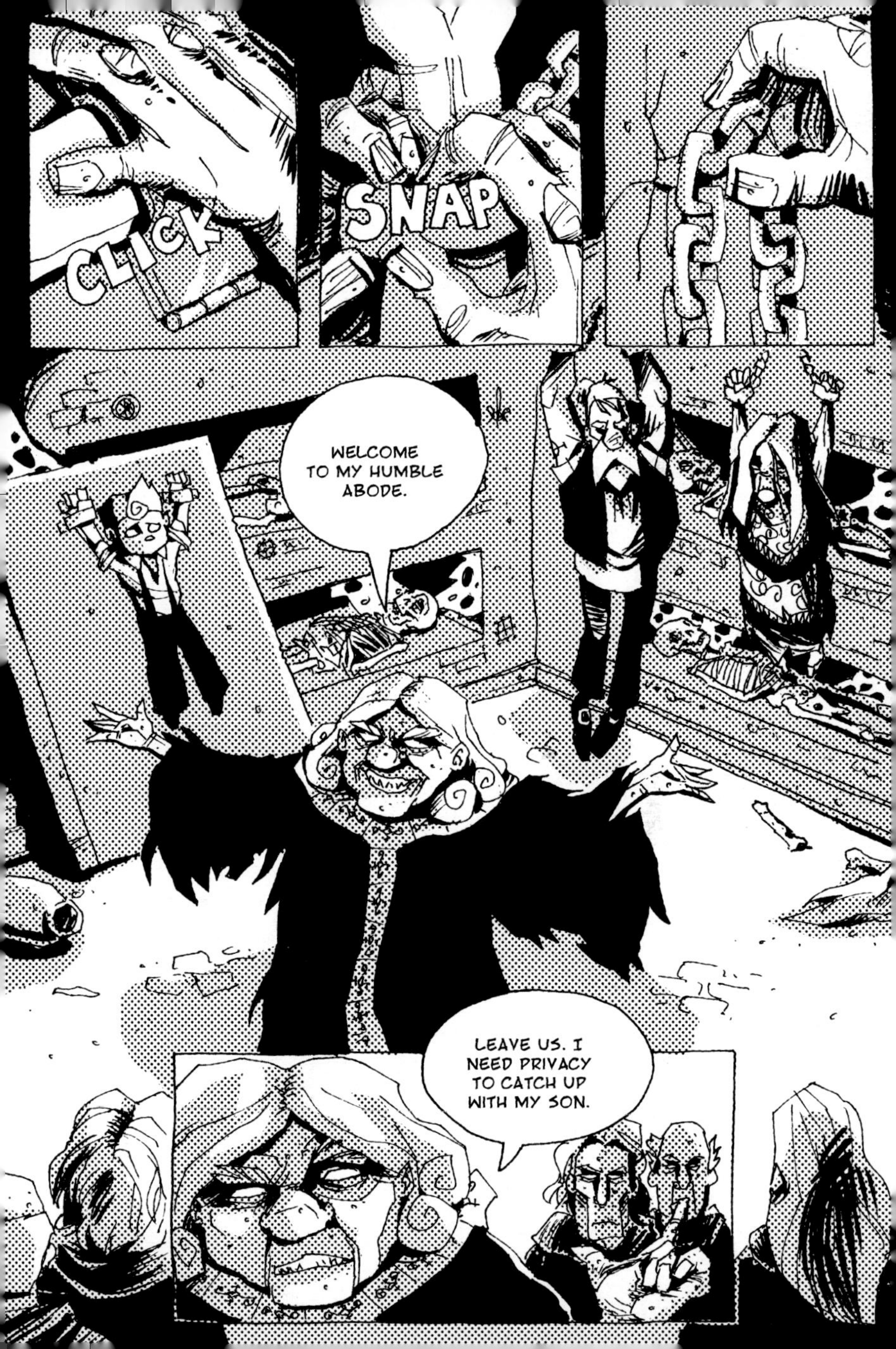
CLICK
SNAP
WELCOME TO MY HUMBLE ABODE.
LEAVE US. I NEED PRIVACY TO CATCH UP WITH MY SON.

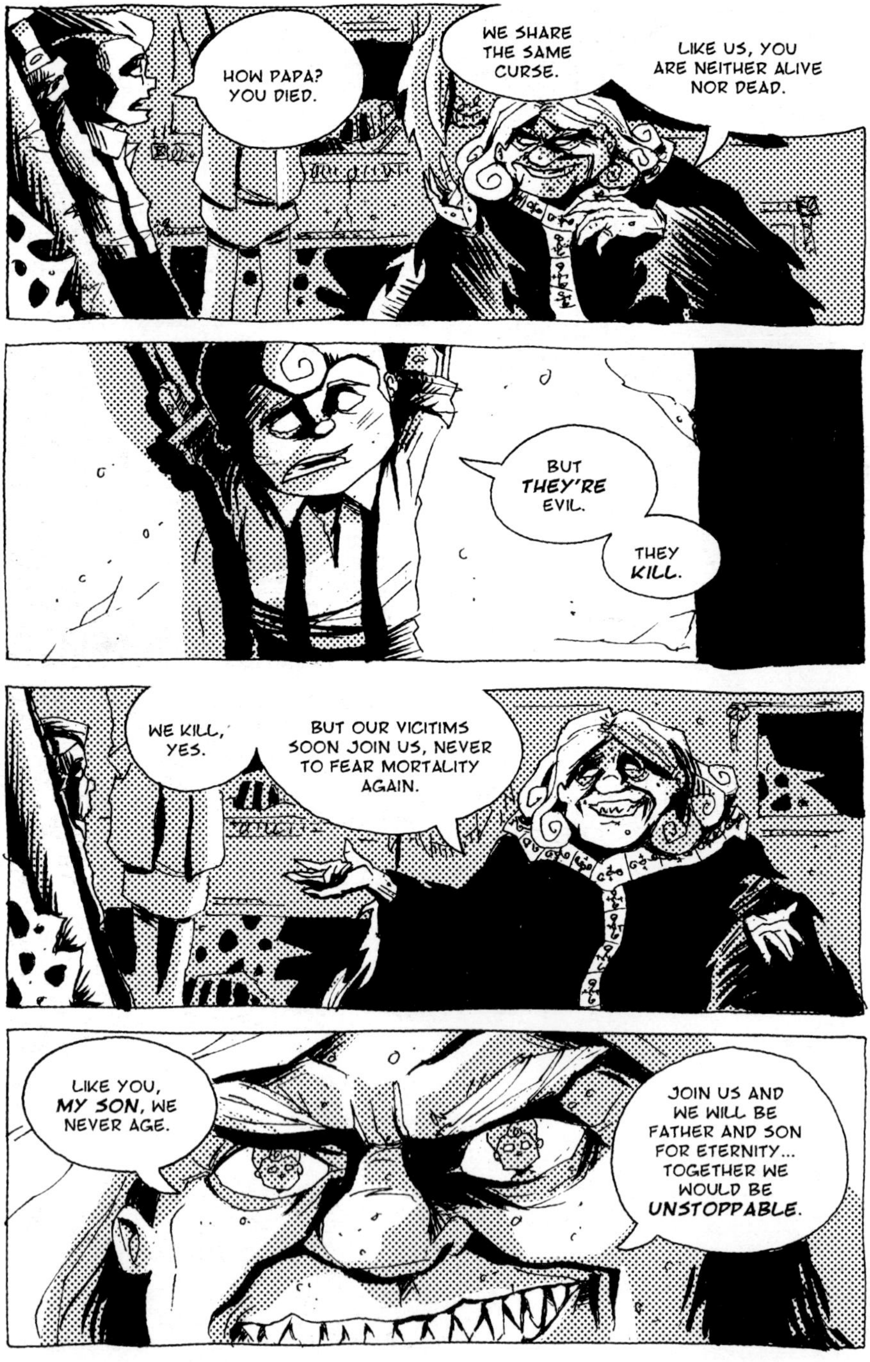
HOW PAPA? YOU DIED.
WE SHARE THE SAME CURSE.
LIKE US, YOU ARE NEITHER ALIVE NOR DEAD.
BUT *THEY'RE* EVIL.
THEY **KILL.**
WE KILL, YES.
BUT OUR VICITIMS SOON JOIN US, NEVER TO FEAR MORTALITY AGAIN.
LIKE YOU, ***MY SON***, WE NEVER AGE.
JOIN US AND WE WILL BE FATHER AND SON FOR ETERNITY... TOGETHER WE WOULD BE ***UNSTOPPABLE***.

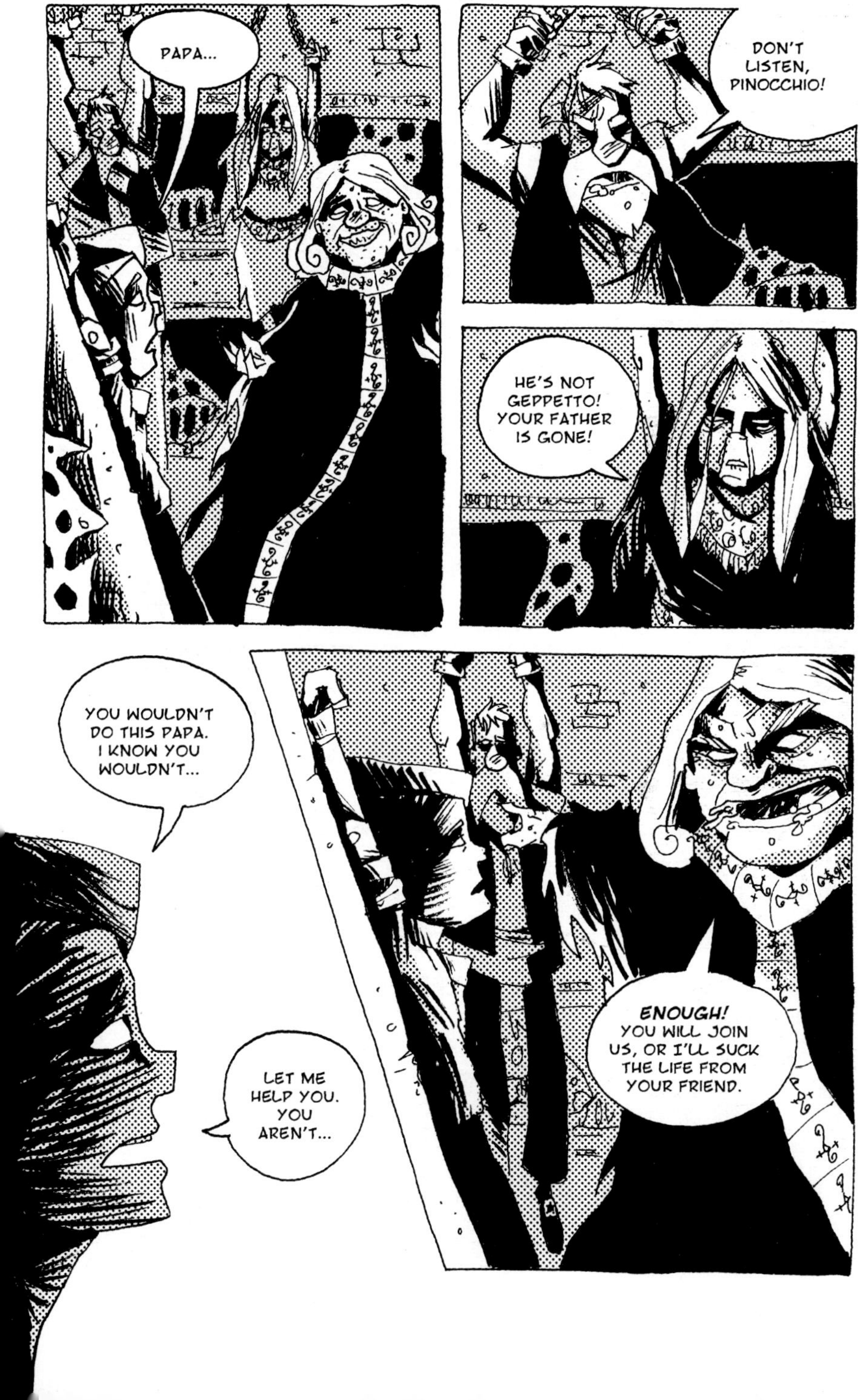
PAPA...
DON'T LISTEN, PINOCCHIO!
HE'S NOT GEPPETTO! YOUR FATHER IS GONE!
YOU WOULDN'T DO THIS PAPA. I KNOW YOU WOULDN'T...
LET ME HELP YOU. YOU AREN'T...
ENOUGH! YOU WILL JOIN US, OR I'LL SUCK THE LIFE FROM YOUR FRIEND.

DON'T WORRY, BOY. OL' GEPPETTO NEVER COULD LICK ME IN A SCRAP.

I MEAN.

IN THIS CASE...

HE DOES HAVE ME CHAINED TO A WALL. BUT I STILL THINK I CAN TAKE HIM.

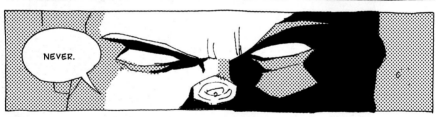

NEVER.

I'LL **NEVER** HELP YOU.

SUCH A SHAME.

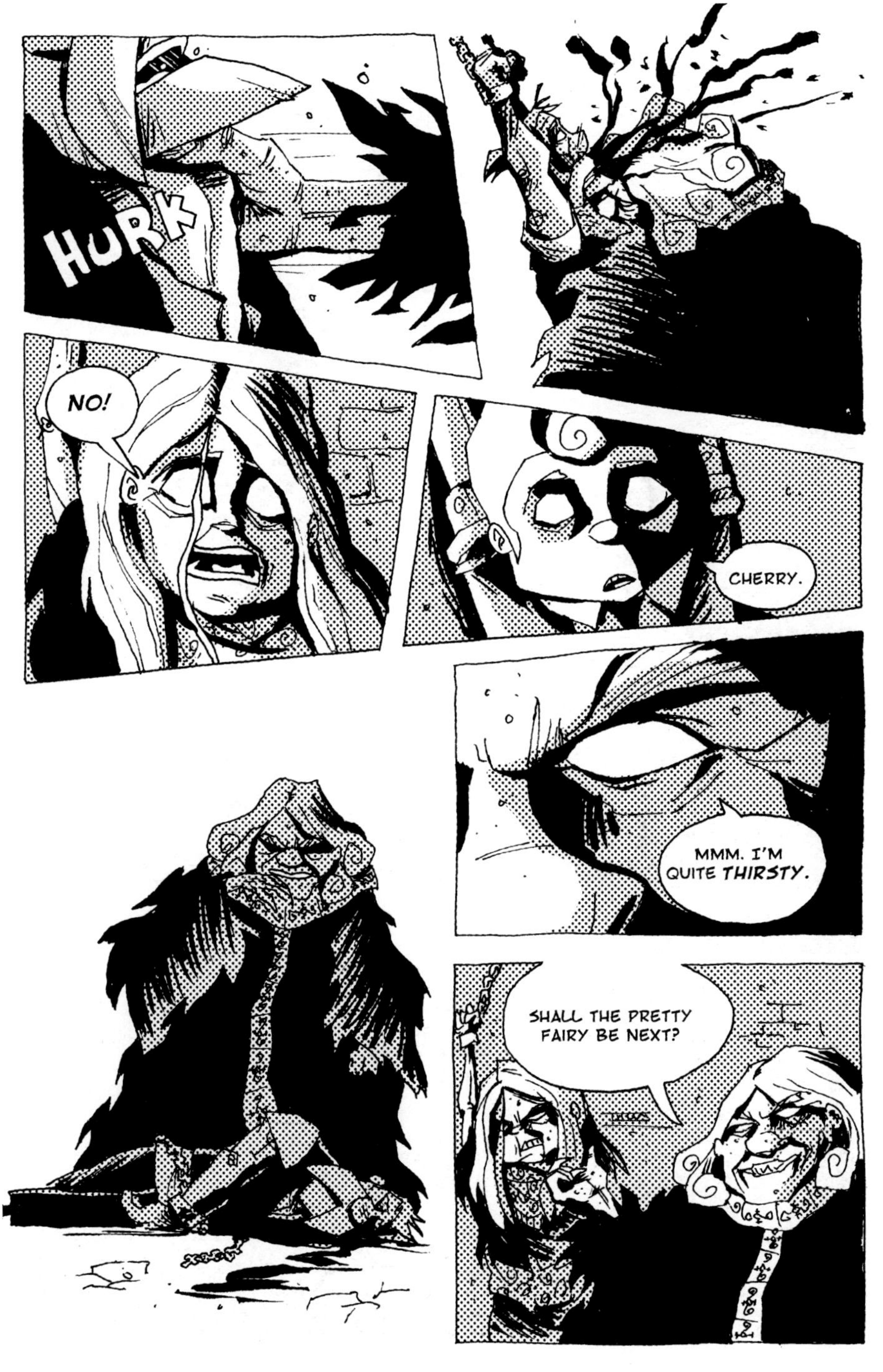
HURK
NO!
CHERRY.
MMM. I'M QUITE THIRSTY.
SHALL THE PRETTY FAIRY BE NEXT?

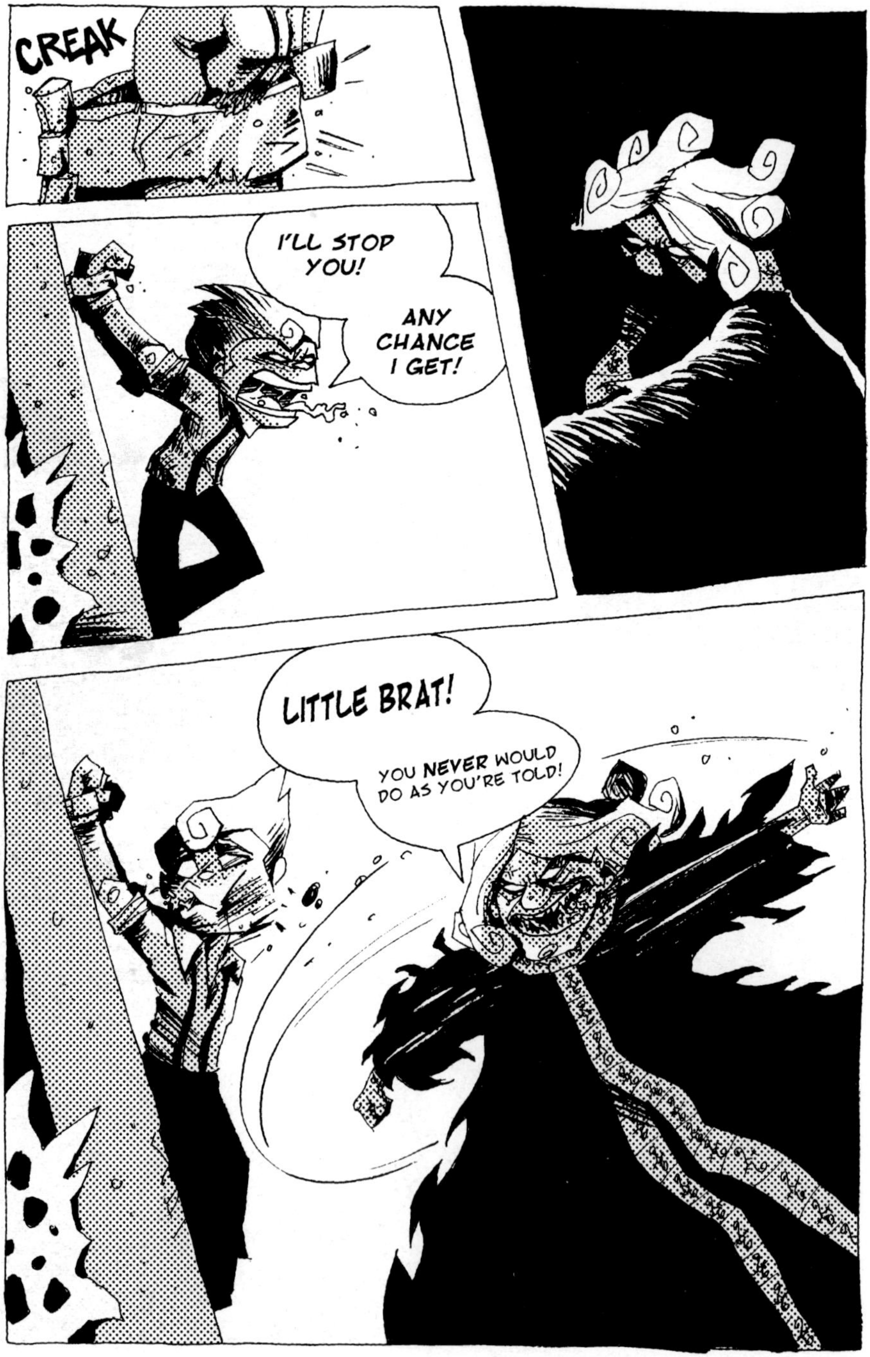
CREAK
I'LL STOP YOU!
ANY CHANCE I GET!
LITTLE BRAT!
YOU NEVER WOULD DO AS YOU'RE TOLD!

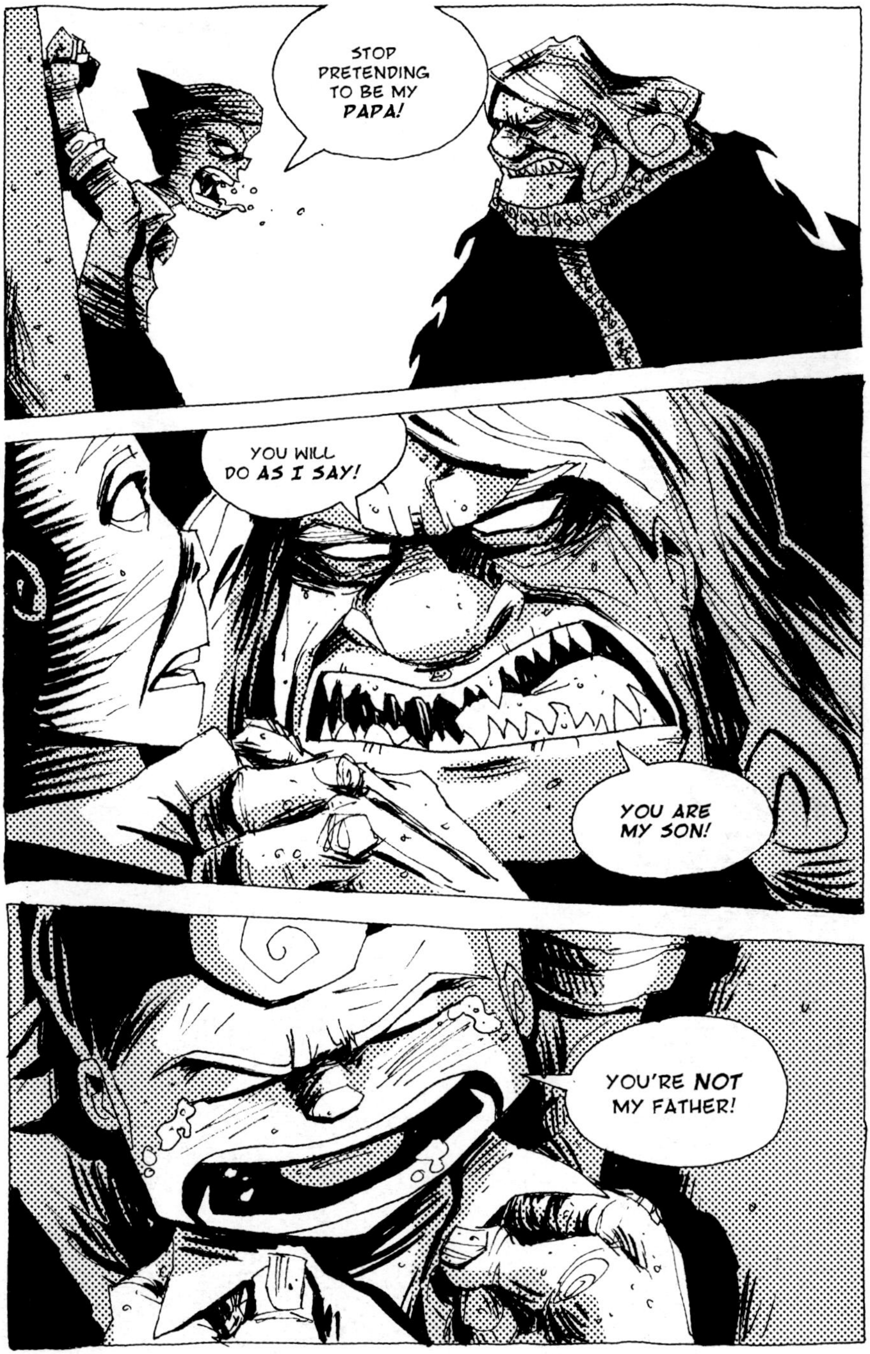
STOP PRETENDING TO BE MY PAPA!
YOU WILL DO AS I SAY!
YOU ARE MY SON!
YOU'RE NOT MY FATHER!

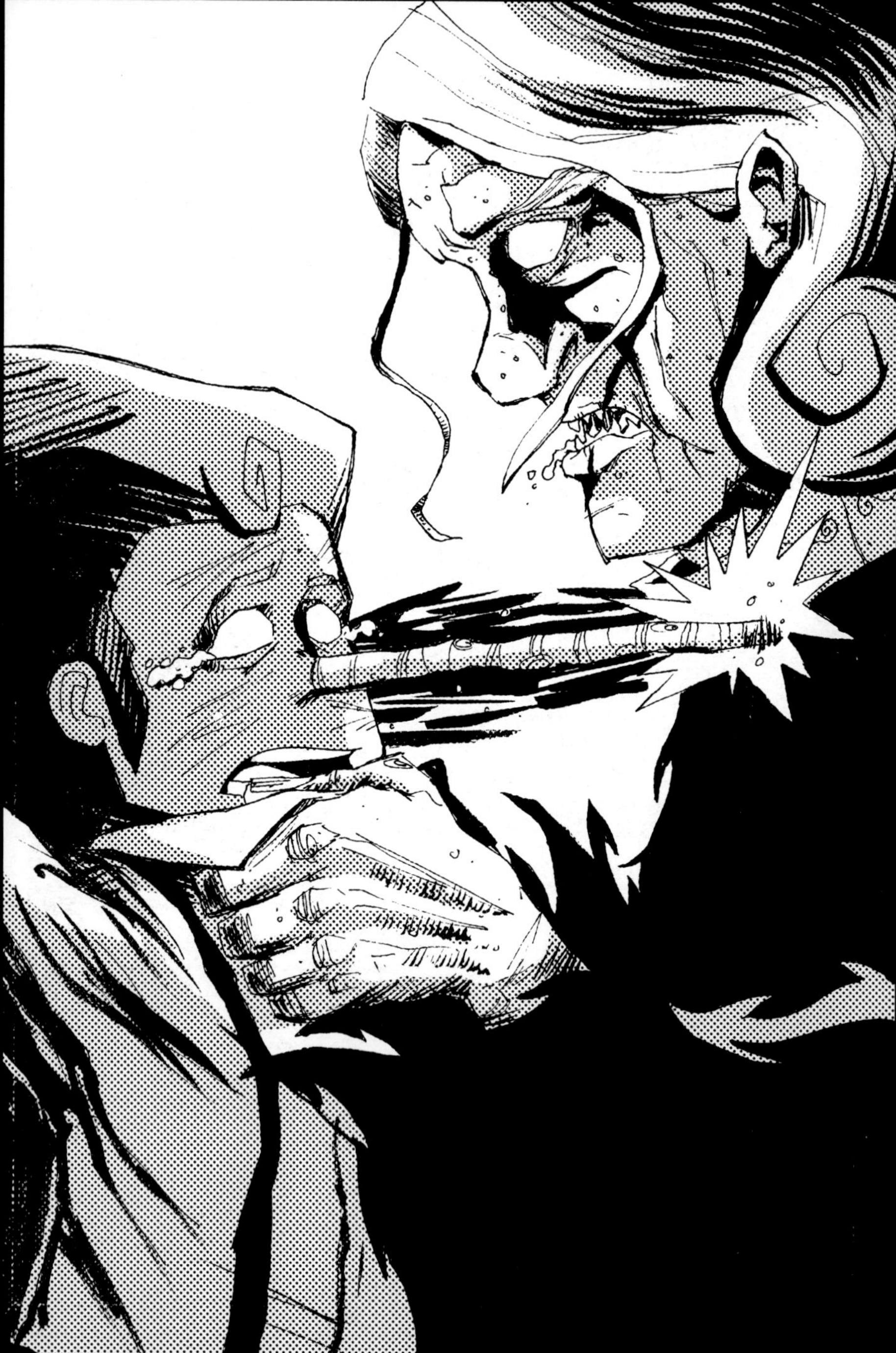

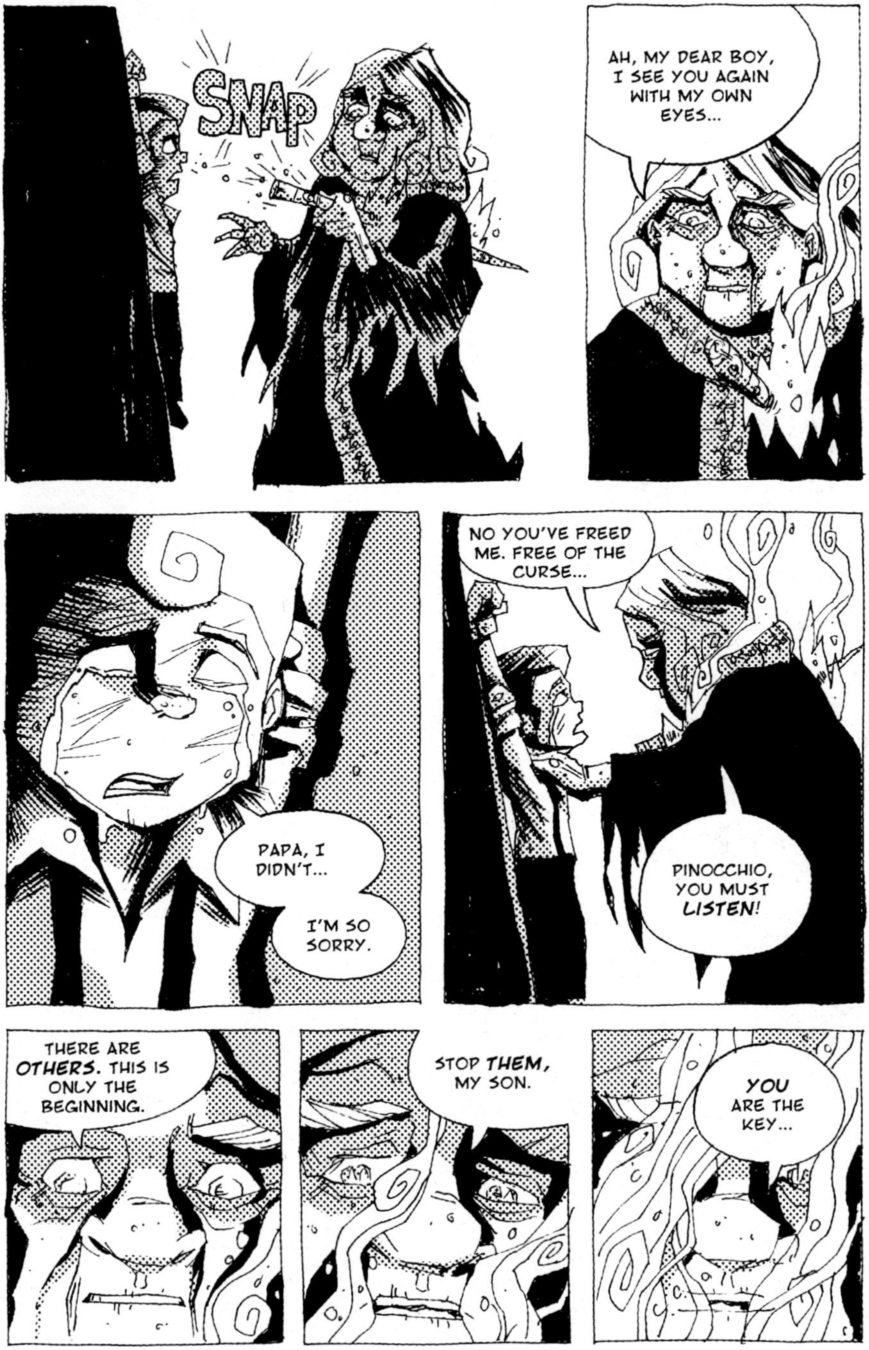
SNAP
AH, MY DEAR BOY, I SEE YOU AGAIN WITH MY OWN EYES...
PAPA, I DIDN'T...
I'M SO SORRY.
NO YOU'VE FREED ME. FREE OF THE CURSE...
PINOCCHIO, YOU MUST LISTEN!
THERE ARE OTHERS. THIS IS ONLY THE BEGINNING.
STOP THEM, MY SON.
YOU ARE THE KEY...

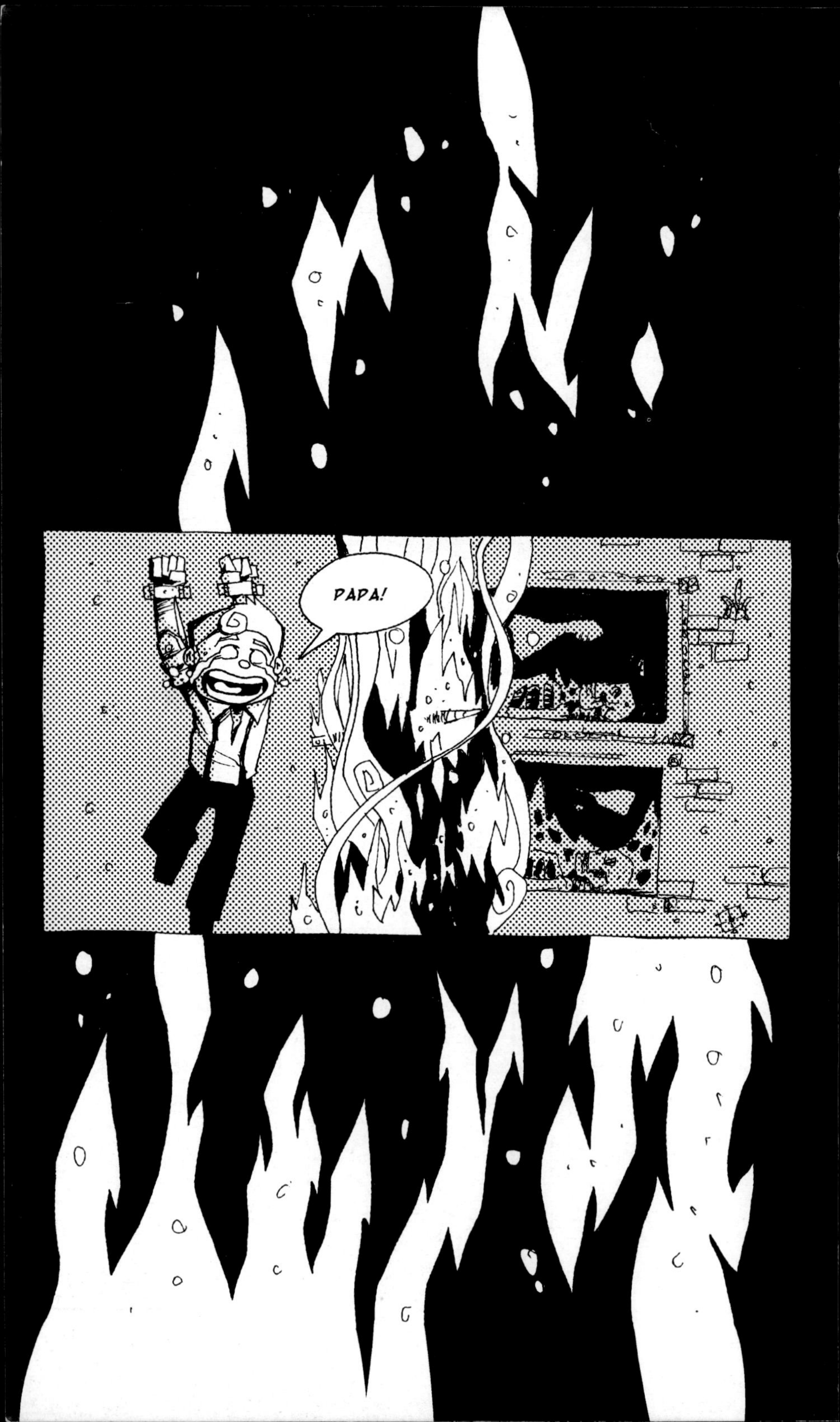
PAPA!

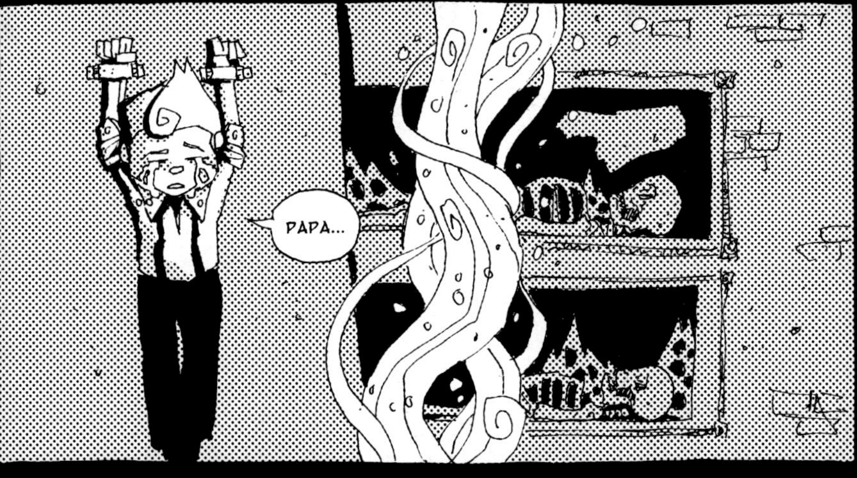
PAPA...

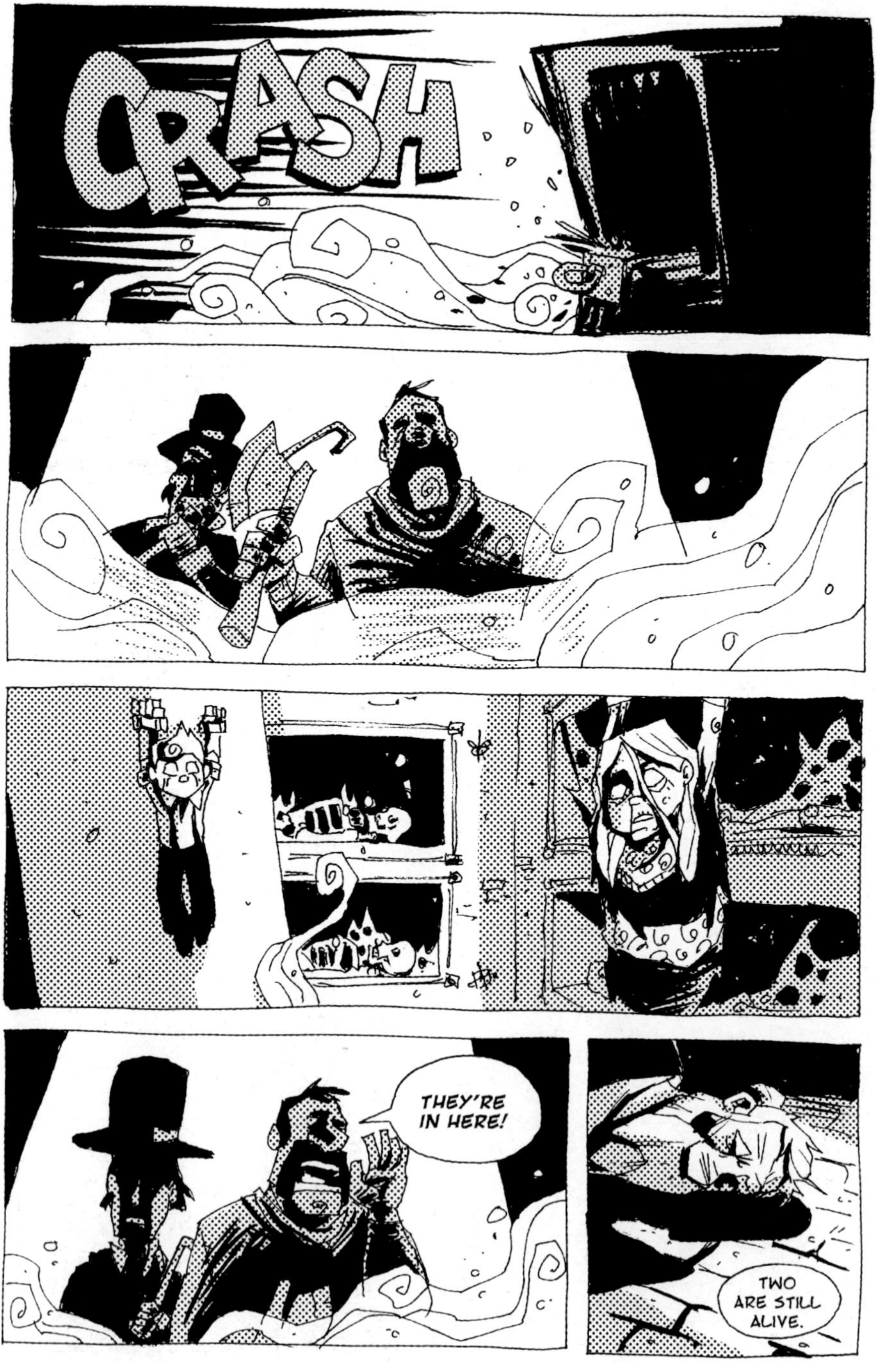
CRASH
THEY'RE IN HERE!
TWO ARE STILL ALIVE.

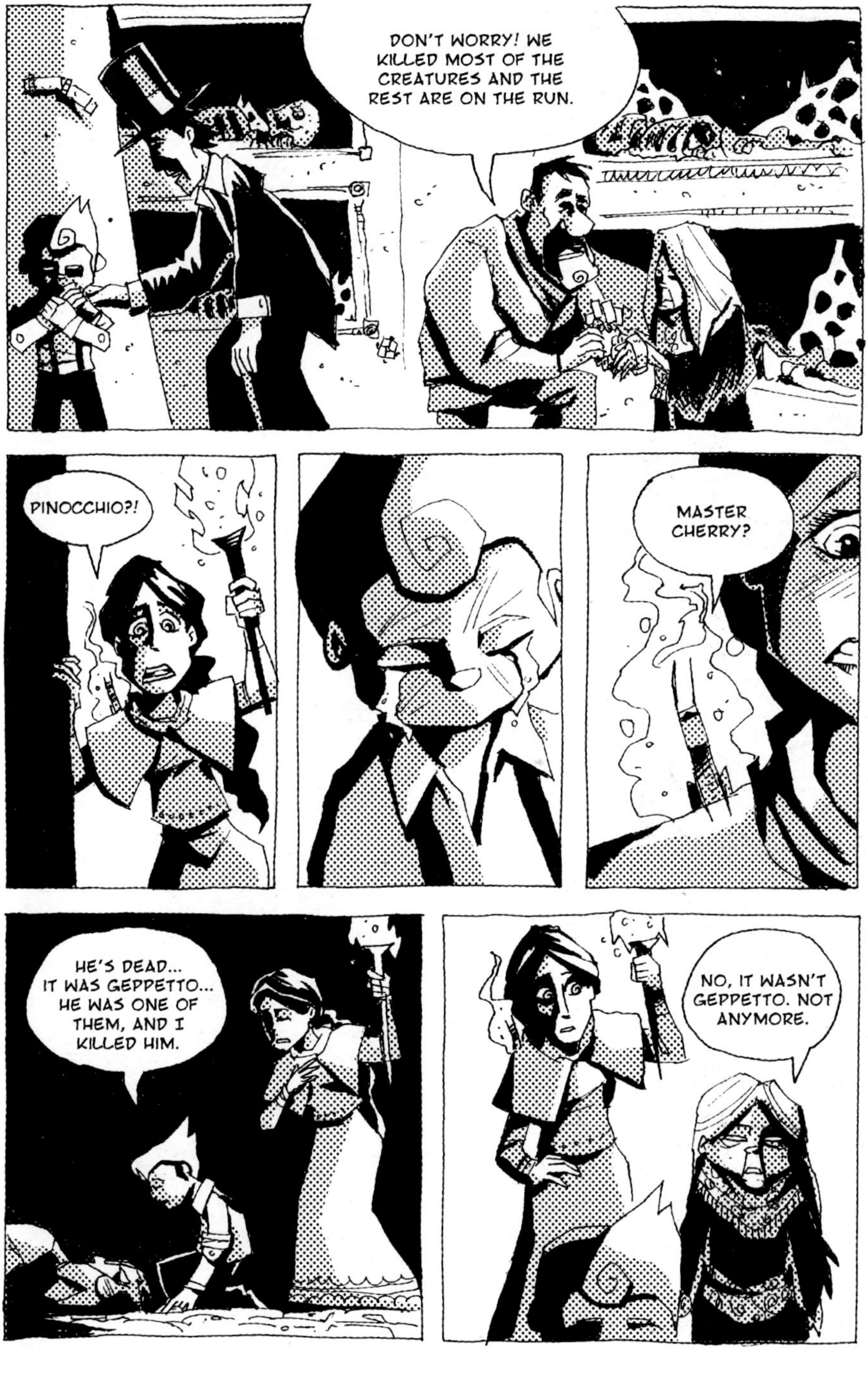
DON'T WORRY! WE KILLED MOST OF THE CREATURES AND THE REST ARE ON THE RUN.
PINOCCHIO?!
MASTER CHERRY?
HE'S DEAD... IT WAS GEPPETTO... HE WAS ONE OF THEM, AND I KILLED HIM.
NO, IT WASN'T GEPPETTO. NOT ANYMORE.

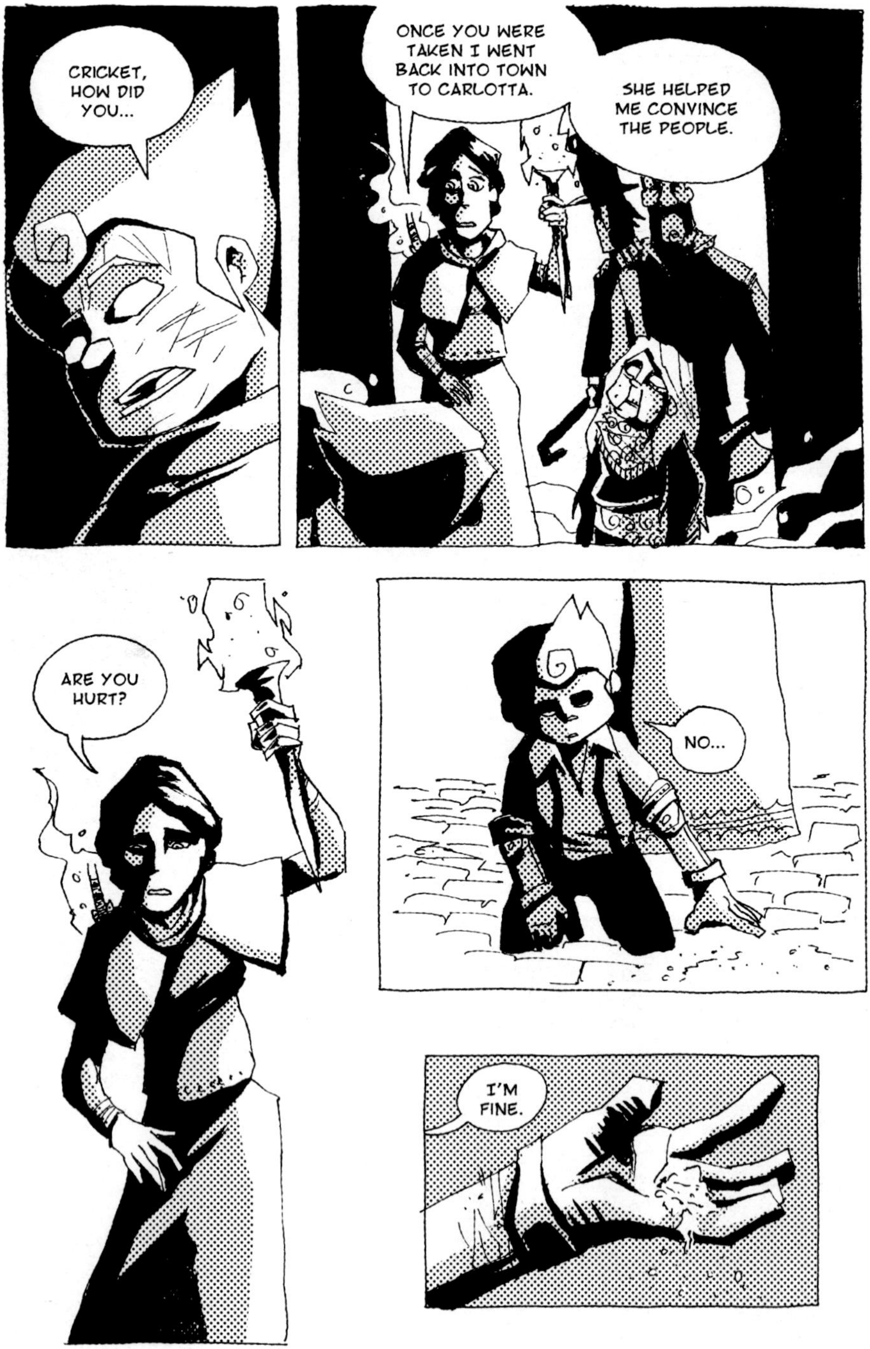
CRICKET, HOW DID YOU...
ONCE YOU WERE TAKEN I WENT BACK INTO TOWN TO CARLOTTA.
SHE HELPED ME CONVINCE THE PEOPLE.
ARE YOU HURT?
NO...
I'M FINE.

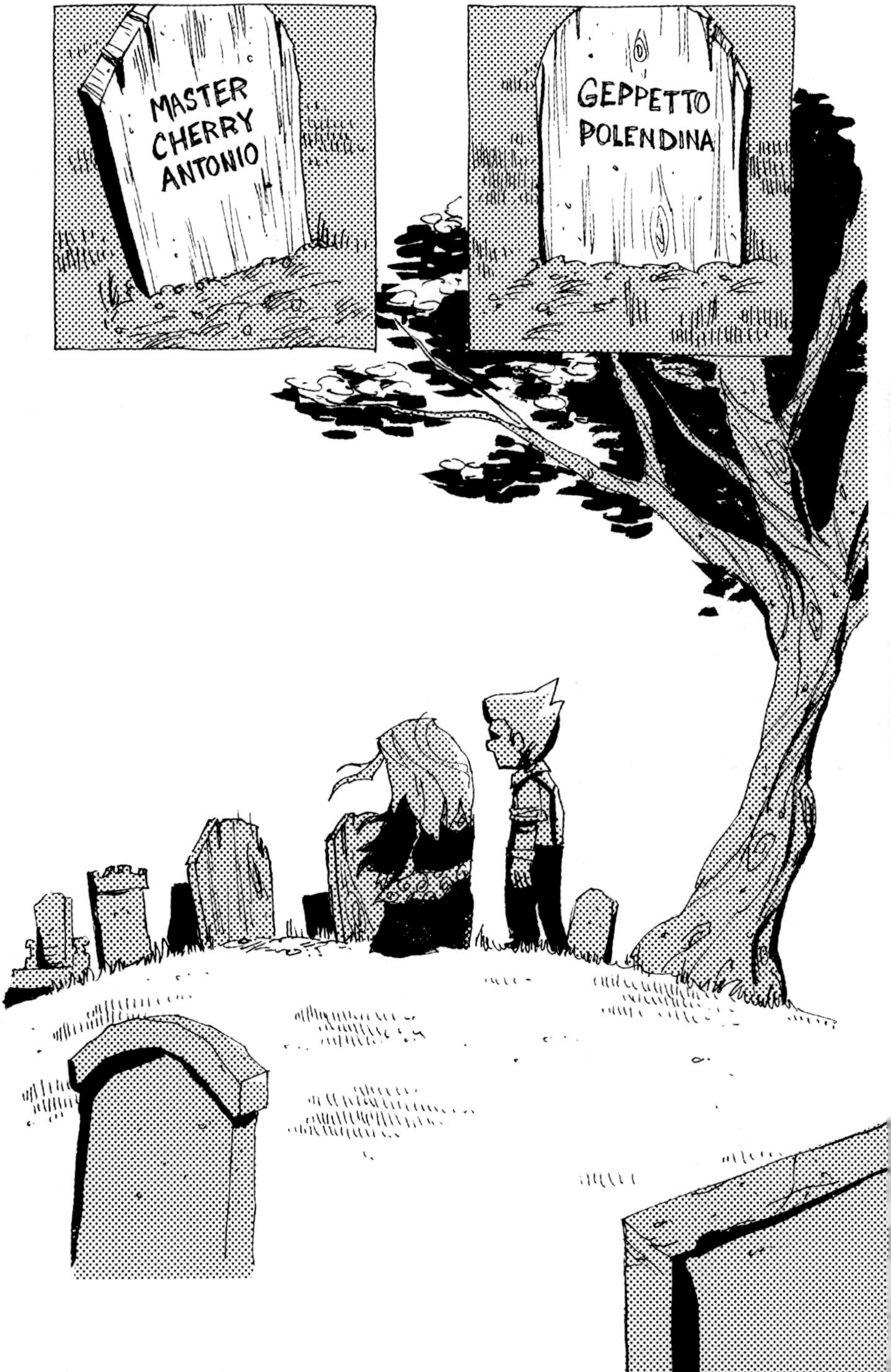
MASTER CHERRY ANTONIO
GEPPETTO POLENDINA

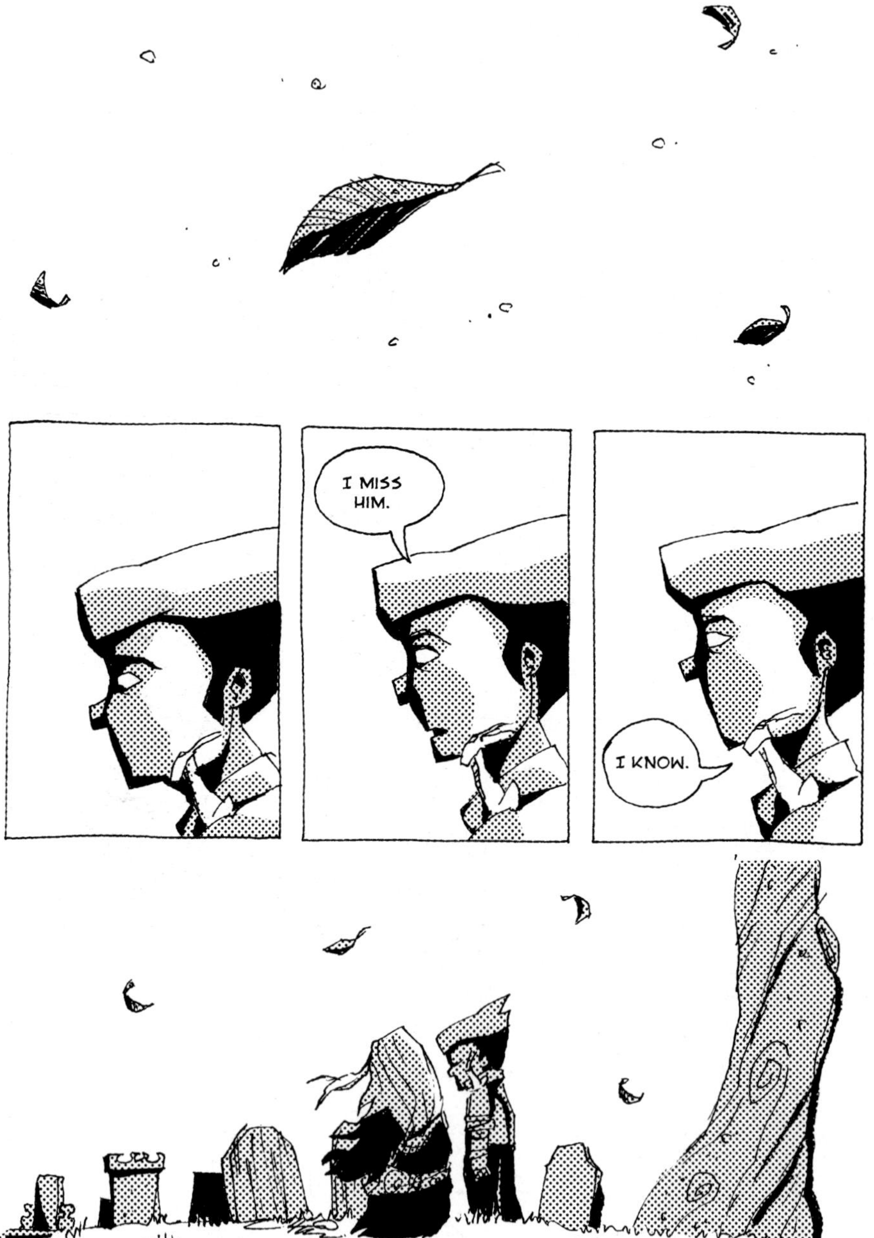
I MISS HIM.
I KNOW.

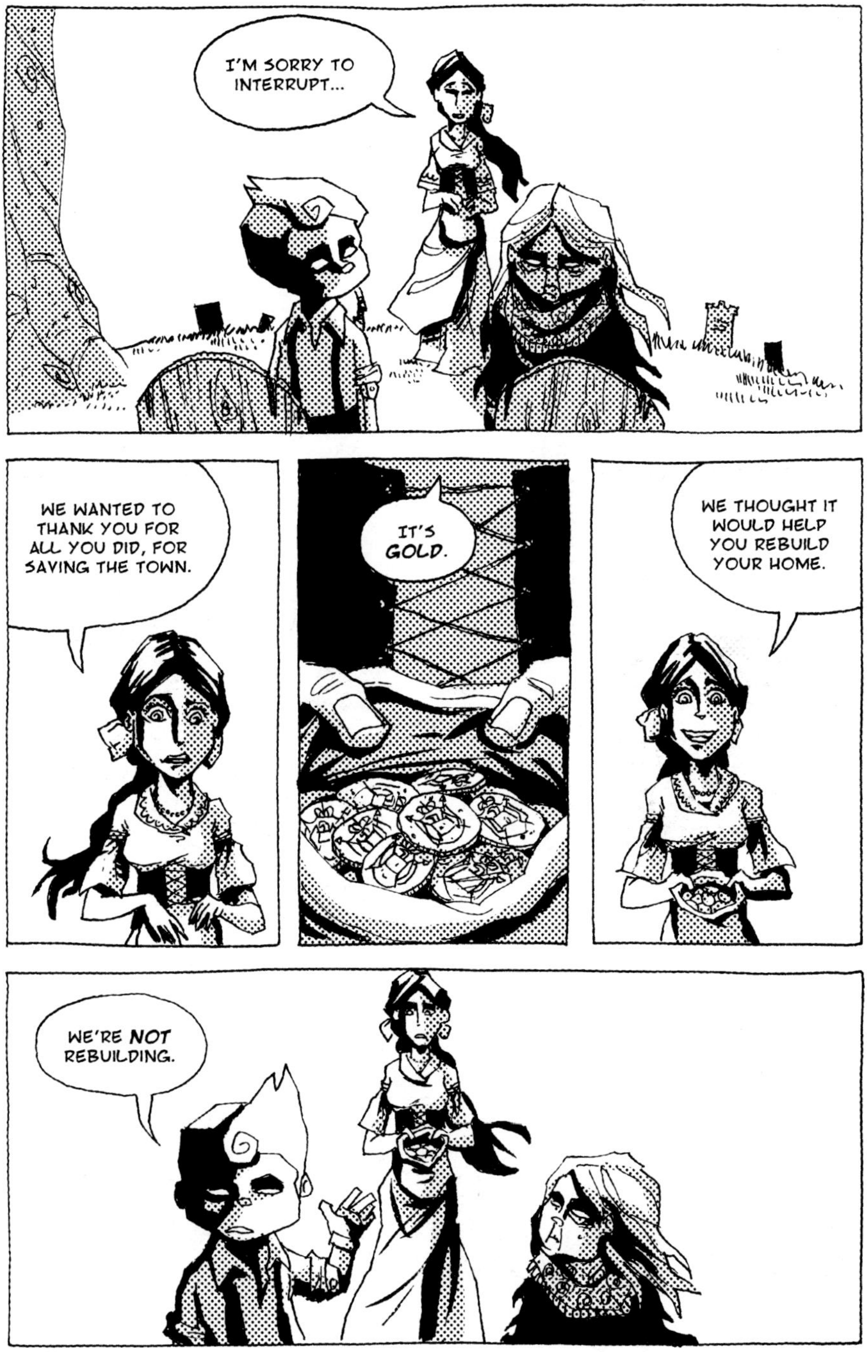
I'M SORRY TO INTERRUPT...
WE WANTED TO THANK YOU FOR ALL YOU DID, FOR SAVING THE TOWN.
IT'S **GOLD**.
WE THOUGHT IT WOULD HELP YOU REBUILD YOUR HOME.
WE'RE **NOT** REBUILDING.

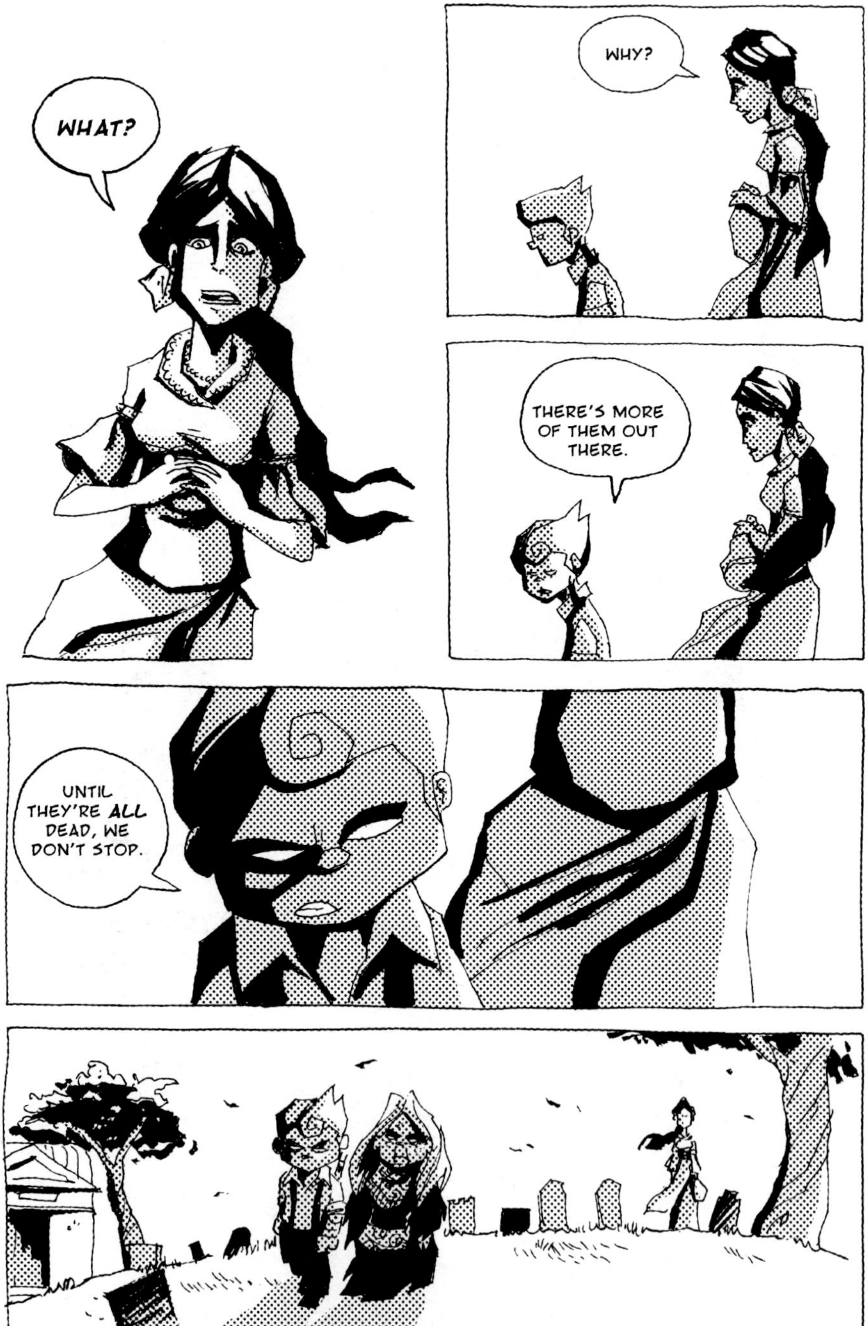
WHAT?
WHY?
THERE'S MORE OF THEM OUT THERE.
UNTIL THEY'RE ALL DEAD, WE DON'T STOP.

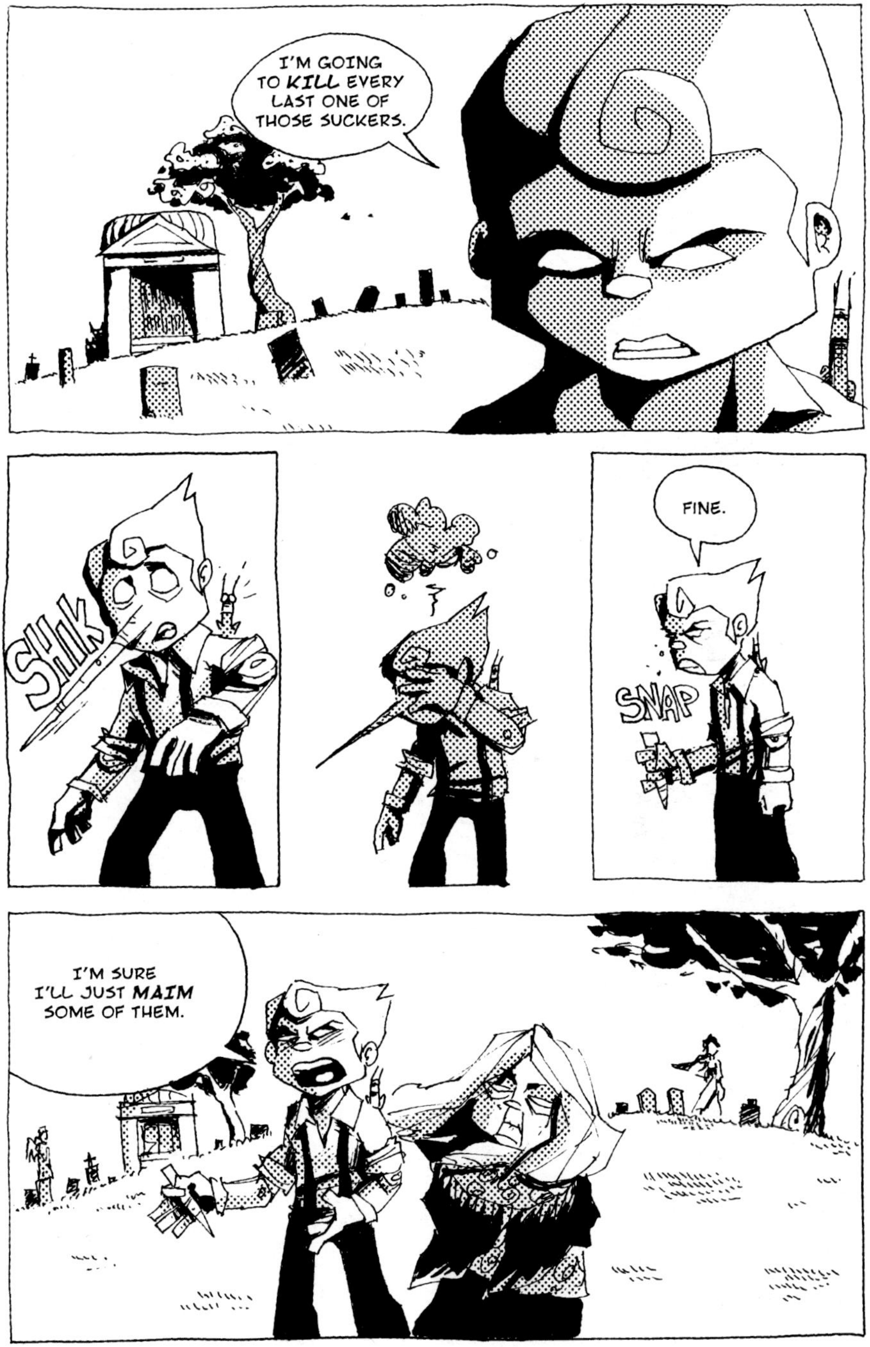
I'M GOING TO KILL EVERY LAST ONE OF THOSE SUCKERS.
SHIK
FINE.
SNAP
I'M SURE I'LL JUST MAIM SOME OF THEM.

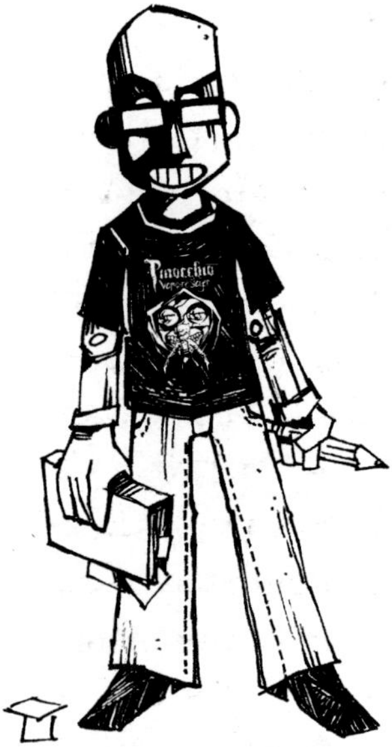

VAN JENSEN

VAN JENSEN GREW UP WANTING TO MAKE COMIC BOOKS. TOLD THAT WASN'T A REAL CAREER, HE WORKED AN ASSORTMENT OF JOBS, INCLUDING A STINT AS A CRIME REPORTER COVERING HOMICIDES LATE AT NIGHT IN THE WRONG PART OF TOWN. AFTER SEGUEING INTO COMIC BOOK JOURNALISM, HE'S NOW MAKING COMICS. FUNNY HOW THINGS WORK LIKE THAT. THIS IS HIS FIRST GRAPHIC NOVEL. HE WAS BORN AND RAISED IN A VILLAGE IN WESTERN NEBRASKA. HE AND HIS WIFE, AMY, LIVE IN ATLANTA, GEORGIA.

DUSTY HIGGINS

DUSTY HIGGINS IS THE CREATOR AND ARTIST BEHIND PINOCCHIO: VAMPIRE SLAYER. HE IS AN AWARD WINNING ILLUSTRATOR AND GRAPHIC ARTIST AT THE ARKANSAS DEMOCRAT-GAZETTE IN LITTLE ROCK, ARKANSAS. HIGGINS CREATED SEVERAL COMIC STRIPS INCLUDING THE ANARCHIST AND GOD, THE DEVIL, AND A MONKEY. THIS IS HIS FIRST GRAPHIC NOVEL ABOUT A VAMPIRE-KILLING PUPPET.

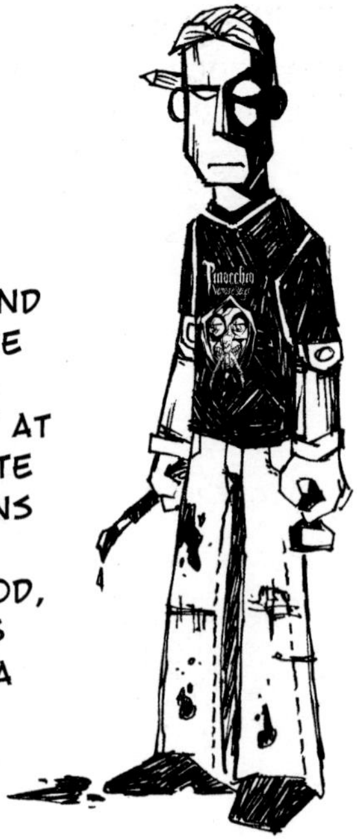